The Complete Medical, Fitness & Health Guide for Men

by LAWRENCE GALTON

Simon and Schuster · New York

Designed by Irving Perkins
Manufactured in the United States of America
1   2   3   4   5   6   7   8   9   10

Library of Congress Cataloging in Publication Data
Galton, Lawrence.
    The complete medical, fitness & health guide for men.

    Bibliography: p.
    Includes index.
    1. Men—Health and hygiene.   2. Men—Diseases.
I.   Title.
RA777.8.G34   613'.04'234   78-15814

ISBN 0-671-22935-4

Contents

*program · Breathing · Exercising when sick · Measures
of fitness · Exercise rehabilitation for heart patients ·
Sports Medicine Tips · Disqualifying conditions for sports ·
Athletic injuries: heat or cold? · First aid · On rubberized
warm-up suits · The ice water myth · Stitch-in-the-side
with exercise · Surfer's ear · Bloodshot eyes from swimming · Hormones and athletes · More on choosing your
sport*

HEART

*On not being fooled by a chest pain · The real thing:
CHD, anginal chest pain, heart attack · How to know if
you are at increased risk · Preventive measures: do they
really work? · The eating factor · The exercise factor ·
Smoking · Water and the heart · High blood pressure ·
Type A behavior · If you have a heart attack · After a
heart attack: early activity · Coronary artery bypass surgery*

Hyperthyroidism · Cushing's syndrome · Addison's disease · Hyperparathyroidism

Urinary

The urinary system · Acute pyelonephritis (kidney infection) · Chronic pyelonephritis · Acute nephritis (glomerulonephritis) · Chronic nephritis · Acute kidney failure · Kidney stones · Bladder stones · Cystitis (bladder inflammation) · Hydronephrosis (kidney distention) · Urethritis

Preface

Two PROPOSITIONS lie behind this book. Men, although they share some of the same concerns as women, have their own—about work, sex, fitness, health and disease, and the relationships among these. And the first proposition is that a book for men about their specific and special concerns should provide more pertinent, straightforward, thorough information and be more useful than a generalized treatise. The second proposition is that even those problems that are not solely male are best and most usefully handled for men in male terms and from the male viewpoint.

I have tried to incorporate in every area of the book the most up-to-date information, the newest insights and developments. This information has come from researchers and clinicians in many fields of medicine, including sports medicine, and from investigators in psychology, sociology, and other disciplines. I have made use of what many have personally imparted in interviews in their laboratories and offices. I have also consulted their published research findings and the findings of many others with whom I have not had opportunity to talk personally.

Space limitations prevent listing all these people here. Many, however, are named in appropriate areas in the text. I am grateful to all of them.

1
Work and Stress

Upsetting Some Myths

In the popular view, success kills. Also in that view, people in high-pressure jobs—who put in long hours and carry heavy responsibility—are unhappy creatures who are jeopardizing their health. But none of this seems to be necessarily true.

A recent Metropolitan Life Insurance investigation covered 6,329 distinguished business and professional men—a one-sixth sample of all those included in *Who's Who in America*. On the average, these men turned out to live longer than men in the general population.

From age 45 on, the successful men had a death rate 30 percent below that of white men in the general population. When compared with men in similar occupations who had not achieved prominence, the *Who's Who* men had a 40 percent lower rate.

Noteworthy, too: The successful men enjoyed the greatest (most favorable) disparity in mortality at ages 50 to 59, contradicting an old notion that the mercilessness with which men drive themselves during their 40's to outstanding positions is reflected in broken health when they are in their 50's.

Among the conclusions of the study: The favorable mortality of the successful reflects in large measure their physical and emotional fitness for positions of responsibility. Reaching the top is survival of the fittest in more ways than one. If you're there, along the way you have proved that you can take the responsibilities, take the pleasures, take the fast pace, take it all and thrive on it. Responsibilities do not make an individual more prone to tension and tension diseases than others. Tension depends more on who is experiencing it than on what is causing it.

THE "EXECUTIVE HEART" MYTH.   The idea that the successful die of heart disease more often than do others is all but abolished by another study as well. Made by Cornell University Medical College investigators, it covered 270,000 men in one of the largest American companies and showed that those who rise to the top are no more susceptible to heart disease than those who fail to work their way into the executive suite; in fact, the executives turned out to have fewer heart attacks than the others. At all ages from 35 through 64, heart attack rates for managers and executives were lower than for workmen and foremen. At all ages, executives experienced only 60 percent of the expected incidence of heart disease.

JOBS HARDEST ON HEALTH.   If long hours, heavy work loads, and unremitting responsibilities hardly sound like the attributes of an ideal job, another recent study shows that men in occupations entailing these seeming hardships are more satisfied, less anxious, and perhaps healthier than those in less demanding jobs. In fact, boredom and lack of responsibility may be hazardous to health, according to a study by the University of Michigan's Institute for Social Research.

In detailed checks of 2,010 predominantly white men in 23 occupations, the researchers found that job satisfaction had less to do with such matters as average number of hours worked each week and the quantitative work load than with more personalized factors such as opportunities to use skills and participate in decision making.

For example, of the 23 occupations in the survey, family physicians ranked highest in the number of hours worked per week (over 55). Men in this profession also put in a large amount of unwanted overtime, had one of the largest quantitative work loads, and reported that their jobs required high levels of mental concentration. Yet they reported the greatest amount of satisfaction with their jobs, low levels of anxiety, depression, and irritation, and few disorders such as sleeping difficulty, loss of appetite, or fast heartbeat.

In contrast, assembly-line workers—without excessively long

hours, large work loads, or particularly great demands for concentration—reported the most boredom and the greatest dissatisfaction with their work load, as well as the highest levels of anxiety, depression, irritation, and somatic disorders. This strong evidence of
strain, the researchers found, is attributable to job insecurity, lack of
social support from superiors and other workers, and lack of opportunity to use individual skills and abilities or to participate in decision making.

This doesn't mean that a person will be happy—or healthy—
just because he takes on a high-pressure job. Different people react
differently to the same work, and the key factor in the mental and
physical health of a worker appears to be what the Michigan researchers call "job fit." As a rule, certain personality types gravitate
toward jobs into which they expect to "fit." One example is the
much-studied "type A" personality, a nervous, hyperactive person
believed to be especially prone to heart attacks. Curiously, such
people often turn up as family GP's, university administrators, and
in other high-powered jobs that, the study indicates, are relatively
free of health complaints. And the Michigan researchers are studying a paradoxical possibility: that coronary-prone types might conceivably live longer in jobs that are demanding than in those
involving less stress.

Stress: Killer or Not?

Many investigators are convinced that not stress itself but the
response to it can be harmful, with the response determined largely
by personality. As one puts it, an imperturbable tycoon may take
in stride the most severe stress while a nervous person could suffer a
heart attack even in a placid job such as assistant librarian.

Dr. Herman E. Hellerstein of Western Reserve University, Cleve-
land, has devoted many years to checking actual heart stresses in
industry and in more stressful occupations. He has checked, among
others, TV broadcasters and entertainers, advertising men, trial
lawyers, sky divers, and surgeons for extended periods, using
sophisticated instruments including portable electrocardiograph
equipment.

Hellerstein sought answers to such questions as: Is a TV news-
caster's heart affected by deadline pressures? How much heart stress
does a lawyer undergo in the heat of a courtroom argument? What

are the strains on a surgeon facing an operating-room emergency and required to make crucial split-second decisions?

The results: surprising. Few subjects, Hellerstein discovered, showed any real great heart responses to job stress situations. The common idea that deadlines and decision making put a burden on the heart was not upheld. The average heart rate during the working period in TV studios was no greater than in a mill or factory. Despite operating-room stress, average blood pressure rise for 39 surgeons was only 15 points; average pulse was 104 beats a minute, and some surgeons even had a drop in pulse rate upon entering the operating room, suggesting that they had done their worrying before entering and once inside concentrated on their work. Occasionally, a critical moment in the operating room did produce a pulse rate increase. One surgeon with a steady reading of 90 had a fleeting reading of 130 when a tube from a heart-lung machine slipped out of a patient's vein.

Hellerstein monitored a very busy internist to study the effect on the heart of a heavily overloaded daily work schedule. The physician had several examination rooms going at the same time, his phone rang constantly, he was often confronted with difficult decisions. For example, he diagnosed a new case of lung cancer during the monitoring. His responsibilities were great. But his heart rate and blood pressure remained normal. Once, however, during the 48-hour monitoring, the doctor's heart rate shot up—when he had to talk by phone with a hospital official. Between physician and official there existed overt hostility.

Hellerstein's conclusions: The pressures of deadlines and heavy responsibilities do not necessarily stress the heart. The personality of the individual and his specific response to job and stress are more significant than the job and stress themselves.

A Hard Look at Stress Itself—and Stress and Work

The world's acknowledged authority on stress is Dr. Hans Selye, director of the University of Montreal's Institute of Experimental Medicine and Surgery. It was he who in 1950 introduced the whole concept of stress.

Selye has defined stress as "the nonspecific response of the body to any demand made upon it." To be sure, the body replies to specific stimuli in specific ways—to cold with shivering, to heat with sweating. But in addition there is always the biological stress reaction—a response in the same manner to things as different as a painful burn or the news that you have won the jackpot in the Irish sweepstakes.

In the stress reaction, the adrenal glands atop the kidneys pour out adrenaline and other hormones—in effect, mustering body energies. The reaction is essentially defensive, but if it is insufficient, excessive, or otherwise faulty, Selye explains, it may cause diseases —so-called diseases of adaptation, the result more of deranged adaptive mechanisms of the body than of direct damaging effects of disease-producing agents.

"If a blow breaks a bone, if a knife penetrates the skin," says Selye, "the resulting damage is due to the injurious agent itself. However, many diseases have no identifiable single cause and can be produced by anything to which our stress mechanism responds inappropriately. Among the best-known diseases of adaptation are gastrointestinal ulcers, high blood pressure, cardiac accidents, allergies, and many types of mental derangement.

"An example will explain in principle how diseases can be produced indirectly, by our own inappropriate adaptive reactions. If you meet a drunk who showers you with insults, nothing will happen if you go past and ignore him. But if you respond, you may start a fight and get hurt, not only by the drunk but also by your own emotional reactions, which increase your blood pressure, accelerate your pulse, and change the entire biochemistry of your body in a dangerous manner."

STRAIGHTENING OUT CONFUSION. Although it makes no sense, an idea has become widespread that stress should be avoided at all cost. It makes no sense because stress, as Selye emphasizes, "being associated with all types of activity, we could avoid it only by never doing anything."

Adding to the confusion has been the recommendation to use tranquilizers and other drugs to "eliminate stress." Some do diminish the distress of excessive emotional instability, but others are ineffective and may even be harmful.

"The spice of life": so Selye terms stress. "Who," he says, "would enjoy a life of 'no runs, no hits, no errors'?"

As for work, the aim of man, he says, should *not* be to work as little as possible. If you're going to enjoy leisure fully, you have to be tired first, just as "for the full enjoyment of food the best cook is hunger."

Ideally, the best bet for avoiding stress in excess is to find an occupation that is play, to pick an environment (wife, boss, social group) in line with your innate preferences. Only in that way is it possible to eliminate the need for constant adaptation that is the major cause of stress.

Personality and Stress

Recently, Navy medics studied 32 pairs of identical male twins, 42 to 67 years old. In each case, one member of a pair had heart disease and the other not, or else one had severe and the other mild heart disease. Since both shared the same inheritance, that factor was out.

The investigators paid particular attention to four possible stress factors: devotion to work, lack of leisure, home problems, life dissatisfactions.

Analysis of the study results showed that men who had experienced coronaries were far more involved with work than the others; those with minimal or no heart disease were best able to relax while away from work; those with more severe disease had a greater number of home problems, often centering around financial arguments; and the more severe the disease, the more the men were dissatisfied with their lives.

But beyond these findings, another significant one turned up: even more important than work, leisure, and home-life patterns was how the individual viewed those and other areas of his life. The study findings suggest that a man who works long hours, takes relatively little leisure time, has domestic problems, and all the while enjoys his life may not be vulnerable to heart disease as a man with similar life patterns who is largely dissatisfied.

This is fully in line with what one distinguished investigator, Dr. Stewart G. Wolf, observed some years ago about the coronary-prone individual: that he is like the mythological Sisyphus who passed the time in Hell pushing a large rock up a steep hill and never quite getting it there. The coronary disease candidate, Wolf argued, is a person who not only meets a challenge by putting out extra effort but takes little satisfaction from his accomplishments.

Which brings us to "behavior pattern A."

The Stressful Behavior Pattern A

A distinctive personality and behavior pattern seems to be characteristic of people headed for coronary heart disease and heart attacks.

Forty years ago, Drs. Karl and William Menninger noted that many patients with coronary heart disease appeared to be aggressive —but under the surface. A decade later, one psychiatrist wrote of a large group of coronary patients that they were hard-driving, single-directed personalities. Another described them as aggressive, compulsive strivers.

But it remained for two San Francisco physicians, Dr. Meyer Friedman and Dr. Ray H. Rosenman, much later to establish an impressive case for the importance of personality and behavior in coronary heart disease.

They consider that there are two major types of personality, A and B, with A being the coronary-prone. If a man with pattern A had to wear an emblem indicating his personality, it might well be a clenched fist holding a stopwatch, Friedman has suggested. The A person is aggressive, ambitious, competitive, has intense drive, must get things done, and makes a habit of pitting himself against the clock. On the other hand, the B person may be just as serious but is much more easygoing, can enjoy leisure, doesn't feel driven by time.

Most of us are mixtures, with characteristics of both types, usually one or the other predominant, and with varying degrees of predominance.

Typically, an A person is briskly self-confident, decisive, never dawdling, even lighting a cigarette briskly. His speech is rarely weak and he tends to use various words of his sentences as battering rams. Commonly, he is involved in many jobs and projects, including many civic activities. If a man's wife has told him to slow down, chances are good he is an A, observes Dr. Friedman.

Typically, too, he is aggressive, with hostile feelings. If he plays games, even with his children, he plays to win. He loves competing with fellow workers. He'd much rather have his associates' respect than affection. Let anyone delay or interfere with something he wants to do and his hostility may be apparent in his voice, even on his face.

Most typically, an A person is conscious always of time, has a great need to try to get more and more done in a given period. He is punctual, unable to tolerate waiting even briefly for a table in a restaurant, can't stand having anyone take a long time to get to the point of a conversation and not uncommonly will interrupt and try to speed the process.

In one study, when a group of lay people were asked to pick out from among their friends those who seemed to fit the type A pattern, they furnished the names of 83 men. Another group, asked to choose 83 men seeming to fit the B pattern, did so. Upon thorough medical check, 23 of the 83 A men (28 percent) had clear evidence of coronary heart disease; only 3 of the type B men (4 percent) had such evidence. Which doesn't mean that generally any type A man will have seven times greater risk of heart disease than any type B man, since the 83 in each category in the study were extremes. But the results of this and many other studies do indicate a greater proneness among the A's.

Breaking Out of the A Pattern

It's no easy matter to change one's whole personality and pattern of behavior. Yet some men manage it; others are able to at least make helpful modifications.

It would appear that anything an A person can do to relax a little, to stop cramming more and more activities into his life, can be helpful.

Dr. Stephen R. Elek, associate professor of clinical medicine at the University of Southern California School of Medicine, who has concentrated for a decade on the effects of stress on heart disorders, especially in the type A individual, has these suggestions for the type A man:

Get a type B secretary and type B aide and cultivate type B friends and associates—and note that they can accomplish a lot while "keeping their shirts on" and not being obsessed by time urgency.

Stop thinking about more than one thing at a time as one way of reducing your excessive emotional stimulation.

Don't accept hurry as an essential of life. Consider the advice of psychologist William James: "Beware of those absurd feelings of hurry and having no time, that breathlessness and tension, that anxiety of feature and that solicitude of results, that lack of inner harmony and ease."

You can't do everything. Put first things first, let the others go. Put in your time where it counts; consider what you're doing that others could do—and let them do it. Give yourself a chance to think. Often, a problem is just the absence of an idea.

Dr. Elek also recommends that you "Recognize the wisdom of not allowing yourself to be upset by the eternal confusion, chanciness and tragic-comic nature of life. Expect it to be so and learn to accept it without bitterness. Learn to treat frustrations like the weather . . . and go on to other things. That way lies the road to serenity."

And "Remember, 'today is yesterday's tomorrow.' Get some pleasure out of it as well as work. Take time out for your family and friends, to listen to great music, and to read. Consider that we differ more from one another by what we have read than by what we have done, for what we have done is often determined by what we have read . . . or not read."

Whether you're a full-blown A man or something less but nonetheless under undue stress, any of a number of techniques of relaxation, some quite simple, can be worth looking into.

Using Meditation to Unwind

At six o'clock any morning, the 59-year-old board chairman of a major company settles into an easy chair, closes his eyes, and begins to meditate. For twenty minutes, he silently repeats his mantra and keeps his mind free of all but the most fleeting thoughts. Before dinner that evening he repeats the process. He is convinced that it tunes up his mind, keeps him from becoming worn out, and helps him keep cool under stress.

Although meditation may not soon or even ever take the place of the double martini as an executive unwinder, it is gaining respectability in the corporate suite. Enthusiasm runs high. A partner in a major New York consulting firm, who does his twenty minutes at six thirty in the morning and again later in the day in his office, is, he says, a "devout skeptic" by nature, and spent $125 for a transcendental meditation (TM) course because he thought it was a "limited downside risk." The most adventurous thing he had ever done before, he notes, "was to change from light to dark eyeglass frames. Now I react very differently to a stressful situation. Occasionally in my work there'll be somebody yelling at the other end of a phone, or something will come up that is really high pressure. I have no anxiety in the pit of my stomach. I can handle it more efficiently and more easily."

Another executive, manager of branch operations for a giant corporation, says, "I don't understand all the physiological things that occur, but I know I'm a lot sharper and more acute. My retention level is higher. I'm not a faddist and I didn't go into this for a couple of years after hearing about it, but it's done wonders for me."

Meditation isn't for everyone. Of six executives in one Connecticut corporation who began meditating, three dropped by the wayside within eighteen months. But proponents praise its benefits and point to studies at Harvard and elsewhere indicating normalization of high blood pressure, reduced smoking and use of alcohol, relief from insomnia, and a variety of curative effects.

TM is learned in a ten-hour course over a one-week period. The technique should be taught by a qualified instructor. It does not involve concentration or contemplation, nor is it a form of self-hypnosis. The individual, after settling down comfortably in a chair for thirty seconds or so with eyes closed, begins freely thinking a specific sound (or mantra).

An Alternative to TM

A simple meditative procedure devised by Dr. Herbert Benson, a Harvard physician who pioneered early research into the physical benefits of TM, appears to be similar to TM, though not identical.

The steps used in what Benson calls "the relaxation response" are as follows:

Sit quietly in a comfortable chair.

Close your eyes.

Relax all muscles of arms, legs, and torso.

Breathe through the nose. As you exhale, say the word "One" silently to yourself to prevent distracting thoughts. The word, Benson finds, serves just as well as the mantra of TM, a word usually derived from Hindu scripture.

Continue for ten to twenty minutes.

Practice the technique once or twice daily but not within two hours after any meal.

Another Simple Relaxation Technique

This one, requiring only a few minutes to learn, has been reported by Drs. A. P. French and J. P. Tupin of the University of California at Davis, who have found it also helpful in many cases in relieving insomnia and in moderating pain, anxiety, and emotional reactions to illness.

Their directions:

Sit comfortably, feet on floor, eyes closed, and let breathing become relaxed, with air gently flowing into and out of the lungs, after which muscles can be readily allowed to relax.

As a second step, relax the mind, letting it drift naturally and gently to some pleasant, relaxing, restful memory. Usually, this is achieved within a minute.

In the third step, present the memory gently to your mind and allow yourself to be there and experience that memory. Don't concentrate on it or think about it in the usual sense, and if your mind wanders off simply bring yourself back, gently and naturally, by presenting the memory to your mind again.

In their experience, the two physicians report, the technique works for many people, resulting immediately in both relaxation and a sense of well-being.

On Exercise and Stress

When he got into medical school at the early age of 18, Dr. Hans Selye recalls, he was so fascinated by the possibilities of research on life and disease that he used to get up at four in the morning to study and attend classes until about six in the evening, with very few interruptions. His mother knew nothing about stress, but he remembers her telling him that this sort of thing couldn't be kept up for more than a couple of months and would undoubtedly lead to a nervous breakdown.

Now approaching 70, Selye still gets up at four and still works until six at night and is perfectly happy leading that kind of life.

But he has made one concession: an hour a day devoted to racing around on a bicycle between four and five in the morning.

Psychological relaxation techniques help master the stress situations of everyday life, Selye says, but exercise is no less valuable.

There is, in fact, a biological principle—that action absorbs anxiety. Research at the University of California directed by Dr. Ernest Michael has shown that you can increase your capacity to withstand stress by taking regular physical exercise.

In the Michael studies, subjects were divided into one group that exercised regularly while the other did not. Each group was then subjected periodically to conditions inducing stress. The exercise group showed markedly greater ability to adjust to stress and to recover quickly. Among the most effective exercises: walking and swimming, because of their rhythmic nature and use of many muscles.

"The studies showed," reports Dr. Michael, "that regular physical exercise not only increases nervous stamina appreciably, but serves another equally valuable purpose: it provides an effective means for the discharge and release of nervous and emotional tensions. Unless these tensions are discharged, pressures on the nerves continue to multiply."

2

Fatigue and Insomnia

On Fatigue . . . as Deceiver

In a classic experiment some years ago at the University of Oklahoma, Dr. Stewart G. Wolf had a group of volunteers hold weights in their extended arms as long as they could. After a period of rest, they were given placebo (dummy) pills which they thought contained a powerful antifatigue drug. The result: a near-doubling of endurance.

Such studies suggest that fatigue levels are set by our minds, that most of us may have far more energy than we normally use or believe we have, that the amount of energy we exert on any activity before fatigue sets in is to some, perhaps even a large extent related to our expectations.

In that sense, and in other ways, we can be deceived by fatigue. It can, of course, stem from sleep difficulties, inadequate rest—and not uncommonly does. But it can also fool us into believing we need more rest when in reality we need the opposite—more activity. It can be caused by physical illness, but it can also fool a physically healthy person into believing that he is ill.

The "Second-Wind" Phenomenon

Years ago, William James, a great American psychologist, gave a lot of thought to what he called the "second-wind" phenomenon and to a corollary proposition: that few men make use of more than only a small part of their possible mental and physical resources.

James' points:

"Warming up" to a job after starting stale is familiar to most of us. The same warming-up process can be striking under another set of circumstances. Working at something, we become, after a time, fatigued. We've had enough and have to stop. But if some unusual need forces us to go on with the work, a surprising thing happens. The fatigue gets worse—up to a point. Then, either gradually or suddenly, it's gone and we are fresher than before. A level of new energy previously hidden by the fatigue-obstacle we ordinarily give in to has been tapped. James observed that there may, in fact, be "layer on layer" of this experience—a third and fourth "wind."

Are there limits? Of course. Yet, James argued, a man who pushes his energies to their extreme often can keep up the pace day after day without wrecking himself. He adapts. "As the rate of waste augments, augments correspondingly the rate of repair," James observed and went on to emphasize: "I say the *rate* and not the *time of repair*." In an Iowa State University experiment, James noted, a group of young men had been kept awake four days and nights after which they were allowed to sleep themselves out. All awoke completely refreshed—and even the man who took longest to restore himself needed only one-third more hours of sleep than he normally had.

In his book *The Energies of Men,* James added these comments: "Everyone is familiar with the phenomena of feeling more or less alive on different days. Everyone knows on any given day that there are energies slumbering in him which the incitements of that day do not call forth, but which he might display if these were greater. Most of us feel as if a sort of cloud weighed upon us, keeping us below our highest notch of clearness in discernment, sureness in reasoning, or firmness in deciding. Compared with what we ought to be we are only half awake. Our fires are damped, our drafts are checked. We are making use of only a small part of our possible mental and physical resources . . .

"Stating the thing broadly, the human individual thus lives usually far within his limits . . . energizes below his maximum . . . behaves below his optimum. . . . To what do better men owe their escape. . . . The answer is plain: Either some unusual stimulus fills them with emotional excitement, or some unusual idea of necessity induces them to make an extra effort of will. Excitements, ideas, and efforts are what carry us over the dam. There seems no doubt that we are each and all of us to some extent victims of habit-neurosis. We live subject to arrest by degrees of fatigue which we have to obey only from habit. Most of us may learn to push the barrier further off, and to live in perfect comfort on much higher levels of power."

How? As James saw it, "The normal opener of these deeper and deeper levels of energy is the will."

But how strengthen willpower? Obviously, there is no one simple answer; many factors are involved. One that is receiving increasing attention: strengthening the body, increasing fitness.

Physical fitness, in fact, as defined by the President's Council on Physical Fitness, is "the ability to bear up, to withstand stress, and to persevere under difficult circumstances where an unfit person would quit!"

After a special study on "Medical Aspects of Aircraft Pilot Fatigue," the American Aerospace Medical Association came to the conclusion that some definite steps needed to be taken to prevent flight fatigue: "First and foremost is the maintenance of one's physical fitness by regular periods of exercise."

The Change-of-Pace Factor

The influence of change of pace on fatigue is also coming in for more attention, with neurophysiological studies providing a better understanding of its importance.

Investigators have been able to pick out brain structures in animals, stimulate them with tiny electrical currents, and show that certain of the structures have a "damping" or inhibitory effect while others make up an activating system. The studies indicate that mood and ability to perform at any given time depend on the degree of activity of the two systems. When the inhibitory system is dominant, the individual is in a state of fatigue. When the activating system is dominant, he is ready to increase performance.

The two systems help to explain why, for example, someone who has reached a stage of physical or mental fatigue but then is exposed to something unexpected—good news or bad, or even a sudden idea —suddenly is freed of fatigue. Suddenly the activating system has swung into ascendancy over the inhibitory because the activating system has been stimulated by the unexpected.

Even after a good night's sleep and only a few hours on the job, not enough to produce physical fatigue, it's possible to become mentally fatigued, bored, if the surroundings are monotonous, the job dull. Then the activating system is dampened and the inhibitory one becomes dominant.

Monotony involves sameness. And even the most thought-provoking, challenging work can become monotonous if it goes on without surcease day after day, week after week, month after month —and even if it goes on hour after hour during a day without change of pace.

Time out, then, is not really time lost. Properly used, it can restore stamina and acuity. Time out, within the working day, can take many forms: a period of meditation, if you like; a short period of reading; even a shift from one kind of work to another. Exercise, too, can provide change of pace, and for some it is possible to spend part of a lunch hour at a gym or athletic club, swimming, playing handball or something else. Even a lunchtime walk is valuable.

A hobby? By all means. Long ago, the distinguished physician Sir William Osler remarked that "No man is really happy or safe without a hobby, and it makes precious little difference what the outside interest may be—botany, beetles or butterflies, roses, tulips or irises, fishing, mountaineering or antiquities—anything will do so long as he straddles a hobby and rides it hard."

A vacation? The ancient Hebrew lawgivers decreed that every seventh year the land should be left uncultivated so it could renew itself. In the Middle Ages, the Christian fathers invented the sabbatical—a layoff every seventh year. Many college professors enjoy sabbaticals. Working journalists rarely if ever get them, but one who took a sabbatical on his own and paid for it himself came back full of enthusiasm.

"If," he observes, "it was rewarding for a medieval friar to escape the hurly-burly of the Middle Ages, it is equally so for anyone who has to wake up every morning face-to-face with modern civilization. With all our progress, life is no more placid than in the days of the Hebrew prophets. The chief reward is that you don't have to face the world every day. If you flee to a mountaintop, or get aboard a small boat, time itself will have a stop. The balm to the spirit is immense. For the human spirit, as for a cornfield, to lie fallow is not the same thing as to lie idle. . . . The spirit, like the earth, grows different things and so has a chance to refresh itself."

If you can't have a sabbatical, you can at least sample the balm of a vacation.

If journalists may be accused of being romantics, hardheaded businessmen rarely are. Says the chairman of the board of one of the major corporations: "We regard the rest period as a vital component of a year's total work situation, and I constantly remind our people that they are not scoring points with the corporation by refusing to take their vacations."

Fatigue and the Worry Factor

"It is amazing," the English mathematician and philosopher Bertrand Russell once commented, "how much happiness and efficiency can be increased by the cultivation of an orderly mind, which thinks about a matter at the right time rather than inadequately at all times. When a difficult or worrying decision has to be reached, as soon as all the data are available, give the matter your best thought and make your decision; having made the decision, do not revise it unless some *new fact* comes to your knowledge. Nothing is so exhausting as indecision and nothing is so futile."

Russell has much more to contribute not only on mental discipline in decision making but also on making use of usually unused unconscious processes in solving problems, aiding decisions, and avoiding fear and worry, which in his view contribute greatly to fatigue.

If, he maintains, psychologists have done a lot of studying of how the unconscious affects the conscious, there has been much less of the operation of the conscious upon the unconscious. Yet the latter process is of vast importance.

It's especially important when it comes to worry. Says Russell: "It is easy enough to tell oneself that such and such a misfortune would not be so very terrible if it happened, but so long as this remains merely a conscious conviction it will not operate in the watches of the night."

His conviction: A conscious thought can be planted in the unconscious if you put enough vigor and intensity into it. You can do the burying deliberately and let the unconscious do a lot of useful work.

"I have found, for example," he says, "that if I have to write upon some rather difficult topic, the best plan is to think about it with very great intensity—the greatest intensity of which I am capable—for a few hours or days, and at the end of that time give orders, so to speak, that the work is to proceed underground. After some months I return consciously to the topic and find that the work has been done. Before I had discovered this technique, I used to spend the intervening months worrying because I was making no progress; I arrived at the solution none the sooner for this worry, and the intervening months were wasted, whereas now I can devote them to other pursuits."

A similar process, he observes, can be used for anxieties. "When some misfortune threatens, consider seriously and deliberately what is the very worst that could possibly happen. When you have looked for some time steadily at the worst possibility and have said to yourself with real conviction, 'Well, after all, I can face it if I have to,' you will find that your worry diminishes to a quite extraordinary extent. It may be necessary to repeat the process a few times, but in the end, if you have shirked nothing in facing the worst possible issue, you will find that your worry disappears altogether and is replaced by a kind of exhilaration."

Russell goes on to add that "This is part of a more general technique for the avoidance of fear. Worry is a form of fear, and all forms of fear produce fatigue. A man who has learned not to feel fear will find the fatigue of daily life enormously diminished."

Fear, in its most harmful form, Russell says, arises when there is same danger we are unwilling to face. "At odd moments horrible thoughts dart into our minds; what they are depends upon the person, but almost everybody has some kind of lurking fear. With one man it is cancer, with another financial ruin, with a third the discovery of some disgraceful secret; a fourth is tormented by jealous suspicions."

And probably all these people use the wrong technique for handling their fear, trying to think of something else whenever it comes into mind, trying to distract themselves with work or amusement.

But every kind of fear grows worse by not being looked at, Russell emphasizes. "The proper course with every kind of fear is to think about it rationally and calmly, but with great concentration, until it has become completely familiar. In the end familiarity will blunt its terrors; the whole subject will become boring, and our thoughts will turn away from it, not, as formerly, by an effort of will, but through mere lack of interest in the topic. When you find yourself inclined to brood on anything, no matter what, the best plan always is to think about it even more than you naturally would until at last its morbid fascination is worn off."

Fatigue from Physical Disorders

Fatigue, of course, can be associated with a considerable variety of illnesses. Often, other symptoms accompanying the fatigue provide clues as to the particular disease or disorder.

Fatigue with fever is common in infectious illness—such as severe colds, flu, atypical or viral pneumonia, and infectious mononucleosis.

Fatigue with headache may occur in advanced high blood pressure, hepatitis, and infectious mononucleosis.

Fatigue often accompanied by appetite and weight loss, and sometimes leg cramps, prickly numbness of hands and feet, breathing difficulty, and swelling and fluid in the tissues, can develop in vitamin B_1 (thiamine) deficiency.

Vitamin C deficiency can produce fatigue along with one or more other symptoms such as weakness, lethargy, bleeding of gums.

Fatigue also may be present in anemia along with any or several of such symptoms as pallor, weakness, ear noises, heart pounding, loss of libido, breathlessness. The most common anemia in women is iron deficiency anemia, which type occurs much less often in men. When it does develop in men, most often it is not the result of inadequate intake of iron, as in women, but loss of iron through chronic blood loss—as, for example, in peptic ulcer, in which it may be slow and unnoticeable but steady.

Pernicious anemia, about equally divided between men and women, results from lack of a factor in the stomach needed for the absorption of vitamin B_{12} and is effectively treated by administration of the vitamin.

Other anemias in men may develop as the result of sensitivity to various drugs such as quinine (an antimalarial), resorcinol (an antiseptic), sulfa drugs (antibacterials), and phenacetin (a pain reliever). Various chemicals such as benzine and naphthol may be responsible. Clues to the causes may appear in the blood samples studied microscopically and in the history of exposure to various agents. Often, the anemia and its symptoms disappear when the cause is identified and eliminated.

Other possible causes of fatigue with anemia include cancer of the stomach, leukemia, all-vegetarian diet deficiencies, and endocarditis, a bacterial infection of the inner linings of the heart chambers.

Hypothyroidism, or underfunctioning of the thyroid gland, can produce fatigue. The disorder may result from many causes including lack of adequate iodine in the diet (iodine is required to produce thyroid hormone), deficient pituitary gland secretion of thyrotropin (which activates the thyroid), wasting of the gland, and in some susceptible people certain drugs and foods (such as cabbage and soybeans).

Although hypothyroidism can be obvious and readily diagnosed when severe, this is not necessarily so in milder cases. When severe, its symptoms may include dry, cold skin, puffiness of hands and face, decreased appetite, weight gain, slow speech, mental apathy, drowsiness, constipation, hearing loss, poor memory. In milder cases, there may be no such overt signs. Tests may include measurement of thyroid hormone level in the blood and the ability of the gland to absorb iodine. A high blood cholesterol level may sometimes be indicative.

Whether mild or severe, the daily use of thyroid hormone preparation is effective treatment.

Fatigue from Depression

Fatigue is a common symptom of the mentally depressed. And mental depression is common—the most common of all psychological ills.

Almost all of us on occasion experience a depressed mood. It often follows loss or separation from a familiar person or place; there are feelings of helplessness and hopelessness which normally subside in a relatively short time. But depression escalates to a serious condition in as many as eight million people a year according to a National Institute of Mental Health survey.

It can be sneaky, wearing disguises, and some studies indicate that elapsed time from onset of symptoms to diagnosis range up to as long as 36 months, during which the depressed, if they receive any treatment at all, may be treated mistakenly for other problems.

In depression, there are a chronic change of mood, an extended lowering of the spirits, a loss of enjoyment of things and activities which, under normal circumstances, make life enjoyable.

Very commonly, fatigue is a major symptom, with easy tiring and lack of drive.

Other major reactions may be experienced (rarely are all present in a particular case) and include difficulty in concentration; sleeping difficulty (particularly a tendency to wake up early feeling exhausted and depressed); remorse over not having done things that should have been done or having done what should not have been done; guilt, with feelings of being unfair to family, friends and others; indecision about major matters and even at times about the most simple; reduced sexual activity; general loss of interest and indifference to people, things and ideas once of importance; irritability and impatience; suicidal thoughts.

In addition, there may be other symptoms, physical ones, and not uncommonly these may overshadow the "blue" mood, so that attention concentrates on them. If medical help is sought, it may be for the physical problems with no mention of the others.

Headaches are common, occurring in about 80 percent of cases. They tend to be worse in the morning than in the evening, often resisting all usual remedies. Appetite loss is frequent. Gastrointestinal complaints can be diverse. Depression often is responsible for abdominal pains and complaints of gas. Some depressed people suffer severely from digestive upsets, nausea, vomiting, constipation or diarrhea and may be mistakenly thought to have ulcers or colitis.

Depression also may cause urinary frequency or urgency, sometimes accompanied by burning and pressure sensations in the bladder area. Some of the depressed experience heart palpitations, chest constriction, and pain in the area of the heart and may believe they have heart disease. Others may experience visual disturbances, ear noises, mouth dryness, numbness or tingling sensations, and skin blotches. In some cases, there is difficulty in breathing, which may arouse fears of lung cancer or emphysema.

Such physical disturbances have come to be called "the somatic mask of depression." They often can be relieved effectively with antidepressant medication.

A considerable variety of antidepressant agents are available today. They include imipramine (Tofranil), desipramine (Elavil), protriptyline (Vivactil), nortriptyline (Aventyl), dosepin (Sinequan), and amitriptyline plus perphenazine (Triavil and Etraton).

Some psychiatrists believe that psychotherapy is essential for cure and that drugs only relieve symptoms. Others consider that drugs help to correct basic malfunctions. The latter acknowledge that depressives, like virtually everyone else, have psychological problems and like everyone else might benefit to some degree from psychotherapy, but psychotherapy obviously isn't practical for everybody and should be reserved for those in whom depression may be complicated by serious neurosis. These psychiatrists also report that often patients find that when depression clears up with drug therapy, most of the other problems become more manageable.

A helpful recent advance, too, is the finding that some depressed patients who do not respond adequately to antidepressants show dramatic improvement with the addition of thyroid hormone to treatment. Among recent studies is one by Dr. Frederick E. Goodwin of the National Institute of Mental Health in which 75 percent of a group of patients unresponsive to standard antidepressant agents improved rapidly when thyroid was added. The hormone was effective, Goodwin reports, even though all of those benefiting had apparently normal thyroid function.

Fatigue and Bipolar Depression

Depressive illness that is all in one direction, down, is known as *unipolar*. But manic, or *bipolar,* depression affects an estimated four million people in this country; they experience episodes of severe depression alternating with periods of great elation (manic behavior). Some in the manic phase are given to flamboyant speech and actions, have feelings of being incapable of doing anything wrong.

Treatment for manic-depressive illness has been discouraging in the past. In their depressed state, patients have often responded to antidepressant drugs. For the manic phase, treatment has relied on electroshock or heavy doses of potent tranquilizing agents. Neither approach has been entirely satisfactory. Heavily sedative, the tranquilizers have kept manics in a kind of chemical straitjacket until the "high" episode departed. Electroshock has produced only temporary benefits. About 75 percent of bipolar victims have had repeated recurrences.

More recently, effective treatment has come from a drug with a checkered past. Lithium was first discovered as an element in nature in 1817. Toward the end of the nineteenth century, lithium salts seemed to break up kidney stones in laboratory test tubes but proved valueless when tried on patients. In the late 1940's, lithium chloride became a popular salt substitute for people on low-sodium diets—until it had to be removed from the market in 1949 because of poisonings.

But in 1949, too, Dr. John Cade, an Australian psychiatrist working with another lithium compound, lithium carbonate, reported that when administered to ten manic-depressives during the manic phase of their illness, it led to normal or near-normal behavior in all within one to two weeks.

By 1967, other Australian and several Danish physicians were reporting similar results. Successful studies followed in the United States, and the drug subsequently became available here for use in manic-depressive illness.

Given in the manic state, it usually controls the manic behavior in five to ten days. It appears to normalize a patient by getting at the underlying chemical problem. Its greatest value is its ability to prevent recurrences not only of the mania but also of the depression. While large doses may be needed for controlling the acute mania, lower maintenance doses are used prophylactically. It also appears to be valuable in some cases of recurrent unipolar depression. Although it does not always eliminate recurrences, it often reduces their frequency and severity.

A Note on Fatigue and What You Eat for Breakfast

A surprising new insight, previously unsuspected, into the fatigue picture indicates that what you eat or fail to eat for breakfast may have much to do with fatigue feelings, fluid retention, or both.

In a study of 138 generally healthy people, both men and women, Dr. Samuel J. Arnold and other investigators in Morristown, New Jersey, found that 79 percent skipped or slighted breakfast, eating at best juice, cereal, bread, and coffee, and getting little or no protein.

Forty-nine of the breakfast-slighters who experienced fatigue, fluid retention, or both, undertook to include in the first meal of the day either the whites of four or five eggs; or fish, meat, or cheese (mozzarella, cottage, or provolone); or artificially flavored gelatins supplemented with at least two tablespoons of brewer's yeast. They also reduced sugar, bread, and cereal intake.

Forty-seven of the 49 experienced clear-cut and, in some cases, dramatic reductions in fatigue and fluid retention.

Urge the investigators: Considering the results, it might be well for physicians to determine what patients have for breakfast and, where necessary, make simple modifications, before undertaking expensive testing, prescribing energizers or diuretics, or implicating psyches.

Sleep and Sleep Problems

Sleep's Purpose

Aptly enough, one of the major investigators in the field has said of sleep science, a relatively young but rapidly blossoming area of research, that "It combines the drama of hunting with the patience of trout fishing."

Concerned with the study of both sleep and sleep disorders, the science has been making considerable progress, but the purpose of sleep is still not definitively established.

Of theories, there are many. Some investigators formulate "single-purpose" and others "multipurpose" theories. Still others postulate that sleep developed during evolution to serve one purpose and that other purposes evolved later to take advantage of a sleep behavior already present.

One view holds that sleep arose originally as a restoring mechanism after periods of exertion. Another holds that it is intended to restore animals in anticipation of preventing fatigue during periods of exertion to follow. In many species, sleep seems timed to permit activity when opportunities to find their particular food are best, with sleep relegated to periods when food would be difficult to find and hunting would be inefficient.

It was once believed that sleep length might be related to length of life. For example, tree shrews, which spend little time sleeping, have 18-month life-spans while bats, which spend five sixths of their lives in sleep, live about 10 years. But a recent, more thorough survey of many species shows no relationship between sleep time and comparative life-span of species.

Could it be, though, that life-span among individuals of the same species is related to sleep time differences? One survey suggests that people who sleep less than six or more than nine hours daily are more likely than others to suffer heart attack or stroke. But this finding may simply reflect the effects of factors that both disturb sleep and predispose to heart and blood vessel disease.

How Much Is Essential

Without adequate sleep, we feel not only physically fatigued but emotionally drained as well. The longest a person can go without sleep, studies have established, is about 240 hours, or 10 days, and volunteers doing that have found the experience a torture. Even after 65 hours without sleep, one volunteer was found in a wash-room frantically trying to wash nonexistent "cobwebs" off his face, convinced he was covered with them.

It's generally assumed that 8 hours is the norm. But investigations reveal a wide range of requirements. One in Scotland, for example, showed that 8 percent of a large sample needed 5 hours maximum, and some got along with less. Fifteen percent needed 5 to 6 hours. The large bulk needed 7 to 8. But 13 percent required 9 to 10, and a few needed even more than 10.

How account for the variations? There have been suggestions that body type is involved: that the endomorph (the soft, fat type of person) sleeps easily and much, while the ectomorph (thin, sensitive and fragile) is prone to insomnia. But there is no definitive supporting evidence.

Scientists, however, wouldn't be surprised if there were a built-in, genetically determined predisposition for more or less sleep. While training and environment are factors in sleep habits as in eating and other habits, still, the old phrase "born that way," referring to genetic inheritance, seems relevant here; i.e., the patterns of sleep many people exhibit or complain about are apparent even in early childhood.

Determining Your Own Needs

One way is to pick a period when you're relatively free of stress— perhaps a vacation period. Go to bed at the same time each night for a period of two to three weeks and get up in the morning without help from an alarm clock. The average length of nightly sleep during such a period is likely to approximate what is normal for you.

The Sleep Stages

Where once it was believed sleep was a state of complete oblivion, now it's known that it's an up-and-down affair, with rhythmic cycles.

As you close your eyes in preparation for sleep, body temperature begins to fall and brain waves show what's called alpha rhythm, a frequency of about 9 to 13 per second. You're still awake but beginning to move into sleep. In stage I sleep, the pulse slows, muscles relax, brain waves slow to 4 to 6 cycles a second; this is light sleep.

In stage II, medium deep sleep, brain waves grow larger and slower. After about 30 minutes, you move into stage III, and the waves slow still more. Deepest sleep, stage IV, comes next but lasts only about 20 minutes, after which you move toward lighter sleep again. As you do you may make some movement, turn in bed, and you reach, almost but not quite, the consciousness level. Now your eyes begin to move under closed lids much as they do when you watch a movie. At this point, you are dreaming, and if you were to be awakened immediately, you would recall the dream clearly. After about 10 minutes of this rapid eye movement (REM) sleep—dreaming sleep—you start the whole cycle over again. Each cycle takes about 90 minutes.

Dreaming appears to be essential. Why is something of a mystery yet. When investigators have wakened subjects every time they started to dream, as shown by REM, but let them sleep at other times, impaired physical and psychological functioning followed.

One theory about dreaming, suggested by a distinguished British psychologist, Christopher Evans, holds that it is a surface manifestation of a complex brain process in which "bits" of information gathered by day are moved from short- to long-term sensory circuits. Somewhat like a computer, Evans believes, the brain has to go "off-line," disconnecting itself from controls, before it can reshuffle the information. If it failed to do so and the reshuffling took place while the brain was awake, what we experience during sleep as gentle dreams might become hallucinations. In fact, Evans suggests, many nightmares may occur when the brain accidentally comes "on-line" during the transfer process.

Sleep Habits and Personality Traits

Do sleep habits reflect personality traits? So it seems from studies of short and long sleepers by Dr. Ernest Hartmann at Boston State Hospital's sleep laboratory. The studies covered men who habitually slept less than 6 hours and others who habitually slept more than 9.

Typically, Hartmann found, the man who sleeps less than 6 hours is likely to be smooth and efficient, a hard worker, extroverted, self-assured, decisive, socially adept, ambitious, content with himself and his life, spending little time in worry, often avoiding problems by keeping busy and denying they exist.

On the other hand, the man regularly needing more than 9 hours of sleep tends to be a nonconformist, opinionated on many subjects, critical of society and politics, given to being something of a chronic worrier, and somewhat insecure. He may be overtly anxious, nonaggressive, somewhat inhibited sexually, not sure of the wisdom of his career choice or life-style.

Hartmann noted that long sleepers' sleep contained about twice as much REM or dream sleep as the sleep of short sleepers. Conceivably, he suggests, they may need to sleep longer and dream more in order to use the greater dream time to resolve psychic problems.

Medical Uses of Sleep Studies

Studies during which subjects are monitored by instrumentation as they sleep in special sleep laboratories are beginning to prove useful for a variety of problems.

IMPOTENCE. Penile erections occur during REM sleep and are normal. In men with psychological impotence, sleep studies show normal REM erection—much greater than in sexual performance. In men with organic impotence, such as that resulting from diabetes, the erections are not as great as in normal men and only as good as that experienced in waking sexual performance. The quality of erection is measured with strain gauges attached to the shaft and tip of the penis. Impotence is often the first symptom of diabetes.

DEPRESSION. Depressed people have lesser amounts of stages III and IV sleep, and the time needed to reach REM sleep (REM latency) is shortened greatly.

There seem to be two types of depressed people. Some do and some do not show a good response to antidepressant drugs such as amitryptyline. Those who do respond also show a return to normal REM latency, normal amounts of total REM sleep time, and less REM as a percent of total sleep time.

Antidepressant drugs such as amitryptyline suppress excessive amounts of REM sleep, and this may be part of their therapeutic action. Some depressed patients have recovered upon being constantly awakened in sleep labs when sleep recordings have shown them to be entering REM sleep. Again, there seem to be two types of the depressed—good and poor responders to REM deprivation therapy. In one study, half of the depressed recovered sufficiently after an average of seven weeks of REM deprivation to be discharged from the hospital. They were deprived of REM by awakenings for six nights out of seven. Only one of those who did not respond to sleep deprivation responded to an antidepressant drug. Most depressives who did not respond to REM deprivation did respond to shock therapy.

HEART AND BLOOD VESSEL DISEASES. An increased number of attacks of anginal chest pain have been found to occur in REM sleep compared with non-REM sleep or with the waking state. In one study, 32 of 39 angina attacks during sleep occurred in REM periods. Routinely, in REM sleep, heart and blood pressure rates increase and become more variable. Physicians are being advised now to avoid giving drugs to cardiovascular patients which are known to suppress REM, such as antidepressants, because REM rebound after drug withdrawal may increase the risk of heart attack, angina, or stroke.

ULCERS. During REM sleep, duodenal ulcer patients have been reported to secrete 3 to 20 times the usual amount of stomach acid. And for ulcer patients, too, physicians are advised to avoid REM sleep-suppressing drugs because of possible later intensification of ulcers during REM rebound after drug withdrawal.

MIGRAINE AND CLUSTER HEADACHES.   Migraine and cluster head-ache attacks tend to occur and awaken the patient during or near REM sleep. Because a body chemical, serotonin, is believed to be involved in triggering REM sleep, methysergide, a drug known to antagonize serotonin, may be prescribed as a preventive of night-time attacks.

Some New Insights into Insomnia

According to some surveys, about half of all Americans over 15 years of age have complained about sleeping difficulty at some time in their lives. About 15 percent say they have chronic trouble, and another one third have recurrent episodes of insomnia.

Seeking to find out more about the sleep of insomniacs and how it differs from that of others, Dr. Ismet Karacan and colleagues at the University of Florida's sleep labs carried out an EEG (electro-encephalogram) or brain wave study with 10 chronic sufferers—8 men and 2 women, aged 30 to 55—and 10 other people, matched for age and sex. The subjects spent several nights in the lab, going to bed and getting up in the morning as they pleased.

The picture for the insomniacs: they took longer to fall asleep, slept a shorter length of time, and lay in bed awake longer in the morning than the others. Although it was expected that the in-somniacs would experience much more wakefulness during the night, there was no actual difference between the two groups in amount of time spent awake after once getting to sleep. It appears that normal sleepers have no recollection of brief awakening periods during the night, but insomniacs, who have difficulty getting to sleep or who awaken early in the morning, remember the loss of sleep well.

Insomniacs also experienced more dream sleep than the others. The intervals between episodes of dream sleep for the insomniacs averaged 58 minutes versus 69 for the others. Insomniacs also took longer to get into deep-sleep stages—60 minutes versus 29 for normal sleepers—and often obtained less deep sleep.

Some New Insights into Sleeping Pills

In a single recent year, five million prescriptions were filled for just one of the more popular of the thirty or so kinds of sleeping preparations available. Yet recent studies indicate that continued use of many of the most widely prescribed pills may only make matters worse.

Some uncertainty has existed about whether "hangover" effects of sleeping pills may be real or imaginary, but a careful investigation at London's Institute of Psychiatry has established that such effects occur even in patients not especially aware of them.

Twelve and 18 hours after using sleeping pills, subjects were given reaction-time and other tests for mental functioning. Regardless of the type of pill used, definite impairment of functioning could be detected in every subject. And although many subjects thought that the tablets "generally improved" the quality of sleep and did not diminish their alertness when awake, the study found that they were simply unaware of their impaired performance.

Moreover, sleeping pills soon lose their sleep-inducing efficacy and may actually impair sleep. When sleep patterns of 10 patients who had been using sleeping pills for months to years and who, despite continued use of the drugs, suffered from persistent insomnia were monitored in a sleep lab and compared with those of 15 other insomniacs not taking drugs, the drug users turned out to have significantly more disturbed patterns than the others. The pill users had fewer periods of REM sleep, as much or even more difficulty falling asleep or staying asleep, and all told had longer periods of wake time.

A phenomenon associated with chronic sleeping-pill use—drug-withdrawal insomnia—accounts for continued use. Upon attempting to suddenly stop taking pills, the insomniac experiences an increase in disturbed sleep, more frequent and intense dreams, and nightmares. Researchers advising physicians about how to help such patients urge that the drug be withdrawn gradually at a rate of one dose every five or six days.

Overcoming Insomnia by Learning How to Fall Asleep

Among their other activities, sleep researchers are beginning to study the relationship between insomnia and bad sleeping habits and how such habits may be corrected.

One researcher, Dr. Richard R. Bootzin of Northwestern University, Evanston, Illinois, considers misuse of the bed to be an especially pernicious habit and provides patients with specific instructions on overcoming it.

A typical case: A man who for four years had gone to bed nightly at midnight and had been unable to get to sleep until three or four A.M., stewing about job, financial, and other problems to the point of often turning on TV to try to stop the stewing.

Bootzin's instructions: Go to bed only when tired, and once in the bedroom, no TV watching, reading or worrying. If sleep doesn't come within a short time, leave bed and room and return only when you're ready to try to fall asleep again. If you still don't succeed, get out of bed and out of the room again, and keep repeating the process until you do get to sleep quickly after getting back to bed. No matter weekdays or weekends and how much sleep you get, set the alarm for the same time every morning. The body needs rest; a regular schedule will help get it.

Typically, the patient in this case had to leave the bedroom four and five times a night. But after two weeks of increasingly associating the bedroom with sleep rather than worry, reading or TV viewing, he was getting two to four hours more sleep a night and at the end of two months was leaving the bedroom no more than once a week.

At another sleep center, insomniacs are instructed to establish a regular hour for retiring and also not to remain in bed if they don't fall asleep. Additionally, they are encouraged to gradually increase activity and exercise levels during the day but not near bedtime hours. Investigators there have found that exercise just prior to bedtime has an exciting effect, but exercise some hours before sleep increases stage IV sleep.

"Nature's Sleeping Pill"

For some years, sleep researchers, particularly Dr. Ernest Hartmann of Boston State Hospital, have believed that there might be some natural hypnotic substance used by the body in producing and regulating sleep.

If there were such a substance, it would have to be one readily available either in food or through natural body processes. It would also have to be shown to produce a normal night of sleep by scientific measurement and to do so at doses equivalent to those that might occur naturally.

L-tryptophan, a naturally occurring amino acid, one of the building blocks of protein, appears to fill the bill. It is present in various foods such as milk, meat, and green vegetables and from one-half to two grams are consumed daily in a normal diet.

In experimental studies in man, the most common side effect of the substance in pure form proved to be drowsiness. And in sleep lab studies with subjects who at home needed 15 minutes or more to fall asleep, that time was halved by a dose of one gram. Moreover, all-night sleep records showed that L-tryptophan produced normal sleep.

L-tryptophan, Hartmann suspects, could well play a role in drowsiness after eating; the usual explanation that blood leaves the head and goes to the gut has never appeared to be very sound.

More recently, too, to test the theory that L-tryptophan may act as a natural sedative, Drs. Clinton Brown of Johns Hopkins and Althea M. I. Wagman of the Maryland Psychiatric Research Center in Catonsville, Maryland, chose 12 insomniacs who often had to spend up to an hour falling asleep. Over a two-week period they reported to the center where, before retiring, they received tablets of L-tryptophan or an inert placebo for comparison.

The insomniacs fell asleep twice as fast with L-trytophan as with placebo and slept about 45 minutes longer than usual without any disturbance in normal stages of sleep.

Dr. Wagman foresees the possibility of early marketing of L-tryptophan as a sleeping pill. Meanwhile, she notes, the traditional home remedy for sleeplessness, a glass of warm milk, contains L-tryptophan.

Sleep Disorders

Sleep disorders of various types afflict a significant number of people. Some contribute to insomnia; some produce other difficulties. Some, such as bed-wetting and night terrors, rarely if ever occur in adulthood. Others, such as sleep apnea (with its frequent cessations of breathing during the night), painful nocturnal erections, and restless legs, are far more common than once supposed. Some are only newly appreciated.

The total incidence isn't known. Only a beginning has been made in determining the incidence of even the most common insomnia. It appears, however, from what data are available, that about 20 percent of the total population suffers from a sleep disorder of some kind.

Sleep Apnea: A Hidden Cause of Insomnia

At Montefiore Hospital and Medical Center, New York City, not long ago, a man who had long suffered from insomnia—knowing only that he had many disturbing arousals during the night, not previously knowing that they were caused by cessations of breathing—underwent a tracheostomy procedure. A tiny hole was drilled in his throat so air could bypass his upper airway tissues and thus allow him to breathe normally at night. Finally, his insomnia problem was over.

Sleep apnea is a condition in which breathing stops frequently during sleep, with the cessations lasting 20 seconds or more. It may lead to several hundred brief or sometimes prolonged arousals during the night and may produce a significant insomnia. The victim does not realize that he has these apneic episodes but may complain of insomnia or disturbed sleep. Apnea may also cause sleepers to spend all their sleep in light stage I or stage II of non-REM sleep so that they do not get enough of stages III and IV. Such apneic sufferers complain of excessive daytime sleepiness. Characteristically, too, they are heavy snorers.

Conservative estimates are that apnea may affect at least 50,000 Americans, about 85 percent of them men, usually 40 years of age or older. And because apnea often produces high blood pressure, researchers believe that the incidence of the condition would be found to be far higher if all hypertensive patients were screened for it.

Apnea is easily detected in a sleep disorders clinic with the instrumentation customarily used for measuring sleep quantity and quality. A clue to it may come when an alert physician questions a patient's bed partner to find out if the patient snores especially heavily and with snorting. The loud, heavy, snorting snore is the resumption of breathing after an apneic episode.

Some apnea victims have many short microsleep periods during the day, lasting only a few seconds. They are able to carry out routine repetitive tasks although sleepy but not complex ones. And frequent microsleeps may produce periods of seeming amnesia and inappropriate behavior, with no recall of activities during such periods.

Some apneic patients are difficult to rouse fully from a night's sleep, even by painful stimuli. When they do awaken, they may be disoriented as to place and time and even have problems with visual perception. These "foggy-minded" periods may last 15 minutes to an hour.

Apnea in some cases has been treated successfully with a drug, chlorimipramine, which currently is available in the United States for investigational use only. Sleeping pills are of no value and may make matters worse because they tend to depress the breathing mechanism.

When apnea is severe enough, a tracheostomy may be performed. An opening is made into the trachea, or windpipe, through the skin to bypass upper airway structures that collapse and obstruct during sleep. The patient can close the opening during the day and so speak normally, and open it only at night for sleep.

Narcolepsy: the Always Sleepy Problem

A sleep disorder mainly characterized by frequent, almost irresistible attacks of daytime sleep, narcolepsy may include other symptoms as well. The sleep attacks, as many as 15 to 20 a day, usually last less than 15 minutes each. A second symptom may be cataplexy, a daytime attack of muscle weakness that may last from several seconds to one to two minutes and may cause collapse of the body. A third symptom is auditory and/or visual hallucinations called *hypnagogic hallucinations* because they occur at the onset of, or on waking from, nighttime sleep. A fourth is sleep paralysis, which occurs at the onset of, or on waking from, nighttime sleep and leaves the patient briefly unable to move his muscles.

According to some estimates, there may be half a million or more narcoleptics in the United States and only about one third have been diagnosed, with 15 years the mean time from difficulty to diagnosis. A tendency to narcolepsy appears to be inherited, and close relatives of narcoleptics are 20 times more likely than the general population to develop symptoms.

Typically, in one study of several hundred narcoleptics, all suffered daytime sleep attacks, while 70 percent also had cataleptic attacks. Twenty-five percent experienced hypnagogic hallucinations, and 50 percent suffered sleep paralysis. Only 10 percent had all four symptoms.

In the sleep laboratory, the most common diagnostic feature of narcolepsy is the presence of REM sleep at the very beginning of a nighttime sleep period, whereas in normal people sleep begins with a non-REM period, and REM appears only after about 90 minutes.

One or more of a variety of drugs may be used to help narcoleptics. Stimulants such as methylphenidate, pemoline, and dextroamphetamine may be prescribed to prevent sleep attacks. Drugs such as imipramine or protriptyline may prevent other symptoms.

Isolated Sleep Paralysis

In addition to being a narcolepsy symptom, sleep paralysis may occur alone and may be a separate sleep disorder. As in the sleep paralysis of narcolepsy, the sufferer is only able to move his eyes and to breathe.

Drug treatment does not seem to be indicated. Affected people often can will termination of an attack by vigorously moving their eyeballs, blinking the lids, and following up with movement of facial muscles and then of more distant muscles.

Painful Nocturnal Erections

Although penile erections normally occur in up to 90 percent of REM sleep periods, in some men the erections are painful and often wake them. The cause of the condition is still unknown, and no effective treatment is as yet available. The painful erections have no effect on normal sexual activity.

Nocturnal Myoclonus (Leg Jerking)

Characterized by a jerking movement of the legs every 25–40 seconds during sleep, myoclonus has been estimated to be involved in 10 percent or more of chronic insomnia cases. The attacks often arouse the sleeper for 5 to 15 seconds. In severe cases, there may be 300 to 400 such arousals during the night, and the sleeping partner may move to a separate bed to avoid being kicked. Some sleep investigators believe that the problem may be caused by improper regulation of the REM sleep mechanism that ordinarily suppresses skeletal muscle tone.

Sufferers usually are unaware of the jerking movements. A drug, diazepam, has been used with limited success. In some severe cases, it has reduced the number of wakings to 20 to 40 a night and has reduced the intensity of the jerks.

"Restless Legs" and Night Leg Cramps

Cramps of the legs and foot muscles, awakening the sufferer from sleep, is a common complaint for which until recently there has been no really effective method of prevention or treatment. Attacks may be relatively mild and infrequent or may occur several times a night, requiring use of heat and seriously interfering with sleep. Treatments such as muscle relaxants, calcium, and quinine have left much to be desired.

A related problem, restless legs, may occur independently or in association with night leg cramps. It is an uncomfortable feeling requiring continuous movement of the legs and finally a need to get up and walk about. An episode may last for several hours.

Several recent reports promise more or less simple relief for many victims. One suggests that caffeine may be an important factor in restless legs. In one study with 55 patients, all benefited from avoidance of caffeine-containing beverages and caffeine-containing medications, coupled with temporary use of the drug diazepam.

Meanwhile, without regard to caffeine, Dr. Samuel Ayres, Jr., Emeritus Professor of Medicine at the University of California at Los Angeles, has reported the value of vitamin E in both restless legs and night leg cramps.

Ayres, a dermatologist who ordinarily would not be concerned with such problems, had a personal interest: both he and his wife were victims of leg cramps, his occurring every five or six weeks, sometimes lasting nearly half an hour, and his wife's occurring several times a week and often several times in a single night.

The possibility of vitamin E as a remedy was suggested fortuitously. A patient being treated with it for a skin problem remarked that since he had begun to take E he had stopped having nocturnal leg cramps which had bothered him for many years.

When both Ayres and his wife tried the vitamin and had a prompt response, he began to make a hobby of the study of muscle spasms. Not long ago, Ayres summarized his experiences with vitamin E in 125 consecutive patients with nocturnal leg cramps.

Of the 125 with cramps, 103 experienced complete or almost complete relief; 20 showed a good to moderate response; only 2 failed to benefit. The cramps had been present for more than five years in 68 cases, were considered severe in 81, and occurred nightly or oftener in 35.

Of 9 patients with restless legs of long duration, including 2 of his own office employees, complete control was achieved in 7; there was 75 percent control in 1, and 50 percent control in 1.

Ayres prescribes vitamin E—in the form of *d*-alpha-tocopheryl acetate or succinate—in doses of 400 international units from one to four times daily before meals. Patients with hypertension or heart problems, or diabetics on insulin, he reports, should be started on much smaller doses. Inorganic iron should be avoided because it combines with and inactivates vitamin E—and this includes vitamins containing iron, and white bread or cereals fortified with iron. Frequent laxatives and mineral oil also are to be avoided. According to Dr. Ayres, there have been no undesirable side effects of vitamin E therapy.

Other Sleep Disorders

A considerable variety of sleep problems are being separated out as entities as the result of the increasing research being carried out in sleep laboratories.

One, for example, the *Kleine-Levin syndrome,* involves periods of severe daytime sleepiness, excessive eating, and excessive sex drive. A drug, lithium carbonate, used in some cases of depression, has been successful in preventing the attacks in some patients.

Another, the *subwakefulness syndrome,* involves frequent micro-sleep periods during the day despite normal amounts of undisturbed nighttime sleep, with sufferers experiencing apparent lapses of memory and difficulty in concentration. The disorder appears to be a defect of the arousal mechanism of the brain. Studies are under way to evaluate the usefulness of a drug, dihydroxyphenylalanine (DOPA).

Some people with excessive daytime sleepiness have been found to have abnormally high levels of a chemical, 5-HIAA, in their cerebrospinal fluid. The chemical is a precursor of the nervous system transmitter substance, serotonin, and its presence in abnormal amounts in the cerebrospinal fluid may indicate higher amounts of serotonin than normal in the brain. Such patients have been treated successfully with inhibitors of serotonin such as methysergide, a compound sometimes used for migraine.

And the list of separate sleep disorder entities keeps growing—a good thing since it promises more effective, specific treatments.

If You Have a Sleeping Problem

Until very recently, insomnia and sleep disorders have received short shrift. Sleep disorders have often gone unrecognized. Insomnia has been treated almost entirely with sleeping pills. The typical physician, according to a recent report, has spent three minutes on insomnia complaints and then has prescribed pills without investigating the causes.

The results of pill use: probably more harmful than helpful. Emphasizes a recent commentary in the *Journal of the American Medical Association:*

"Once regular use of hypnotics begins, giving them up becomes arduous. Regular use might be more reasonable were they more than temporarily effective. Unfortunately, however, chronic hypnotic use does not get the patient to sleep any faster but rather increases nightly awakenings, abolishes deep sleep, and continues to affect sleep patterns for five weeks after drug withdrawal. The ready drug prescriptions available, it seems, not only have led to a scourge of drug habituation, but may well have lessened the quality of sleep obtained by insomniac patients. Additionally, it has bolstered the unrealistic notion that one ought first to resort to drugs to alleviate chronic insomnia. The patient relying on hypnotics is often left with his original insomnia plus a drug problem."

What should go into investigating a case of insomnia or sleep disorder?

If you have a problem, your awareness of the facts just presented may give you a clue to its nature. Additionally, an alert family physician or internist should seek to uncover possible medical, behavioral, or emotional causes.

A medical examination may reveal an allergic condition such as asthma; an endocrine disorder such as hyperthyroidism; a painful disease such as angina, ulcer, or arthritis; or a neurological disturbance. In such cases, the medical disorder needs to be brought under control.

Questioning by the physician of a sleeping partner may elicit reports of kicking in bed; stoppages of breathing; or loud, snorting, intermittent snoring. Emotional problems from dissatisfaction in work, marriage, or family life may be detected in interviews. The physician himself may be able to help with some of these.

USE OF A SLEEP DISORDERS CLINIC.   When a patient is referred to a sleep disorders clinic for more thorough evaluation, his medical history will be obtained together with results of any recently performed physical examination and laboratory tests. The clinic may send the patient a diary to be kept for several weeks in advance of his visit, with notations about his sleep-wake habits, hours of work, diet, any drugs being taken.

At the center there may be further tests and studies. Polysomnogram (electronically monitored) sleep studies may follow. Sometimes, sleep recording of a daytime nap may be all that is needed. All-night sleep recordings for several nights may be required to identify, for example, the type and severity of sleep apnea. In rare cases, several days of 24-hour recording may be needed.

The clinic can then recommend or perform such procedures as prescription of medication for the diagnosed problem, withdrawal of some medications already being used, and in special cases a tracheostomy if indicated for a severe sleep apnea. Clinic physicians also can continue to consult with the patient's own physician for extended management of the sleep complaint.

The American Association of Sleep Disorders Centers—and more and more such facilities are being set up in university and other major medical centers—has established minimal standards of facilities, personnel, and capabilities for membership. It will furnish a list of accredited centers to referring physicians.

One night in a sleep laboratory costs about $200 to $300. Unfortunately, insurance does not always cover the expense, at least not as yet, although that may change as the significance of sleep disorders continues to be increasingly recognized.

3
Getting Fit...Keeping Fit... Sports Medicine Tips

"Ready, Set, Sweat"

It has been called a startling development for a nation that has invented electric golf carts and even pushbutton car windows. Viewing the phenomenon, one weekly newsmagazine not long ago pronounced: "Now physical fitness is upon us like a wet spaniel." According to some surveys, a record 87.5 million American adults, 18 and over, now claim to engage in athletic activity, some with quixotic resolve, some with evangelistic fervor and tenacity, some considering it fun, some regarding it as a struggle, all convinced that there is something to owning a healthy body.

One very visible sign of the fitness boom: some 8 million joggers observable in big city parks and even on sidewalks as well as suburban byways. Plus an army of runners, some 29 million tennis enthusiasts, almost half a million platform tennis players, 3 million racquetball activists. And more and more major U.S. companies urge, almost to the point of compulsion, at least executives to pour out some sweat in often-lavish in-plant facilities, with many opening up facilities for lesser employees.

There are now books galore—more than 1,000—on fitness, a $2-billion-a-year supply industry, and testimonials to benefits that range from cures for insomnia and impotence to altered states of consciousness, Zen-like peace, and "a super feeling, like being immortal."

But accompanying all this: no small amount of confusion and some hazards and even downright dangers.

How It Helps

That physical exercise and fitness can provide many benefits and improve the quality of life seems clear enough.

Exercise can help significantly in removing excess weight—not startlingly at a 2-pound-a-week rate or anything like that (unhealthy, anyhow), but at a consistent and valuable rate—and it can help significantly as well to keep weight at an ideal level. It also alters the composition of body tissues, increasing the proportion of muscle and decreasing the proportion of fat.

Vigorous physical activity is a good, perhaps the best, antidote for mental and emotional tension; it is difficult, if not impossible, to remain tense during vigorous activity.

With regular physical activity, muscles that may have been weak and sagging become stronger, better toned. Along with an increase in muscular strength and endurance, there may also be an increase in coordination and joint flexibility, leading to a marked reduction of minor aches and pains. Postural defects, too, may be corrected and there is likely to be an improvement in general appearance. Feelings of listlessness and fatigue are likely to be replaced by sensations of alertness and energy.

The human body is reported to be capable of generating 14 horsepower with maximum effort. It generates only 0.1 horsepower at rest. In sedentary people, there is some muscular atrophy, or wasting away. Undermuscled for their weight, they may lack the strength and endurance needed even for sedentary work. In addition, it has been suggested that the unused horsepower, so to speak, may go into building up tension, with the tension then becoming a factor in producing fatigue and sometimes other complaints as well.

Sometimes, it is possible to obtain new or added insights into the value of something by depriving people of it. At the State University of New York Downstate Medical Center, Brooklyn, Dr. Frederick Baekeland carried out one such deprivation study. His subjects: 14 normal college students accustomed to regular exercise. Baekeland monitored their sleep in a sleep laboratory on nights during a period when they were engaging in their customary exercise, and again on several nights during a one-month period when all exercise was prohibited. Not only did the subjects complain that they didn't sleep as well during the month without exercise; the monitoring with instruments showed clear changes in the pattern of sleep indicating increased anxiety. Baekeland also noted that during the month without exercise, the students experienced increased sexual tension.

It has been observed that if man, sociologically speaking, has become a pushbutton modernist, he nevertheless remains, physiologically speaking, a caveman—and for maximal health he needs exercise; his whole body is keyed to it.

The Heart Protection—and Life-Prolonging—Questions

Does exercise prevent heart attacks? Does it improve the chances of surviving a heart attack? Does it prolong healthy life?

Unfortunately, the answers to these questions are not definitively established. There are intimations that the answers may be yes but no solid scientific proof.

True, many studies—those in England with bus drivers and conductors on double-deckers (page 153), others here in the United States with longshoremen (page 153), and still others—indicate that people who exercise heavily seem to have fewer heart attacks and live longer than others leading more sedentary lives. But such studies fall short of providing a conclusive answer. A question that remains is whether such people are healthy because they exercise or whether they exercise because they are healthy.

Numerous studies have indicated that heart patients in medically supervised exercise programs have fewer recurrences of heart attacks on average than similar patients not in such programs. But a question remains of whether the benefits are all the result of exercise or come, too, from overall changes in life-style such as dieting and giving up smoking.

But if clear-cut answers are not yet available, many physicians and investigators who believe in the protective value of exercise can and do point to clear evidence of what exercise of the right kind actually does for the heart and blood vessel system.

Exercises such as jogging, running, swimming, and bicycling encourage the heart to work hard, and the heart muscle, as with a muscle anywhere else in the body given exercise, increases in strength. After a sufficient period of exercise training, the heart muscle efficiency increases—and the heart can pump more blood with less effort. Moreover, as it pumps out more blood with each stroke, it can rest comparatively longer between beats.

A "cardiovascularly fit" person has a lower heart rate even when he is not being active—and can exercise vigorously for a long time without feeling tired and can respond to sudden physical or emotional demands without his heart racing or his blood pressure shooting up precipitously.

Exercise training also tends to produce some lowering of blood pressure and of the level of fats (triglycerides) in the blood. It also reduces the tendency of the blood to form clots that could trigger a heart attack.

Certain other possible benefits of exercise have not yet been proven. They include the development of collaterals (supplemental blood vessels to the heart), so that if a main vessel is blocked by a clot, the heart muscle would still receive blood and oxygen. Another is the expansion of existing coronary vessels feeding the heart, so that if a clot did form and produce some blockage, it would be less likely to be complete, shutting off all flow through the vessel.

On the basis of the established benefits, an increasing number of physicians along with the American Heart Association are convinced that exercise is wise, prudent.

How It Can Hurt

Rushing into jogging or any other vigorous activity, including tennis, racquetball, and other demanding sports, can be dangerous to anyone not in good physical condition—for one thing, because of the considerable likelihood of sprains, strains, and other injuries in the unfit.

It can be especially dangerous for people with already damaged hearts and fat-clogged arteries. Many men over the age of 35 have coronary artery disease even though it is still "hidden," its presence not yet manifested by symptoms. A sudden exercise spurt may throw the heart rhythm out, triggering a heart attack.

Others for whom sudden, strenuous exercise could be particularly dangerous include those with untreated high blood pressure, congestive heart failure, uncontrolled diabetes, or skeletomuscular diseases.

The First Step

As a general rule, anyone over 35 should undergo a stress test before embarking on an exercise program. The test involves peddling a stationary bike or walking vigorously on a treadmill while your breathing, blood pressure, and the electrical activity of your heart are monitored. It measures the body's capacity for effort and detects otherwise silent heart disease that may not yet have signaled itself in daily life and may not be detectable by tests taken at rest.

If the heart has difficulty under the burden of increased activity, the stress test may produce chest pain, a change in the heart's electrical activity as shown on the electrocardiogram, blood pressure changes, or breathlessness. That doesn't mean that an exercise program cannot be undertaken. Exercise, in fact, may be prescribed as part of treatment. It does, however, indicate urgently that exercise should be undertaken with medical guidance.

More and more physicians now give the stress test in their offices, and many believe that it should, in fact, be part of a regular checkup for people over 45 whether or not they exercise.

Many community hospitals as well as medical centers and a number of private organizations currently provide medically supervised exercise programs for heart patients and for the general public as well. They offer stress testing, followed by an expert evaluation of individual exercise capabilities and a prescription in detail for exercise conditioning.

The principles used in prescribing are applicable, too, if you've received a go-ahead after a medical checkup which has included stress testing and plan to undertake a conditioning program on your own.

The Buildup

An exercise program should start slowly and over a period of weeks or months should gradually increase in strenuousness until a level that conditions the heart is reached. This conditioning level corresponds to about 70 to 85 percent of your maximum heart rate. Your physician can tell you your maximum heart rate on the basis of the stress test, or you can approximate it by subtracting your age in years from the number 220, assuming you are in good health.

Thus, if you are 45, the maximum rate would be 175. And, accordingly, the heart rate to be aimed for in your exercise program—your "target zone"—would be 70 to 85 percent of that, or in the range of 122 to 148 beats a minute. Within that range, you would be exercising at an appropriate level; below it, there would be little if any conditioning effect; above it, the burden on the heart could be excessive and dangerous.

Determining whether you've reached your target zone is simple enough, although it may be awkward at first and does take a little practice.

The heart rate, or number of heartbeats per minute, is generally the same as the pulse rate. So you can arrive at your heart rate by taking your pulse. A common way to do that is to press the index and middle fingers of one hand on the upturned wrist of the other hand at the thumb side where you can feel the pulse beat.

Count the number of pulse beats that occur in exactly 10 seconds, preferably using a watch with a large sweep second hand. Then multiply the number of beats by 6. The pulse rate should be taken within the first 15 seconds after stopping exercise.

If you are out of condition, you will find that it takes relatively little vigorous activity in the beginning to raise your pulse rate to the target zone. But as you go along and your conditioning improves, you will be adjusting your exercise program every few months, finding it necessary to work harder to bring your pulse rate into the target range because your cardiovascular system is becoming increasingly efficient and able to tolerate exercise with fewer heartbeats.

Which Exercises?

The kinds of exercises valuable for the heart are those involving sustained, repetitive, rhythmic motion such as jogging, bicycle riding, and swimming. Static exercises, which involve short, rapid, forceful movements, such as weight lifting and isometrics (in which muscles are tensed but held in relatively fixed position), can certainly strengthen the particular muscles involved and may improve your build but have little if any helpful effect on the heart, since they don't provide the steady, sustained effort needed for cardiovascular conditioning.

Generally, all exercises or activities that call for frequent and repeated use of large muscle groups can be valuable for cardiovascular conditioning. In addition to jogging, biking and swimming, they include running, running in place, brisk walking, rowing, rope-skipping, stationary cycling, and a number of sports.

Sports such as golf, bowling, softball, and baseball are unlikely to be of much value because they involve long pauses or only occasional vigorous efforts. On the other hand, sports that involve considerable running or repeated continuous movement can be valuable and these include basketball, handball, squash, skating, hockey, cross-country skiing, soccer, and hiking. Tennis? Yes, if it's a fast-paced singles match between players of comparable ability. But doubles or slow-paced singles may not help much. The right kind of calisthenics can be useful—not slow bending and stretching but continuous, rhythmic.

Brisk walking is not to be pooh-poohed. It can provide effective conditioning, especially for those in poor physical condition and for elderly people.

How Often?

Virtually all physiologists and other experts agree that exercise programs should be carried out at least three times a week, with no more than two days between workouts. This frequency is effective for both building fitness and maintaining it. For the first half year or so of training, it may be best not to exceed this frequency; going beyond may in some cases lead to muscle and joint discomfort. After that, you can if you like—and many men, once accustomed to training, find it no chore at all but rather pleasurable—exercise every day.

How Long?

A workout generally should run 30 to 50 minutes, including a warm-up period of 5 to 10 minutes and a cool-down period of 5 to 10 minutes.

The Warm-Up

A gradual warm-up, using light exercises, is important for several reasons.

Muscles themselves are limbered. The heart and lungs are prepared for exercise, given a chance to get ready to function more effectively.

At the same time, the central nervous system is tuned up. Many muscles of the body are paired. One of a pair works in one direction; the second, in the opposite direction. One muscle, for example, bends the knee or elbow; a second straightens the knee or elbow. If one muscle is to move efficiently and safely, without undue strain and risk of injury, the other should relax its tension properly. The nervous system controls this and should be readied by warm-up to do so.

In a sense, the warm-up is something like the procedure a pilot goes through after taxiing a plane out to the runway. He guns up the motors, checks responses to controls. By means of simulated load conditions, he brings components up to optimum temperature and pressure ranges. The procedure is for safety. The warm-up similarly is a safety measure.

The warm-up period should extend 5 to 10 minutes. If you're going to jog, for example, you can warm up with calisthenics or by walking, gradually increasing the pace and then breaking into a slow jog. If you're going to be bicycling, you can start leisurely, gradually increasing your effort.

The Cool-Down

No less important than warming up at the beginning is tapering off and cooling down at the end of a workout.

One reason: During active exercise, the heart pumps out more blood than usual to keep muscles supplied. Having brought fuel and oxygen to the muscles, the blood enters the vein system for return to the heart and lungs for refreshening. And, during exercise, the contracting muscles, as they press on the nearby veins, produce a kind of pumping action that helps return the blood quickly to heart and lungs.

If exercise is stopped suddenly, the heart goes on pumping extra blood for a time—but the muscles no longer pump on the veins, blood return is slowed, and blood may pool in the legs, producing temporary shortages elsewhere and leading to faintness.

A second reason: It has been observed that cramps and stiffness are more likely to develop when exercise is halted abruptly. A tapering off period can help prevent these discomforts.

To taper off, just keep moving about in relaxed fashion. Walk about, lazily bend and stretch as you walk, gently move arms. You need 5 to 10 minutes of this.

Don't rush into a hot shower immediately after a workout or even immediately after the tapering-off period. If you go right into the shower, your body temperature will still be up from the exercise, the hot water will impede heat dissipation, and you will come out of the shower still sweating.

Moreover, for a time after exercise, a lot of blood still goes to the legs. If you fail to taper and cool off sufficiently, the hot water will dilate skin blood vessels and may increase the blood pooling effect so that less blood returns to the heart, which then can send only less-than-normal amounts to the brain, and fainting may occur. Sometimes, too, an abnormal heart rhythm may develop.

Allow yourself another 2 or 3 minutes beyond the tapering-off period to cool off, radiating some of the heat you have worked up.

A good rule to follow is to wait before taking a shower until your pulse rate has returned to within 10 to 15 beats of what it was before exercise.

A Starter Program

For the first month or so, it's a wise idea to keep your intense exercise period down to about 10 to 12 minutes, especially if you're over 35 and haven't had regular exercise for several years.

One starter program, which has been used successfully with about 90 percent of people by a New York City facility, Cardio-Metrics, that specializes in medically supervised exercise programs, provides a choice of two sequences: 2 minutes of exercise followed by 2 minutes of relative rest such as slow cycling or walking repeated 6 times or 3 minutes of exercise and 2 of the relative rest repeated 4 times. Joggers, however, are often advised to jog for a minute and walk for a minute, and repeat the sequence 10 to 12 times. Such "interval" training can be just as effective as continuous training and helps to minimize the risk of aches and pains in untrained muscles.

When you have chosen an interval sequence you like, take your pulse immediately after stopping the first 2- or 3-minute interval of exercise. If the rate is in the target zone, fine; maintain that level of exercise. If it is lower or higher, you can accordingly exercise a little faster or slower until the pulse rate is where it should be.

After a period of time, perhaps one or two months, as your cardiovascular efficiency progressively improves, you're likely to find it necessary to work harder during the exercise intervals in order to keep your pulse rate in the target zone. And as you become better conditioned, you can also gradually increase your active exercise time and decrease the relative rest intervals.

Breathing

During exercises against resistance, such as in lifting weights or isometrics, there is a tendency to hold the breath. Don't.

When the breath is held, pressure builds up inside the chest and abdomen. The increased pressure interferes with return of blood from the body to the heart. Then, when breathing begins again, the pressure falls suddenly and decreases heart output. As a result, for a time blood flow to the brain may fall off enough to cause fainting.

During exercise against resistance, the proper procedure is to exhale while exerting force—for example, blow out while lifting a weight—and then inhale on completion, or when the weight is brought down.

This applies to sit-ups, chin-ups, and similar activities as well as isometrics.

Exercising When Sick

Physical exertion should be avoided during and for a few days after an illness, including the common cold.

Physical fatigue is deleterious during poor health. Fatigue can interfere with body defenses and may make an illness worse.

Measures of Fitness

Commonly in the past, fitness was equated with muscularity and eye-popping physique. Emphasis was on achieving an impressive frame, with strength the major goal rather than resilience or stamina.

Not today. The primary goal of the modern fitness approach is cardiovascular health. Even Charles Atlas, who built a thriving business on putting biceps on a stereotype—the bullied, 97-pound, bag-of-bones weakling—took to jogging faithfully and, quite likely, had he lived, would have adapted the new cardiovascular approach in the courses he sold.

How do you know if you're fit or not? Various indications and tests have been suggested.

Often, a trained athlete will have a resting pulse rate below 50 per minute. For a man in good condition, it doesn't have to be that low but it should be less than 70, some believe.

Another suggested measure: Take the pulse immediately after standing quietly in one place for 2 or 3 minutes. If it increases more than 15 beats a minute over the resting pulse rate, or goes above 100, it indicates poor condition.

Another check: Carry out an exercise such as running in place for about a minute, lie down and immediately take the pulse. If it exceeds 100 a minute, it indicates poor condition.

In addition to what it may indicate in terms of fitness, the resting pulse rate, a number of studies suggest, may indicate greater or lesser likelihood of heart attack and of death from other causes.

In the government's famed Framingham Study, which has been following some 5,000 residents of that Massachusetts community for more than 20 years, the heart attack death rate has been almost four times greater for those with pulse rates over 92 than for those with rates less than 67.

Another long-term study in Chicago has been covering more than 1,300 men, all employees of a utility, who were 40 to 59 years old and free of coronary heart disease at the start in 1958. The resting pulse rate was under 70 for 603 men, 70 to 79 for 480 men, 80 to 89 for 161, and more than 90 for 85 men. The 10-year mortality rate per 1,000 has ranged from a low of 8 in the men with the lowest pulse rates to 41 in those with the highest pulse rates for sudden death, from 33 to 82 for deaths from coronary heart disease, and from 98 to 211 for deaths from all causes.

Pulse rate aside, as one useful definition of fitness, Dr. Kenneth Cooper of Dallas, a conspicuous spokesman for the modern fitness approach, posits the requirement of running-jogging-walking a mile and a half in 12 minutes. It's arbitrary yet does provide some kind of norm to measure yourself against.

It sounds easy enough—1½ miles in 12 minutes—especially in an age of sub-four-minute miles. Yet some authorities guess that less than 10 percent of American men over 21 could do it.

To some degree, substantiation for that pessimistic guess is provided by the experience of Life Extension Institute, a New York-based organization concerned with health improvement particularly among many businessmen clients.

In its stress-testing procedure, the institute has a man walk on a treadmill for six consecutive 3-minute periods. The angle of incline and speed of the treadmill increase gradually at the beginning of each period. As a gauge of fitness, the stress test can be considered to roughly approximate covering 1½ miles in 12 minutes. But the experience at the institute is that 80 percent of men tested do not get past even the second period of the six involved in the test. Which would indicate that 80 percent are not fit by any standard and could not begin to meet the 1½-miles-in-12-minutes standard.

Exercise Rehabilitation for Heart Patients

No less than for its possible value in helping to prevent heart trouble, exercise is getting increasing attention as a means of rehabilitating heart patients, including those who have suffered a heart attack.

Although it is not yet clear whether exercise prolongs the life of a man with coronary heart disease, several studies suggest a beneficial effect and most researchers agree that the quality of life is improved, sometimes markedly.

Until recently, less than half of the 600,000 patients each year who survive heart attacks have been successfully rehabilitated. Exercise, when properly used for heart patients, has been found to allow for increased heart efficiency, with beneficial effects on blood fat levels, high blood pressure, and glucose intolerance, and with improvement in the state of mind and the ability to relax.

Even more so than for others, for heart patients dynamic or isotonic exercise, where muscles change length, is preferred over static or isometric exercise where there is no motion but only a change in muscle tension. The major problem of static exercise is reduced blood return through the veins, which can be hazardous in a man with coronary heart disease.

After a heart attack, many physicians now favor beginning rehabilitation when pain is no longer present, heart rhythm is normal, and the resting pulse is under 100. That can mean starting leg exercises in bed twice a day as early as the second or third day after an attack. Thereafter there is gradual progression: a couple of days of sitting on the side of the bed or in a lounge chair, arm exercises about the sixth day, walking around the bed about the eighth day, walking about the room two or three times daily by the tenth day, walking in the corridor twice a day by the twelfth day, and walking 50 yards twice a day by the fourteenth day. The early rehabilitation program is guided by comparing the evening resting pulse rate with the morning resting pulse rate to see that the former does not exceed the latter by more than 20 percent.

Three to four weeks after a heart attack, an intermediate program may be started. It consists of walking twice daily possibly supplemented by other moderate activities. Usually, care is taken to see that no activity is begun sooner than 45 minutes to an hour after a meal, that the pulse rate does not exceed 100 per minute, and that any fatigue associated with activity disappears in a reasonable time (10 to 20 minutes). Many physicians consider it safe for sexual relations to be resumed.

After 10 to 12 weeks, a patient may be encouraged to participate in a medically supervised walking-jogging program. A stress test is administered, and the exercise program is based on pulse rates of 70 to 85 percent of the maximum heart rate attained during the test. Another stress test may be administered after three months and then yearly.

A home program may be planned for the patient with exertional pulse rates kept below 70 percent of the maximum at the last stress test. In one such program, for example, the patient starts with walking and jogging a mile, with no more than two jogging intervals of one twentieth of a mile each. Jogging then may be increased about once weekly by one twentieth of a mile, until the patient is jogging a mile in 12 to 15 minutes, provided breathlessness disappears and the heart rate returns to resting levels in 12 to 15 minutes. The activity is carried out three to five times a week. All the exercise sessions are preceded by warm-up and followed by a cooling-down period.

There are, of course, variations of such programs.

Sports Medicine Tips

Increasing interest in fitness and sports is bringing more and more expertise to bear on problems associated with athletics and other physical activities. In some countries now—in fact, in most European Communist nations—sports medicine is a recognized medical specialty. Recently, the United Kingdom has become the first western European country to establish a formal qualification in sports medicine.

In the United States, while there is no specialty as such, more and more physicians are interested and there are a number of organizations in the field. The American College of Sports Medicine is currently recognized as the national association for the country. The American Medical Association, too, has an active Committee on the Medical Aspects of Sports.

The result: development of helpful guidelines for physicians, coaches, and participants and useful information that in some cases replaces old myths.

Disqualifying Conditions for Sports

Under what conditions of illness is it unwise to participate in sports? In some given condition, is it okay to engage in one kind of game but not in another?

The AMA's Committee on the Medical Aspects of Sports has taken a hard look at these questions and come up with some helpful tips. It has classified sports into four categories:

Collision: Football, rugby, hockey, lacrosse, etc.
Contact: Baseball, soccer, basketball, wrestling, etc.
Noncontact: Cross-country, track, tennis, crew, swimming, etc.
Other: Bowling, golf, archery, field events, etc.

Except possibly for findings by physicians in individual cases that would indicate otherwise, the committee has these suggestions:

No sports at all if, and as long as, you have an acute infection (respiratory, genitourinary, infectious mononucleosis, hepatitis, active rheumatic fever, active tuberculosis); inadequately controlled diabetes; jaundice; severe pulmonary insufficiency; certain cardio-vascular problems (mitral or aortic stenosis, aortic insufficiency, coarctation of aorta, cyanotic heart disease, recent carditis, or high blood pressure from an organic or physical cause); symptomatic musculoskeletal abnormalities or inflammations; kidney disease.

On the other hand, no type of sport is necessarily barred if you have controlled diabetes; if you have had previous heart surgery for congenital or acquired heart disease and your physician and operating surgeon judge you fit; if you have a controlled convulsive disorder and your physician approves.

All but "other" sports are advised against if you have hemorrhagic disease (hemophilia, purpura, and other serious bleeding tendencies); inguinal or femoral hernia; functional inadequacy of the musculoskeletal system; a convulsive disorder not completely controlled by medication.

Only noncontact and "other" sports are advised if you have only one functioning eye; enlarged liver; certain skin problems (such as boils, impetigo); enlarged spleen; absence of one kidney; previous surgery on the head.

Only collision sports are advised against if you have a history or symptoms of previous severe head injury or repeated concussions.

Athletic Injuries: Heat or Cold?

Even among physicians, there has been some confusion about whether to apply heat or cold for such injuries as contusions, ligament sprains, muscle strains, and fractures.

Cold, by all means, is the treatment of choice; early use of heat may, in fact, have adverse effects, according to physicians and physical therapists at the Milton S. Hershey Medical Center, Hershey, Pennsylvania.

The application of ice controls edema (or swelling) and hemorrhage, and can be an important factor in rehabilitation and return to activity. With cold, blood vessels constrict, then later dilate again. The constriction diminishes hemorrhage through damaged capillaries in the injury area. And with cold, metabolic processes within damaged cells slow down, diminishing need for oxygen and nutrients carried in blood, and the reduction of metabolism reduces the production of edema.

With heat, on the other hand, both blood flow and metabolic rate are increased, increasing inflammation and edema, both undesirable responses.

Whatever the type of injury, ice should be applied immediately, with the ice pack held in place with an elastic bandage wrap for a minimum of 30 minutes.

First Aid

From the Committee on the Medical Aspects of Sports as well as other experts come these suggestions:

BONES AND JOINTS.

Fracture: If there is any suspicion of a fracture of back, neck or skull, no movement; physician needed at once. If a fracture elsewhere, splint and refer to physician. Never force a protruding bone back into place.

Dislocation: Support joint, apply ice bag or cold cloths, refer to physician.

Bone bruise: Apply ice bag or cold cloths, protect from further injury. If severe, refer to physician.

Broken nose: Apply cold cloths, refer to physician.

MUSCLES AND LIGAMENTS.

Bruise: Apply ice bag or cold cloths, rest injured area, protect from further injury. If severe, refer to physician.

Cramp: Stretch the affected muscle gently, massage or have someone else massage it. If a cramp occurs on a hot day, sip dilute salt water.

Strain and sprain: Elevate the injured area, apply ice bag or cold cloths, use a pressure bandage to help reduce swelling, avoid weight bearing, and refer to physician.

BLOWS.

Head: If the blow is followed by disorientation, memory loss, dizziness, headache, incoordination or unconsciousness, refer to physician at once. Keep victim lying down; if victim unconscious, give nothing by mouth.

Teeth: If loosened, do not move, cover with sterile gauze, refer to dentist at once. If completely knocked out of socket, save teeth, refer to dentist at once.

Eye: Apply ice bag or cold cloths. If vision is impaired, however, especially on gazing upward, refer to physician at once.

Testicle: Rest on back, apply ice bag or cold cloths. If pain persists, refer to physician.

Solar plexus: Rest on back, with clothing around waist and chest loosened, moisten face with cool water.

WOUNDS.

Cut and abrasion: Hold area briefly under cold water, cleanse with mild soap and water, apply sterile pad firmly to stop any bleeding, protect with looser sterile bandage. Refer to physician if extensive.

Puncture wound: Treat as for cut and refer to physician.

Heavy bleeding: Apply direct pressure (with pressure bandage if available), elevate area if possible, apply cold to further reduce bleeding. Refer to physician.

Nosebleed: Sit or stand, cover nose with cold cloths. For heavy bleeding, place small cotton pack in nostrils, pinch nose. If bleeding continues, refer to physician.

Blisters: Clean with mild soap and water, protect from further injury. If blister is broken, trim ragged edges with sterile instrument.

HEART ARREST.

When definite heart stoppage has occurred, a sharp blow with the fist to the chest area over the heart may start the heart again.

If not, even as a physician is called immediately, start external cardiac massage and mouth-to-mouth resuscitation.

For external cardiac massage, place heel of one hand on lower half of middle chest, other hand on top of first, and with elbows straight exert firm downward pressure, compressing chest bone $1\frac{1}{2}$ to 2 inches, holding for half a second. Repeat 60–70 times a minute.

For mouth-to-mouth resuscitation, place victim face up, with head tilted back, clear the airway, pinch nose, blow into mouth until chest rises, remove your mouth and let victim exhale. Then replace mouth on his, pinch nose again, and repeat. Repeat 15 times a minute.

If a single person is applying first aid, 15 heart compressions should be alternated with 2 mouth-to-mouth resuscitation efforts. If two people are working, one should carry out the cardiac compression while the second applies mouth-to-mouth resuscitation after every 5 heart compressions.

On Rubberized Warm-Up Suits

Despite a popular notion, wearing rubberized warm-up suits while exercising will not help shed pounds permanently and may be harmful.

During exercise a large amount of heat is produced by the body and should be transferred to the environment, primarily by the evaporation of perspiration, in order to keep body temperature within a tolerable range.

Rubberized clothing can make you sweat more, and some weight loss does occur; but it is only temporary, since the loss is due to dehydration, and weight is regained as soon as the fluid level in the body returns to normal.

Rubberized clothing can be hazardous because it leads to over-heating, causing a large amount of blood to be diverted to the skin for cooling. This, along with excessive fluid loss (through sweating) which leads to reduction in blood plasma volume, puts an inordinate strain on the cardiovascular system.

The Ice Water Myth

A common belief that it's unhealthy to drink ice or very cold water when overheated from exertion or on a very hot day is not valid, acording to two sports-involved American Medical Association consultants. At Alvarado Medical Center, San Diego, Dr. John L. Boyer took body temperatures of subjects after strenuous physical activity and then immediately after they drank large quantities of refrigerated drinking-fountain water in the gymnasium and found no significant temperature change due to the cold water. Observes Dr. Allan J. Ryan of the University of Wisconsin, Madison: "I am aware of no evidence that drinking ice water is harmful to athletes in the course of their participation in sports." Because ice water stimulates rapid emptying of the stomach, brief cramps might result, Ryan notes, but this would not be a serious effect.

Stitch-in-the-Side with Exercise

The sharp pain that may pop up in the liver or spleen area during vigorous physical activity has nothing to do with the liver or spleen and does not mean that activity should be restricted.

Instead, such stitch-in-the-side pain, reports a sports medicine authority, stems from entrapment of gas in the colon and contractions of the colon that occur during exercise when the bowel has not been properly emptied beforehand. If necessary, for people who are particularly susceptible, an intestinal antispasmodic medicine may be prescribed for use one to two hours before starting vigorous activity as a means of preventing the cramping.

Surfer's Ear

Surfer's ear, a bony growth inside the ear canal, can be brought on by exposure to cold ocean water and big waves over a period of years; and if it becomes large enough, the growth can cause a "plugged ear" and can affect hearing. Known as ostosis or hyperostosis, the growth sometimes occurs in active swimmers but is much more severe in surfers because the turbulence of large ocean waves can force more water into the ear canal of a surfer than that of an ordinary swimmer. A surgical procedure for removing the bony growth without damage to the eardrum is now available. It takes a lot of steady surfing—seven to ten years—to develop the growth, and the occasional weekend surfer probably has little risk. If you surf a lot, you can avoid the risk by wearing custom-fitted, molded ear plugs that entirely fill the ear cavities. A small cord should be attached to the plugs and strung around the neck if they should pop out when you turn a flop in a big wave.

Bloodshot Eyes from Swimming

After swimming in chlorinated pools, many people develop bloodshot eyes, and some may also experience burning and tearing for several hours after a swim. But even though chlorinated water, and sometimes fresh unchlorinated water, may inflame the eyes, no instance of permanent eye damage has ever been reported, even among professional swimmers who, in addition to competing frequently, often practice many hours a day. Suggests one physician, a member of the AMA Committee on the Medical Aspects of Sports: putting a few drops of methylcellulose in the eyes is often valuable for relieving irritation and even as a preventive agent to help reduce irritation to a minimum.

Hormones and Athletes

Some athletes resort to taking anabolic steroids—hormonelike compounds related to the male hormone, testosterone—as a means of building muscle and improving performance. But do the compounds help? And can they harm? Physicians knowledgeable in the area report that the steroids often do produce weight gain and muscle growth, but these are due to water retention—and careful studies show no improvement in either physical fitness or athletic performance in those taking the drugs as compared with those not using them. As for risks, there have been some cases of prostate enlargement in young men using steroids in large doses for long periods of time, and occasionally a loss or diminution of libido has been reported.

More on Choosing Your Sport

Not long ago, the President's Council on Physical Fitness and Sports called on seven medical experts to evaluate fourteen popular forms of exercise and rate them in terms of health benefits, based on (1) heart and lung endurance, (2) muscular strength and endurance, (3) flexibility, (4) balance, (5) weight control, (6) muscle definition, (7) digestion, and (8) sleep.

The experts evaluated each form of exercise on the basis of regular participation and vigorous activity—defined as a minimum of four times a week and not less than a half-hour at each session.

They found the following activities, in order, to be the most beneficial:

1. Jogging
2. Bicycling
3. Swimming
4. Skating
5. Handball or squash
6. Skiing—Nordic
7. Skiing—Alpine
8. Basketball
9. Tennis
10. Calisthenics
11. Walking

12. Golfing
13. Softball
14. Bowling

Jogging, running, swimming, and bicycling, of course, as noted previously, are particularly effective for helping to improve cardio-vascular fitness. Skating and other activities can be useful for the purpose, too, when vigorous enough.

Some special notes:

Handball requires fast movement and can be better than tennis in terms of increasing endurance and improving heart function and breathing. It's exacting—not for anyone who is unconditioned.

Skiing uses arm and leg muscles, improves balance and agility. It may not, however, do much for endurance, particularly when downhill runs are short and a chair lift is used. Climbing is a help but some preconditioning is needed to avoid undue stress on the heart. Best for total body strengthening: cross-country skiing, both uphill and down.

Tennis singles can be a strenuous sport. If you haven't played very recently or at all, you would be well advised to do some exten-sive brisk walking and jogging to get both your heart and leg muscles in shape before tackling the game. Tennis can build endurance in skilled players—and even more so in the unskilled, who have to run all over the court reaching for the ball. Doubles tennis tends to be considerably less valuable in terms of endurance; continuous play may help a bit.

Golf is good exercise but commonly doesn't help much in terms of improving physical fitness. Time and motion studies of golfers who played an average of 54 holes a week have shown that only a little more than one third of the playing time was spent walking; and except for a few minutes of hitting the ball, the rest of the playing time was spent waiting—at the tee, on the fairway, on the green. Some studies suggest that it may take 12 hours of golf to produce the same conditioning effect as a one-hour brisk walk. Brisk walking between shots can help. If you want, you can try jogging between shots; some golfers actually do so.

Bowling is fun, good for improving coordination of vision and mind, sometimes helpful for relieving postural backaches that may come from long hours at a desk. But it's too intermittent and not nearly taxing enough to help with endurance and heart conditioning.

4
Sexual Matters

Some Basic Facts and Fancies

SEX AND LONGEVITY. Asceticism, according to an ancient theory, is the father of longevity. Anchorites are reputed to have lived to far-advanced age virtually as a matter of course. The anchorite Paul, for example, is supposed to have achieved age 113, contenting himself with "water, a few dates, and a bit of bread that Providence sent him every day."

There have been numerous advocates, if not of total abstinence, at least of major restraint in sexual activity as assuring long life. All the way back to antiquity, there has been debate about some "best" frequency of intercourse for health founded on the proposition that it's wise not to "squander a given amount of capital energy that cannot be replaced."

Is there any valid scientific evidence that sexual activity leads to an early grave? None. Octogenarians and nonagenarians and even centenarians can be found very much alive and active after a lifetime of anything but abstinence. And there are those who would argue now that, if anything, an active sex life may well be life-prolonging since it may ease, absorb, or compensate for the so-called stresses of modern living.

SEX AND AGE. Must sexual activity stop at some point because of age? No evidence at all that this is so. At least, not because physical aging dictates it.

At the Reproductive Biology Research Foundation, St. Louis,

psychologist Alexander P. Runciman studied the sex lives of 100 men and women ranging up to 89 years of age. His findings: Some of the oldest had plenty of active libido going. Others not sexually active had the physical capacity but were influenced by psychological factors, often using "advanced years" as an alibi for ending sex.

THE PEAKS. Sexual drive for men reaches its peak in early adulthood and gradually declines after that. But for women the peak is not generally reached until the 30's and then remains relatively stable into the 60's or beyond.

Folklore has it that if a newly married man were to put a pea in a jar each time he has intercourse during the first year of marriage, it would take more than five years to empty the jar if, after the first year, he were to take a pea out each time he has intercourse.

WHY MEN PROGRESSIVELY LOSE SEXUAL RESPONSIVENESS. According to some serious research, there are many factors, any one or several of which may operate in an individual man.

Boredom is one. As one investigator puts it: "Year after year a wife may wear the same type of nightgown, and her husband may climb into bed and kiss her in exactly the same way. They may touch each other in the same places for the same length of time. They may say the same things and climax in the same way. They know what to expect. No wonder they lose interest."

According to another investigator, boredom may often stem from the fact that the female partner "has lost sight of the necessity for working at the marital relationship with the same interest in stimulating and satisfying her male partner that she originally may have demonstrated at the outset of marriage." The boredom-inducing wife may have lost herself in the demands of children, social activities, an individual career, or other interests extraneous to marriage.

Preoccupation is another factor. Most men, beginning about age 40 or even before, begin to reach competitive heights in their work, become engrossed in striving for preeminence. They may have less time for marriage. Many, moreover, make no attempt to talk about their occupational concerns at home. With the falloff of communication, sex becomes less and less of a natural occurrence and more and more something requiring a major effort of physical and mental reorientation.

Mental or physical fatigue may be accountable. Either can reduce or eliminate sexual tension and so deter sexual responsiveness.

Overindulgence in food or drink has a tendency to repress sexual interest.

WHAT'S NORMAL FREQUENCY? Popular wisdom holds that a "normal" married couple has sex twice a week on the average, with the peak in frequency occurring at the beginning of marriage and declining to almost none after middle age.

But the patterns of sexual activity among married couples are as varied as the couples themselves.

Recent studies indicate that while intercourse frequency among married couples has generally increased in the past decade, it is common to find couples who share a lot of love but little or no passion or for whom sex has become virtually nonexistent for weeks or months at a time.

Actually, a lot of confusion has arisen from the long-held notion that sex is an instinct, a driving force that has to be satisfied. Ergo, many pepole have worried because they don't seem to be as interested in, and driven by, sex as others. They think there must be something inherently wrong with them. But there may be nothing wrong.

Obviously, biological factors influence sexual behavior. But such terms as "urge," "need," "impulse," suggesting it is all a matter of a driving force, were applied before modern research into human sexual behavior. That research indicates that although sexual behavior may have an instinctive base, it also is very much a matter of acquired taste and habit, considerably dependent upon learning experiences which could account for wide differences in behavior.

Not long ago, in a reassuring talk to a British audience over BBC, Derek Wright, lecturer in psychology at the University of Leicester, pointed out that "If sexual desire is learned and cultivated, then obviously there is no biological standard of sexual behavior against which to assess ourselves. Norms in this matter are completely social. If we want to ignore them, we can. The sexologists have sought to liberate us in the area of our sexual relationships. Now, to my way of thinking, liberation in sex means being able to take it or leave it. The biological-energy idea claims that it's impossible to leave it, but when we recognize that it is to a large extent learned, we begin to realize that it is also a matter of choice whether we have it or not."

"POTENCY CONSUMPTION." Despite some notions to the contrary, intercourse doesn't "eat up" potency and abstention doesn't increase virility. To be sure, intercourse several times a day may decrease the amount of sperm emitted with each ejaculation. But potency isn't exhausted. There may come a point where a rest is needed—more likely from satiation than potency exhaustion.

SOME NEW LOOKS AT MASTURBATION. The long-prevalent idea that masturbation, especially in youth but at any other time as well, can be harmful, producing some kind of physical damage, has long since been outmoded, though it hangs on.

And some sex experts now go beyond the placid reassurance that "it won't harm you if you are moderate about it."

Dr. Philip M. Sarrel of Yale Medical School, joining with Dr. H. R. Coplin of Amherst's psychology department, not long ago wrote in the *American Journal of Public Health:* "Concerning self-stimulation, we disagree with the injunction that 'it won't hurt you if you don't do it too much'—what is too much?—and affirm that for some individuals, women included, it can enhance the development of sexual response; under some conditions it can serve as a substitute for coitus, can temporarily relieve honest sexual tensions, and need not result in self-devaluation."

Dr. William H. Masters, of Masters-Johnson fame, has pointed out that many married men and women masturbate on occasion, for good reason and with no harm done. The reasons may include sickness, separation, just plain impulse. Adds Masters: "We know that many women will masturbate with the onset of their menstrual cycle if they are having dysmenorrhea—severe cramps. An orgasmic experience frequently will relieve the spasm of the uterus and the cramps will disappear. Many women learn this trick. Does it work for all? Of course not, but it helps some women and so they masturbate, which seems sensible."

Virtually everyone has used masturbation. In the original Kinsey studies, 92 percent of all men interviewed owned up to practicing masturbation at some time; 88 percent of unmarried men aged 12 to 20 admitted practicing it. And some 50 percent at age 50 said they masturbated. The practice among women is no less general.

SOCIAL ATTITUDES AND SEXUAL PRACTICES. The first has always influenced the second—often to a startling extent.

Dr. Judd Marmor of the University of California notes that in the first millennium of the Christian era in many parts of Europe, virginity was not prized, marriage was a temporary arrangement, extramarital affairs were taken for granted, incest was frequent, women aggressively invited intercourse, and bastardy was a distinction, implying that some important person may have slept with one's mother.

In feudal times, the feudal lord's prerogative was to deflower any bride, and in some societies all the wedding guests copulated with the bride. Such practices were considered helpful for the marriage because any pain of initial coitus couldn't be associated in the bride's mind with her husband.

"It was not," says Marmor, "until the Medieval Church was able to strengthen and extend its control over the peoples of Europe that guilt about sexuality began to be a cardinal feature of Western life. Even the early Hebraic laws against adultery had nothing to do with fidelity but were primarily concerned with protecting the property rights of a man (the wife being considered property). Married men were free to maintain concubines or, if they preferred, multiple wives; also there was no ban in the Old Testament on premarital sex. The Medieval Church, however, exalted celibacy and virginity. . . . At one time it went so far as to make sexual intercourse betwen married couples illegal on Sundays, Wednesdays, and Fridays, as well as for forty days before Easter and forty days before Christmas. (By contrast, Mohammedan law considered it grounds for divorce if intercourse did not take place at least once a week.)"

Sex and the Heart

Sex involves exertion. It increases blood pressure, pulse rate, and the work of the heart. Any man who is fat, flabby and out of condition, and who tops that off with trying to engage in sex after a big meal with lots to drink, is likely to do a lot of huffing and puffing and maybe even consider the exertion too much of a strain.

But is sex ever too much for the heart, too fatally much? Although "death in the saddle" does occur, it is extremely rare—even among men with heart trouble and a history of heart attack.

Yet, commonly, men with and without heart trouble histories who experience racing heartbeat and physical exhaustion during sexual activity limit the activity for fear of dying during intercourse —and when they do have sex, many either ejaculate prematurely because of anxiety to get it over with or are impotent.

The solution for even the man who has heart trouble and has had a recent heart attack: provided he is physiologically capable, and commonly he is, he should exercise to help condition himself physically to resume his normal sexual pattern.

There has been a growing conviction among many medical men that exercise is valuable for generally lowering the heart rate in the postcardiac patient, but definitive scientific data have been lacking, largely because of practical difficulties presented by such research.

Recently, however, a study in which ECG (electrocardiographic) recorders were used to monitor the coital heart rate of a group of postcardiac men before a four-month exercise training program and after completion of the program has shown that exercise not only significantly decreases the heart rate during sex but also may dispel accompanying anginal (chest) pain as well.

In the research study, carried out by Dr. Richard A. Stein, a cardiologist at the State University of New York Downstate Medical Center in Brooklyn, a group of men 12 weeks after a heart attack and their wives participated. Each couple was told to plan for intercourse on a certain night; and on the afternoon prior, the husband went to the hospital where electrodes were attached to his torso and arms and he was given an ECG recording device to take home. An hour before intercourse, he plugged the electrodes into the device and wore it over a shoulder until retiring, when he could place it on a nearby night table.

After two self-monitoring coital experiences, the men began the exercise program designed to train them. Three times a week they worked out for 30 to 40 minutes—in their cases, for research purposes, on a bicycle ergometer at the hospital. (The bicycle ergometer, a stationary bicycle with adjustable resistance calibrations for various amounts of energy expenditure, is a precise method of measuring and prescribing exactly how much work a heart patient can do before his heart rate reaches a certain level). Periods of three to five minutes of pedaling were interspersed with three to five minutes of rest, an interval method useful in training people in the shortest possible time with the least amount of fatigue and greatest improvement in fitness.

After 16 weeks, the men again monitored their ECG's during intercourse. There was a clear reduction in the peak heart rate during intercourse. There was also a dramatically decreased sense of anxiety and increased sense of confidence on the part of both the men and their wives. Notably, too, some of the men who had experienced anginal chest pains during intercourse prior to training were free of it afterward, and one who had been taking nitroglycerin before coitus to alleviate pain found that he no longer needed it.

Not all heart patients can participate in this kind of exercise program—particularly those with uncontrollable abnormal heart rhythms or certain other problems. But for most, exercise can make a major difference—in general health and fitness as well as in sexual fitness and enjoyment.

If that's true for them, it's certainly likely to be true for other men experiencing sexual difficulties because of having gone physically, but not unalterably, to pot.

Hormones and Sexuality

The relationship between male sexual behavior and the male sex hormone, testosterone, is still far from being an open book.

Some things are clear. Until puberty, the minute amount of testosterone produced by the testes seems to have little sexual importance. In fact—and this may be surprising to many—the levels of the male hormone in the immature boy and girl are approximately the same, accounting perhaps for their rather similar gross bodily configurations.

At puberty, testosterone levels in the boy increase sharply, penis and testes enlarge, motile sperm are produced, bodily growth accelerates, and pubic, facial, and underarm hair sprout.

No question about the importance of the hormone, then, in initiating puberty. But when it comes to its role in adult male health and disease, there are complications and subtleties and fewer hard facts than are needed for understanding.

Again, no question about this: without testicular hormones, the male fails to exhibit sexual behavior. In either a castrated man or a man with hypogonadism, or whenever there is quite obviously inadequate testosterone circulating in the blood, treatment with testosterone will restore sexual behavior.

But what exactly the effects of testosterone are on erection and the many other aspects of sexuality are still unknown. And there is no available evidence to indicate that testosterone blood levels—within the normal range—are correlated with sexual behavior in any fashion.

Some facts come out of rat studies, and they may possibly have some bearing for man. The animal investigations indicate that testosterone acts not only on the genital region but also on spinal cord reflexes and the brain.

At the genital level in rats, testosterone controls growth of the penis, but there is no evidence that penis size in the adult can be increased by hormone treatment.

In rats, and dogs as well, nervous reflexes at the level of the spinal cord are also facilitated by testosterone. Responses in the animals to genital stimulation have been found to be suppressed by castration and restored by testosterone.

In animals, too, specific parts of the brain have been found to be sensitive to testosterone, so that in castrated rats after the disappearance of sexual behavior, implants of the hormone in the sensitive areas restore full ejaculatory behavior.

But what about the relationship between the amount of testosterone and the variations in sexual behavior in a normal population? Does a male who shows a greater amount of sexual activity have higher blood levels of the hormone than one who is less active? Animal studies show that the percentage of the castrated able to reinitiate full sexual behavior increases with increased size of hormone doses, indicating a direct relationship between how much is given and the probability of normal copulatory behavior. But the studies also show that less hormone is needed for sexual behavior than for full growth of such organs as prostate and seminal vesicles. And to many investigators, this suggests that there's a considerable "margin for error" in the amount of hormone needed for sexual behavior.

Rat experiments have thrown some light on impotence and hormone levels—at least in rats. Among healthy, otherwise normal rats, some do not mate; they are "noncopulators." Studies have shown that, to be sure, these rats have lower levels of circulating testosterone than the others—but higher levels than needed to maintain sexual behavior in normal rats that were castrated and then treated with testosterone. The implication, as Dr. Julian M. Davidson of Stanford University points out, is that impotence in the rat may have something to do not only with the amount of hormone circulating but also with low behavioral sensitivity to it.

There are difficulties in relating animal observations to man because in man psychic, social, and cultural influences may be of greater importance than biological ones. Obviously, more intensive investigations in man are needed and are now possible because of the relative ease with which circulating testosterone can now be measured.

Such investigations could provide answers to many questions. For example, after about the age of 50, a decline in sexual capacity in men is fairly common. Some have attributed this to the overall aging process. But testosterone levels are also declining in late middle age. Whether the decrease in hormones at that time is responsible for increasing probability of complete or partial impotence is not yet clear for either animals or men.

Another confusing situation has to do with the possibility that intercourse stimulates testosterone secretion. Several recent studies have suggested this on the basis of postcoital increases; others have failed to find such increases. Says Dr. Alan J. Cooper, a leading British sex expert, Honorary Consultant Psychiatrist at St. Mary's Hospital, London: "Despite the dearth of definitive knowledge, my hunch is that testosterone levels mirror sexual activity; i.e., low levels are a consequence of sexual abstinence and high levels follow frequent sexual outlets."

Actually, as Dr. Davidson observes, increased levels of testosterone have been found following mating in bulls, monkeys, rabbits, and rats; and in rats there is some evidence that the phenomenon may be of importance in preventing regressive changes in old age.

And what of something of almost paramount interest to many aging men: Can testosterone therapy restore potency?

Generally, there have been poor treatment results using various testosterone formulations and even newer man-made testosterone-like agents—"aphrodisiac mixtures"—even when urinary testosterone levels (and presumably testosterone production rates) are appreciably reduced.

Acknowledging this, Britain's Dr. Cooper nevertheless considers that if there is a place for testosterone treatment, it is "probably in the older age group." Cooper reports seeing "dramatic improvements in such cases."

But he also notes: "Whether this is due to any specific action on potency or the anabolic effects [anabolism is the constructive phase of body metabolism in which body cells are active in growth and repair] of the hormone, or the expectation of improvement consequent upon receiving a 'powerful drug,' is debatable. If pushed, I would have to say that, in my opinion, the suggestibility of the patient, together with the charisma of the prescriber, are probably the most important factors. To illustrate this point, I have had some spectacular successes using a combination of forceful, even hypnotic reassurance . . . and an interesting mixture of testosterone, pemoline, strychnine and yohimbine, which comes in a sexy gold capsule. Whoever designed this knew a thing or two about male psychology; because, seriously, suggestion can be powerful medicine in the right cases."

Alcohol and Sexual Function

Heavy drinking can increase libido but it can also decrease or sometimes even abolish erectile and ejaculatory ability. Studies have shown that heavy alcohol intake can be followed by increased time to onset of erection, decreased duration of erection, and increased time to onset of ejaculation.

And chronic alcoholism may lead to persistent impotence. In one series of 17,000 patients, 8 percent were totally impotent, and impotence persisted in one half of these even though alcoholic intake had ceased months or years before.

Although alcohol's mechanism of action hasn't been established, very recent studies have provided a new insight: that prolonged drinking appears to alter male sexual behavior by stimulating the liver to dramatically step up its destruction of testosterone. The studies—by Dr. Emanuel Rubin of Mt. Sinai School of Medicine and Dr. Charles Lieber of the Bronx Veterans Administration Hospital in New York, along with other investigators—aimed, to begin with, at answering questions about how alcohol destroys the liver and damages other organs in the body.

By 1975, they were revealing that the alcohol damage occurs

even with a good diet. When animals—in this case, baboons—were fed the equivalent of a fifth of liquor every day for up to four years, cirrhosis and other liver damage turned out, contrary to what generations of medical students had been taught, to result directly from the toxic effects of alcohol and not from poor diet.

More recently, the investigators turned to what alcohol does to testosterone. The first experiments, in animals, established that long-term alcohol consumption doubled the production by the liver of an enzyme that destroys testosterone.

Once the animal studies were completed, the investigators extended them to humans, with the help of five intrepid volunteers—three normal, nonalcoholic men, and two alcoholics, who volunteered to stop drinking and then resume it under supervision.

For four weeks, the volunteers got the equivalent of a pint of whiskey a day in the form of pure alcohol diluted in fruit juice. It was given in small doses every three hours, and the amount in the blood never reached the legal limits of intoxication and no volunteer became drunk. But blood and liver tests showed unmistakably that the liver enzyme activity was increased two to five times and that the body did not compensate by forming more testosterone.

Reports Dr. Rubin: "The findings go a long way toward explaining the sex problems of alcoholics. It is not a reaction peculiar to some chronic alcoholics. Anybody who drinks continuously can get the effect. This is a pure effect of alcohol in any form you take it—whiskey, wine or beer. The total amount of alcohol is the only thing that counts."

Adds Rubin: "We don't want to tell people they cannot have a drink. We're talking about the damage that results from prolonged alcohol consumption."

Aphrodisiacs

Drugs of various kinds, reputed to be sex stimulants or aphrodisiacs, have long been used.

Two functions intimately associated with sex stimulation in men are muscular tension and the holding of blood in the vein system of the penis so that the veins engorge and distend the penis. Both depend on activity of the autonomic or involuntary nervous system. Some of the old-fashioned aphrodisiac drugs such as yohimbine, from the bark of an African tree, owe their reputation to their effect on the autonomic system, although there is little convincing evidence for an actual aphrodisiac effect.

But there are others, including opium and many opiumlike synthetic drugs, which are reputed to exert their aphrodisiac effect by action on the central nervous system to produce a euphoric state with its unusual sense of well-being. In both India and China, opium has been used for centuries on account of both its stupefying influence and its reputed aphrodisiac properties. Centuries ago, too, Mohammedan physicians were freely prescribing opium, particularly to newlywed men, in the hope of increasing their "seminal and muscular powers."

Today, in Egypt and South America, other narcotic drugs such as hemp are used because of a widely held belief that they induce erotic dreams, supposedly leading to stronger libido and longer copulation.

Investigators report that in this country as well as elsewhere, the modern problem of drug abuse, dependence and addiction in men, particularly as regards opiumlike and hallucinogenic drugs, has its roots first and foremost in personality disorders, not infrequently associated with sexual inadequacy or impotence. Observes one authority, Dr. T. Mann, professor of reproductive physiology at the University of Cambridge in England: "There can be little doubt that impotence, sometimes imaginary rather than real, can be an important motive in pushing a man into the ranks of drug abusers. Frustrated, often humiliated, and always guilt-ridden, the impotent man turns to drugs, hoping that some drug or other will eventually help him to overcome his inability to cope with the opposite sex and to fulfill his desire for sexual gratification. In believing that, he is, unfortunately, grievously mistaken. In the long run, opium addiction frequently produces an effect exactly opposite to that intended, namely, a loss of sexual drive and a decrease in fecundity."

Drug-Induced Sexual Problems

Many therapeutic agents—drugs valuable for such purposes as lowering high blood pressure and treating mental depression, anxiety, and peptic ulcer—sometimes, in some men, may cause decreases in libido, impotence, and other sexual disturbances. How they do so isn't always clear, although they may block autonomic nervous system control of the sex act, have adverse effects in the brain, or influence blood vessel responses.

Knowing about such disturbances is important. If you have any reason to suspect that one or more drugs you may be taking for good reason may be having adverse effects on your sex life, you shouldn't hesitate to take this up with your physician. In some cases, there may be no alternative, but often there is. Sometimes a reduced dosage of a drug may help. Sometimes, it is possible to substitute another drug which may not produce the adverse effect or may do so to a far lesser degree.

ANTIHYPERTENSIVE DRUGS (FOR HIGH BLOOD PRESSURE). One of these, clonidine (Catapres), only infrequently may cause impotence, urinary retention, and some breast enlargement in men. Impotence, decreased emission, and failure of ejaculation may sometimes occur with use of the drugs hexamethonium chloride (Methium), mecamylamine hydrochloride (Inversine), and trimethaphan camsylate (Arfonad).

Some antihypertensive drugs of the rauwolfia alkaloid class—Raudixin, Harmonyl, and Serpasil—may sometimes decrease emission, delay ejaculation, decrease libido, and cause erectile difficulties. Another agent, guanethidine sulfate (Ismelin), especially in large doses, may cause reduced emission and delay or failure of ejaculation in half or more of patients. Methyldopa (Aldomet) may, in up to as many as one fourth of patients, cause some difficulty in ejaculation and reduction of emission; and reduced libido and potency have also been noted.

NARCOTICS. Morphine, heroin, and other narcotic drugs tend to decrease libido and sexual activity. Addicts may have a delay or failure of ejaculation with normal erections.

DRUGS FOR MENTAL DEPRESSION. Certain antidepressant drugs known as monoamine oxidase (MAO) inhibitors—Parnate, Nardil, Eutonyl, and Marplan—may occasionally cause delay in ejaculation and impotence. Other antidepressants of the class called tricyclics—Tofranil, Presamine, Norpramin, Pertofrane, Elavil, Aventyl, and Vivactil—may either increase or decrease libido; some men experience impotence.

TRANQUILIZERS. Some of the drugs used as tranquilizers, as aids in anxiety states, and, in some cases, for psychotic conditions and other purposes, such as controlling otherwise unyielding nausea and vomiting, can affect sexual behavior in men.

Members of the class known as phenothiazines—such as Thorazine, Permitil, Prolixin, and Mellaril—may cause decreased libido, impotence, and inhibition of ejaculation. Others of the class called thioxanthenes—Taractan and Narvane—have effects similar to those of the phenothiazines, but difficulty in ejaculation is less common. Another type of drug, Haldol, has also been reported to cause impotence in some cases.

And increases in libido in some men and decreases in others have been reported with the use of Librium, Valium, and Serax.

CHOLINERGIC BLOCKING AGENTS. These drugs, which may be used for various purposes, such as relieving spastic conditions of the gut and peptic ulcer, include atropine, belladonna, Banthine, and Pro-Banthine. In high doses, they sometimes produce impotence and failure of ejaculation.

Impotence

Impotence, the inability to achieve or sustain an erection, is a far more common problem than most men realize. At some time in their lives, most men experience it. For many it is a one-time occurrence. Others may experience periodic episodes. For still others, it is a chronic problem.

It can be one of the most emotionally devastating things to happen to a man, causing severe anxiety, depression, marital discord, and may even lead to suicide. Yet it is the most treatable of sexual problems.

Any organic factors, to be sure, that interfere with the nervous, blood vessel, or muscular components of sexual response can cause trouble. These can include drugs, as already noted, and also disease, injury, or chronic pain. Severe diabetes can cause impotence; so can diseases and disorders of the nervous system. But in the overwhelming majority of cases, the problem is psychosomatic.

Commonly, it starts in this fashion: Almost inevitably, sooner or later, every man has a discomfiting experience. His body refuses to cooperate with his emotions. Because of fatigue, or some worry or stress, he can't cope when he tries. The experience is so common as to be considered within the normal range of male sexual functioning.

Unfortunately, many men think they are the only ones to whom this happens. The first time it occurs, a man may become anxious and begin to question his manhood. In his next sexual encounter, his anxiety about what happened the previous time may actually cause a repetition of the difficulty and may set up a vicious cycle of psychogenic impotence.

Writing in the *New Physician*, Dr. Martin Weisberg of Jefferson Medical College, Philadelphia, offers one kind of typical story. After a busy day at the office, a man stops for a few drinks on his way home, has a few cocktails at dinner, and maybe has a nightcap, too. In bed he has trouble getting an erection. The reasons are physiological: fatigue coupled with the depressant effect of the alcohol. The whole next day the man and his wife think about the events of the previous night. She wonders if he may be fooling around or maybe it's her fault. He wonders if he is sick, or gay, or maybe she is gay.

Observes Weisberg: " 'Well,' they both say to themselves, 'it's not going to happen again tonight.'

"She prepares a superb dinner and wears his favorite gown. He puts on her favorite cologne and picks up their favorite wine. They are going to be better than ever tonight. To make sure, after their bodies get in bed, their minds get up and take box seats on the bedposts. There they sit with stopwatches, score sheets, rulers and the *Guinness Book of Records*. He is going to have the hardest erection he ever had. She is going to be the best she has ever been. They both try as hard as they can, only to discover that you can't *make* sexual response happen—you have to *let* it happen. . . . This scene may be repeated a few more times before the couple gets tired of failing and just stops trying."

Some men recover their equanimity and sexual prowess when they understand how anxiety can inhibit sexual ability. Just as anxiety can have reverberations in the gut, causing spastic pain, it can act to prevent the increase in hydraulic pressure needed in the penile vein system if erection is to take place.

Some become aware, with a bit of prodding by a physician, that they have partial or full erections on occasion when half-asleep or aroused by some erotic literature. That helps restore confidence and promote a relaxed attitude in the next sexual encounter.

A new development could help others to become convinced that their problem is not physical but psychological. It's a test called NPT, for "nocturnal penile tumescence" monitoring. It measures the frequency of penile erection during sleep. If erections occur, as they normally do, during the deepest period of sleep, the cause of impotence can be assumed to be psychological. If little or no penile enlargement occurs, the cause is probably organic. In studies with several hundred impotent men, NPT monitoring proved to be the most useful diagnostic tool available. The studies have been carried out in the sleep laboratory, but it is possible for patients to be given a small, portable version of the NPT monitor to use at home while they sleep, with the results returned to a physician for evaluation.

When necessary, psychotherapy can be helpful in restoring a man's confidence. Or sex therapy may be used.

Sex therapy can be quite simple and relatively brief. A first principle, since sexual failure usually leads to fear of failing again, which leads to anxiety, which often leads to another failure, is to eliminate the performance anxiety, and this can be done by temporarily eliminating performance. No erections? Then stop trying. No intercourse. The couple may be told they can't even touch each other's genitals. There is no longer a need to perform. They can touch each other otherwise, and he doesn't have to worry that if he kisses her she is going to think he wants intercourse, and it won't work, and he'll feel bad, she'll cry, and they'll both be depressed.

Forbidding intercourse also lets a couple learn to pet again—not to get each other ready but to touch for the sake of touching. The couple may be told to pleasure each other, nongenitally, every day and to tell each other what feels good and what doesn't.

After several days, with much of the anxiety about performing on the wane, the next step is genital pleasuring—but not aimed at erection, only for telling each other what feels good and what doesn't. When a couple is comfortable with genital pleasuring, they may be encouraged to try nondemand intercourse. The penis is permitted into the vagina—not thrusting or writhing, only to appreciate the feeling. Later, slow pelvic moments can be started.

When, finally, both partners are ready, orgasm happens. As one therapist puts it, the partners usually come in with their heads sheepishly hung and announce: "We cheated. We didn't mean to do it but we accidentally had orgasms." The pressure was off enough to let natural sexual response sneak up. At that point, cure is complete.

The same method of treatment used for a physically healthy man with psychological impotence may sometimes work for one with impotence associated with diabetes or other physical cause. More often than not, the impotence is partial rather than complete, and fear of failure enters the picture. A diabetic man, for example, who has an occasional impotent episode can be frightened into total impotence. With sex therapy, his potency may be at least partially, if not perfectly, restored.

CASUALTIES OF THE LIBERATED WOMEN. There have been reports recently in medical and psychiatric journals that more young men than ever before are complaining of impotence, with some indications that the phenomenon may be related to women's lib.

There was a time when the man was the sexual aggressor, expecting the woman to be little more than a passive partner. But in today's liberated world, the woman not only often may initiate the sexual encounter but has expectations of her own. As one male college student complained: "When you get one of these liberated women in bed, you damn well better perform the way they want, or that'll be the end of the relationship."

Thus, a young man today may find himself, or think he finds himself, being judged on his performance. "There is a reversal of former roles," Dr. George L. Ginsberg and two other New York psychiatrists recently reported. "The role of the put-upon Victorian woman is that of the put-upon man of the 1970's. Inhibited non-orgastic women can often hide their lack of response, but men without erect penises cannot feign intromission. This challenge to manhood is most apparent in a sexually liberated society where women are not merely available but are perceived as demanding satisfaction."

In the case histories of impotent young men there is a common theme—inability to satisfy their partners. An initial failure leads them to doubt themselves, leading to greater anxiety on the second encounter, and making impotence all the more likely.

It may be, according to Dr. Philip Sarrel, of Yale University's sex counseling service, that some of the men encountering problems today aren't really all that interested in going to bed with a woman under today's circumstances. "These are guys," says Sarrel, "who, in the past, would have been able to get out of it by relying on the conventional values that said you shouldn't go to bed with a woman before marriage. Now they're being pressured to have intercourse."

For them, as for older men with psychological impotence problems, the solution may lie in understanding of the role of anxiety, reassurance, and sometimes sex therapy.

HELP FOR ORGANIC IMPOTENCE. Until recently, relatively little could be done for severe organic impotence—impotence due to physical impairment. Within the past few years, however, a new surgical procedure called a penile implant has been found to be successful for men with otherwise implacable impotence arising from diabetes, spinal injury, urological malformation, and other disorders.

The procedure involves implanting a cylindrical silicone prosthesis in the penis and a pumplike device in the scrotum and, under the abdominal muscle, a reservoir which holds 70 cubic centimeters of a radiopaque solution.

The pump, reservoir, and penile implant are connected with silicone tubing through which the solution can flow. By compressing one side of the pump, solution can be released from the reservoir to inflate the prosthesis and produce erection. Similarly, by compressing the other side of the pump, the solution can be returned to the reservoir, deflating the penis. The opaque dye is used so that in case of future injury or accident, x-rays can outline the implants to detect possible damage. The whole prosthesis causes no change in the appearance of the genitals.

Postoperatively, a man is able to function sexually in about three weeks, and if he has had normal orgasms prior to surgery, his orgastic potential remains the same. The surgery only corrects the erectile problem.

Urologists throughout the country have performed hundreds of the implants with reports of high success rates. Currently, an implant is recommended only for men whose impotence is organic, since the procedure destroys the natural mechanism for erection.

If the impotence is psychological, the chance of restoring normal sexual functioning is great, and an implant is contraindicated.

Ejaculatory Problems

These include premature ejaculation and ejaculatory incompetence (or retarded ejaculation).

In premature ejaculation, a man lacks control of his sexual response, causing him to ejaculate before either he or his partner is satisfied. Various theories have been offered to try to explain the problem. Some investigators think it may be a kind of developmental stage that all men go through. Others consider it conditioned. Commonly, early sexual activities take place in back seats of cars and on living room sofas, with some risk of sudden interruption, making it important to get it over with before someone walks in. As a result, some men learn to ejaculate quickly.

To men troubled by the problem, it often seems hopeless. Yet it can often be remarkably easy to overcome.

Sex therapists use various strategies to teach a man to become sensitive to his genital sensations and to use the feedback mechanism to gain control over the ejaculatory response. His partner may be asked to stimulate him manually until he feels the ejaculatory urge. At that point, he asks her to stop for a few seconds until the urge diminishes. Stimulation is then resumed. After repeating this sequence three or four times, he is encouraged to ejaculate.

In the usual course of events, after about three days of this, there is usually the feeling of some control beginning to develop. In the next step, the couple may be instructed to use a lubricant, such as Vaseline, which simulates the natural feel of the vagina, and to repeat the technique. Next, the couple may be asked to try intercourse with the woman in the superior position so she can control and stop her movements when he nears ejaculation—and again ejaculation should be allowed to occur only when the man has approached and backed away from it three or four times.

It is not unusual after about two weeks of this for a couple to be able to maintain intercourse for about ten minutes with the woman in superior position. Thereafter, the man may assume the superior position with equal success.

Another technique that may be used in the "training" procedure is the "squeeze"—which simply calls for the partner, after stimulating the man to the point of near-ejaculation, to place three fingers around the head of the penis and squeeze for three to four seconds until the urge to ejaculate diminishes.

In retarded ejaculation, or ejaculatory incompetence, a man is able to get turned on, get an erection, penetrate the vagina, but then is unable to ejaculate or have an orgasm. It can be the result of an organic problem but far more often is psychological in origin, and is often readily treatable.

All that may be required is a kind of desensitization to having orgasm inside a vagina, achieved by having the partner stimulate him almost to the point of orgasm before mounting. After a time, the problem disappears, although in some men it may return with a change of partner and require desensitization again.

Sexual Problem Clinics

Until quite recently, few physicians were trained in the treatment of sexual problems. In 1960, for example, less than half a dozen medical schools offered courses on the subject. Today most do.

There still remain many physicians with no training, experience, or even interest in sexual problems. But the numbers of the competent are increasing.

Today, sex therapy can range from friendly counseling and education of both partners by family doctors, to treatment by specialists such as urologists, psychologists and psychiatrists, to treatment offered in special sexual problem clinics.

The clinics are modeled on the prototype established by Dr. William Masters and his psychologist associate, Mrs. Virginia Johnson, now Mrs. Masters, at the center of the Reproductive Biology Research Foundation in St. Louis.

The treatment offered by the clinics—and by many of the private psychiatrists, psychologists, gynecologists, and other physicians who have been trained in St. Louis or by the clinics—is designed to be rapid, positive, direct. It avoids any long, depth-sounding traditional analytic approach which, in effect, decreed: "Let's put sex aside, over here, for now; and let's explore guilt feelings, personality problems, childhood trauma and other factors which presumably foment the sexual distress and must be overcome first."

The new treatment considers the immediate problem, what can be done in simplest fashion and briefest time to solve it. It is not for all kinds of sexual problems—but it is for those that are, by far, the most common and harassing.

Says Dr. Helen Kaplan, associate clinical professor of psychiatry, Cornell Medical Center, and head of the Payne Whitney sexual treatment and study program in New York City: "There are three major types of sexual problems. We deal with one type in the clinic—sexual dysfunction. A dysfunction renders a person incapable of intercourse or of obtaining great pleasure. Impotence, premature ejaculation, retarded ejaculation, orgasmic difficulties in the female which are called frigidity and vaginismus—these are all dysfunctions and highly amenable to brief treatment." (Vaginismus is involuntary contraction of the muscles around the entrance to the vagina, which can make intercourse painful and may even make penetration impossible.)

"A second category of problems is called deviation—a pejorative term but I use it only descriptively. A person with a deviation has excellent function and great pleasure from sexuality, but the conditions under which he has sex are peculiar or, in our culture, 'immoral.' If the only way a person can have an erection and enjoyable orgasm is by using an animal or a shoe or by looking out the window, or with a person of the same sex, that is a deviation.

"Deviations are not nearly as amenable to brief treatment. This is a field now in the process of being explored. A dysfunctional person is very much aware of a lack of pleasure and of a need. He is highly motivated for treatment. If you get him to function, this reinforces treatment. But a deviant who wishes to be treated—and I emphasize that I use deviant only as a descriptive term; I am not at all convinced that all people with deviant sexual patterns are sick or should be treated—is getting so much pleasure out of what he or she is already doing that it is more difficult to substitute another form of sexual activity.

"The third category is controversial—sexual problems which reflect psychopathology, or mental disturbance. This is controversial because many psychiatrists believe that all sexual problems are reflections of deep disturbances. We have not found that to be true; neither have Masters and Johnson. Some people who are perfectly normal in every other way have premature ejaculation or are nonorgasmic. It is simply not true that everyone with a sexual dysfunction is sick and requires psychiatric care. But there are some patients, a relatively small number, who do have sexual problems that are manifestations of serious underlying disturbances. For them, rapid treatment does not work and may be risky. Tampering with just the sexual problem in their case may lead to a breakdown. So we screen patients carefully to make certain we take none who may be harmed by brief treatment but who could be helped by more extensive therapy."

While the clinics that have been established in many areas of the country owe a debt to Masters and Johnson, they are not slavish imitations. They don't hesitate to modify the St. Louis methods, test the modifications, and use those that simplify and speed treatment or make it available to more people.

The work of Masters and Johnson is now so familiar it needs only brief mention here. In 1966, Dr. Masters and Mrs. Johnson published *Human Sexual Response,* which revealed—if readers were willing to penetrate the deliberately difficult prose (enough were to make the book a best-seller)—the most daring series of laboratory studies ever conducted for the scientific investigation of sex. Nearly 700 men and women had been directly observed during intercourse or masturbation. In great detail, the many phenomena occurring in the body before, during, and following orgasm were recorded. New knowledge of sexual physiology, of how the body functions during sexual activity, replaced folklore and much medical mythology as well.

Soon, Masters and Johnson were showing that the new knowledge gained through the study could be applied to helping couples overcome such common difficulties as impotence and frigidity. Sexually troubled people, it seemed, often shared one thing in common: a great tendency to be distracted from natural sexual performance by fears about it. An impotent male, for example, rather than participate unself-consciously in the sexual act, virtually steps outside himself and acts much like a spectator, concerned over whether he will be able to have an erection and, if not, what his partner's reaction will be. Neither partner realizes that the other is mentally standing in an opposite corner, observing the bedding scene in a spectator role.

Yet, most couples could be helped with surprising facility, Masters and Johnson found, by two basic innovations they introduced. No matter which partner has the problem, both partners had to be involved in treatment; it was the relationship between the two which was the real patient. And the treatment had to be carried out by two therapists, a man and a woman. The idea of dual-sex therapy teams came from studies that had convinced Masters and Johnson that neither sex could fully understand the sexual responses of the opposite sex. There had to be one of each to act as a "friend in court" for the partner of the same sex. A male therapist could better explain a husband's problem to his wife; a woman therapist could better clarify a wife's treatment program for the husband.

In the intensive treatment program worked out at the St. Louis facility, a couple spend two weeks in St. Louis, living at a local hotel and visiting the clinic daily. After several days spent obtaining a sexual history of each partner, another two or three days are spent educating the couple in how to use the physical senses, especially touch, to give and receive pleasure; and during this time, sexual intercourse is banned so the couple feel no demand to perform sexually. For the rest of the two-week period, instructions are given in techniques to be tried in the privacy of the hotel room.

All in all, 80 percent of patients have benefited—a record unprecedented in all previous sexual therapy attempts. Treatment has helped 50 percent of men impotent since adolescence and unable to consummate marriages, 80 percent of men who became impotent later in life, 80 percent of women who had never achieved orgasm before, and almost 100 percent of men with premature ejaculation.

The newer clinics differ somewhat. At Long Island Jewish Hospital–Hillside Medical Center in New Hyde Park, New York, the clinic was the first to be offered as a hospital-integrated community service. It is available for married couples who are seen by male-female therapy teams. Instead of daily sessions during a two-week period away from home, patients continue to live at home and carry on usual activities. Treatment may extend over several weeks or months, depending upon the need and convenience of patients. Some patients may be seen on weekdays; others in the evenings and on Saturdays. Each session lasts about an hour, and the number of sessions required ranges from 12 to 20.

The first two interviews are carried out by individual therapists. In the first, a female therapist interviews the wife while a male therapist sees the husband. In the second session, the therapists switch. Thereafter, husband and wife are seen jointly by a male-female therapist team.

At Payne Whitney, the sex therapy clinic functions as part of an outpatient department. The average number of sessions, each lasting 30 minutes to an hour or more, is 8, and the range is from 2 or 3 to 11 or 12. Usually two sessions a week are scheduled, and telephone contact in between sessions is available if needed. The Payne Whitney clinic treats couples but also accepts many patients who come without partners. Treatment is provided by individual therapists rather than teams.

With their modifications, the clinics have in common reliance not just on therapeutic sessions with patient or couple but also on activities to be carried on at home. They provide specific suggestions for types of stimulation, exercise, and gradually progressive sexual experiences, and deal with any obstacles that may emerge.

The suggestions provided by many of the clinics are the same as or similar to those already noted under impotence and ejaculatory problems.

A note here, in case it may be useful in your situation, on methods used in the more common problems of women—vaginismus and inability to achieve orgasm: The muscle contraction or spasm of vaginismus may result from a painful first coital experience or a traumatic gynecological examination. Or it may be psychological in origin, directed against sexuality. Yet, almost invariably, whatever the reason, the clinics have been successful in treating vaginismus, even vaginismus that has prevented consummation of a marriage for many years.

"Physical examination," says one therapist, "is especially important in vaginismus, and all the more so when there is associated impotence in the husband, because we can show the man what the problem is and relieve him of a burden of guilt. When you can demonstrate that not even a baby speculum can penetrate, he can quickly understand why his penis could not. And this can be helpful, too, for the woman who—such has been our culture—often has mistakenly blamed the man because sex was supposed to be his responsibility.

"Usually, when a man finds out it is not his fault and gets involved in helping his partner dilate herself, and when both also get involved in nondemand touching of each other, he gets an erection. We reinforce the experience, emphasizing that it demonstrates there is nothing wrong with his ability to cope and that constant frustration has led to his impotence. So far, in almost every case, somewhere between therapy session 9 and session 12, such a couple has been able to have intercourse."

At another clinic, where there has never been a failure in a vaginismus case, a therapist explains: "It's a matter of deconditioning. When you have a conditioned reflex—for example, when a child or a dog has been beaten and conditioned so there is cringing every time you raise your hand—you can decondition the reflex by raising the hand and never punishing at that time or by giving candy every time you raise the hand. Soon, child or dog will not shudder when the hand is raised.

"This is precisely what we do. If a woman becomes accustomed gradually, while in relaxed condition, to have something penetrate —it can be her own finger one day, her finger wiggled around the next day, and the following day her husband's finger but not in a sexual context—deconditioning can be accomplished. Sex does not take place until the deconditioning is achieved. But that may take only two or three weeks or sometimes even less. If the conditioning has been extreme, the deconditioning may have to start further back—with simply imagining something entering the vagina. But it can then progress."

In some women, there may be a complication: along with the vaginismus, a woman may also have developed a phobia about intercourse, a fear of being seriously injured if penetrated by a penis. Some women have another kind of phobia—about orgasm. They have an idea that they cannot, must not, let go; if they have an orgasm they may die. In French, orgasm is *petit mort,* "little death." Orgasm can be a seizurelike experience. Some women fear it intensely.

In such cases, the first effort is to desensitize to the fear. The process is somewhat like desensitization for allergy except that instead of injections of gradually increasing doses of the allergy-producing material to build up immunity, the patient, while relaxed, is asked to imagine intercourse until finally the imaginary sex act, which at first can produce fear reactions, no longer does so. Once this is achieved, deconditioning of the vaginismus can start.

Many women whose primary problem is failure to achieve orgasm are helped by brief treatment. A nonorgasmic woman and an impotent man, the clinics find, may share one thing in common: both have been under pressure to perform. Often, when a woman is nonorgasmic, her partner has tried hard to make her orgasmic and, in doing so, despite the best of intentions, has only made matters worse by making her feel under demand.

In such situations, just as it is for impotence, sensate focus can be remarkably helpful. "This kind of physical closeness," says one therapist, "is no artificial maneuver. Actually, it has proven to be something all people want but have denied because they have lived with the assumption that if they touch, it must lead invariably to something more. Most people we have treated, no matter for what kind of sexual dysfunction, now appreciate it so much that they spend some time every night, and in many cases during the day as well, in physical contact of some kind with each other. And when it is a nonorgasmic problem, such closeness provides, in the very best sense, the opening wedge, the necessary relaxation, the freedom from constant demand that can help markedly in overcoming the problem."

Many women, while unable to achieve orgasm with penis contained, are able to achieve it by self-manipulation or when manipulated by a partner. Others are orgasmic with intercourse but do not know how to be with self-manipulation. The clinics treat both types.

One problem the clinics have to contend with is confusion about types of orgasm in women. Some people latch onto the Masters-Johnson study data and interpret them as indicating that there is no such thing as vaginal orgasm; that clitoral orgasm is the only thing. Some even turn it around and put it the other way.

But what Masters and Johnson really found was that from the physiological point of view, whenever a woman has an orgasm, the same things seem to happen to her. Whether you manipulate the clitoris without getting anywhere near the vaginal area, or manipulate the vaginal area and don't touch the clitoris, the outer third of the vagina becomes engorged with blood, the uterus contracts, and the total body response is the same.

"There do seem to be some differences in feeling that women experience with penis contained as against clitoral manipulation," explains a woman therapist. "Not necessarily better feelings but different feelings. And we try to get this across to women. We explain that we will do all we can to enable them to be orgasmic with penis contained and with clitoral manipulation so they can have a choice of being orgasmic either way. And this then relieves some of the pressure to perform in an unrealistic way."

A woman who has never in her life had an orgasm in any way can be more difficult but far from impossible to treat. The clinics encourage sexual fantasizing. They suggest stimulation techniques, sometimes including the use of devices such as vibrators.

"We started to treat such patients with their partners," one clinic therapist says. "But it can take so much effort to get a woman over her initial stages of frigidity, so many hours of stimulation, that we found this to be destructive to sexual relationships. So we now work with the woman herself initially until she can have a masturbatory orgasm. Then we work with the partner as well. We have found this to be far more effective and less anxiety-provoking."

Often the clinics are able to help couples without a specific problem such as impotence or nonorgasm but who are concerned about a decline of sexual interest and enjoyment.

"The prime difficulty very often," one therapist emphasizes, "is that they are afraid to tell each other what to do—to assert themselves. To say, 'I'd like you to kiss me here.' Or, 'Tonight, I want to be the active one.' Or, 'Tonight, I just want to lie here and have you do this and that.' They are afraid to say what they would like, to tell each other, to reinforce each other's positive behavior. We teach them to. We may say to them: 'Now, go ahead, here and now, tell each other what you would like.' Both may start blushing and stammering, and it becomes apparent to all of us how difficult it is, and we work it through."

Says another therapist: "Most people don't know how to communicate in a very direct way. Apparently, almost all of us have been trained to behave on the basis of what we think the other person is thinking, and we hesitate to make ourselves vulnerable by expressing how we feel and then asking how the other person feels. And while this is particularly the case in sexual relationships, you see it pervading whole relationships. Couples are always second-guessing one another. A man may want to try something but will be afraid to even suggest it because he thinks his wife may not want it. And she may be thinking, I wish he would be more assertive, because I would like to try this and I am a little afraid to try. So they live within their own worlds, not having the freedom to exchange what they really feel. This is as true out of as in bed. Most couples don't know how to share what they feel; instead, they share how they react to situations. If one partner, for example, does something that makes the other angry, the latter usually doesn't say, 'I feel hurt or angry,' but rather explodes, 'You bitch (or bastard), why did you do that to me!' And then the battle starts.

"We work a good deal of the time to get a basic expression of real gut-level feelings. We may even start with something as simple as asking them, for the next 24 hours, in each other's presence, to start every sentence with 'I think' or 'I feel' or 'I need.' We feel sexual functioning is one way in which two people communicate, and we work on the communication problem in and out of bed. And it is rewarding both in and out of bed when two people find out how much simpler it is to be direct with each other."

Self-Help for Sexual Difficulties

Many sex therapists—those in clinics and those in private practice who often use the same techniques—agree that it is possible for some people to help themselves, to apply the principles used by therapists on a do-it-yourself basis.

People who understand the principle of treatment for premature ejaculation, for example, may well be able to apply it successfully. If they understand that impotence often results from fear of failure, they can take that into account. A nonorgasmic woman can learn to explore her own body and her fantasies and not expect that some man on a white charger will come riding up to magically overcome her problem.

Says one therapist who was trained by Masters and Johnson: "I think it is possible for some people to do much for themselves. One of the interesting things that sometimes happened in St. Louis was that a couple would call and be given a date to come to the Foundation—and before that time arrived they had solved their problem for themselves. Just having made the date seemed to take off enough pressure for them to face the problem and work at it, using principles they had read in the Masters-Johnson book. Not all people can do this, but some can."

Getting Help Without Getting Bilked

Sex research, sex training, sex education, and sex therapy programs have been blooming profusely around the country and—as you might expect, and perhaps even more than you would suspect —there are a good many weeds among the blossoms.

People without training are getting into the act. Some "educational seminars," for example, offer little more enlightenment than a weekend of dirty movies. Some "sex therapists" treat their clients to sadomasochistic practices, homosexual seduction, sexual participation by the "therapist," and thinly veiled prostitution under the label of "surrogate partners."

Just a few years ago, Dr. Masters verbally strafed proliferating sex clinics, calling the great majority of them "institutions operated for money by pure charlatans." He charged that "Out of the 3,500 to 5,000 sex therapy clinics operating in the United States, not 50— by any stretch of the imagination—can be considered legitimate. The public is being incredibly bilked."

Added Masters: "If every patient demanded information on the educational background of his or her therapists, this would immediately close half the sex therapy clinics in the United States."

There may be the same problem with many private practitioners.

There is some debate on exactly what constitutes proper training for a sex therapist. But there is general agreement that a would-be therapist should start with a degree in a discipline requiring clinical and counseling skills and should then undergo a course of specialized training, lasting perhaps six months to a year. The obvious candidates for advanced training are doctors, psychiatrists, psychologists, marriage and family counselors, psychiatric nurses, social workers and clergymen. Full-fledged training programs are being conducted; most are university based.

Various organizations— the American Association of Sex Educators and Counselors, the Eastern Academy of Sex Therapy, the National Association for the Scientific Study of Sex, and the American Medical Association—have become concerned about proper training, qualification, and accreditation.

If you're considering a sex therapist or clinic, your physician may be able to help by recommending one or assisting you in checking credentials. If he can't or won't, don't hesitate to ask pertinent questions of the therapist or clinic about background and training.

It's been observed by some that if you have a bad experience with a mediocre or totally inadequate therapist, it's not likely to do any great harm. Brief therapies designed to treat specific symptoms probably do have less potential for harm than long-range ones designed to explore total personality, for the simple reason that if you don't find yourself cured of the symptoms within some ten to twenty sessions, you know you ought to quit and go elsewhere. Still, the loss of time and money counts.

Infertility in Men

An estimated 15 percent of all couples planning to start families have problems initiating pregnancies, and in one third of these the difficulty is directly attributable to male disorders.

The normal male ejaculate contains from 140 to 400 million sperms, and 60 percent or more of that number should be vigorously motile and capable of making the long trip to the fallopian tubes. With lesser numbers of sperms, even with 100 million per ejaculate, the percentage of them, even if healthy, completing the journey and reaching the egg may be too small, and a man may be infertile.

Along with adequate sperm production, male fertility requires unobstructed passage of sperms through the seminal tract and their satisfactory deposition within the vagina.

The possible causes of impaired sperm production include undescended testis or testes, prolonged fever or other causes of increased testicular heat (even possibly the wearing of tight jockey shorts which retain heat), drug toxicity, disorders of the thyroid, pituitary or adrenal glands, and such conditions as hydrocele and varicocele.

Obstruction of the seminal tract may result from orchitis (an inflammation of the testicles that may be caused by injury or mumps or other infection, including venereal), epididymitis (an inflammation of the spermatic cord and tissues, usually secondary to prostate infection), and inflammation elsewhere in the tract.

Defective delivery of sperms into the vagina may be the result of premature ejaculation or anatomic problems, including narrowing of the urethra.

Infertility in a man is often treatable after careful investigation to establish cause or causes. Diagnosis may require thorough physical examination, semen analyses, thyroid and other studies.

Infections of the prostate or elsewhere can be cleared up. Gland disorders respond to appropriate hormone treatment. Inadequate sperm production sometimes responds to several months of oral methyltestosterone treatment.

A hydrocele, if present, can inhibit sperm production through pressure effects; it can be repaired. In this defect, a sac or bag of watery fluid surrounds a testicle. It may cause little or no discomfort and may appear at any age, resulting from excessive accumulation of fluid as a consequence of overproduction or diminished resorption of fluid. The operation is relatively simple. Under spinal or general anesthesia, through an incision in the scrotum, the sac is emptied and its wall removed, and the patient is usually out of bed in a day and home within a week.

Similarly, a varicocele, if present, may require surgical treatment. In varicocele, veins of the spermatic cord are dilated and varicosed. There may be no symptoms at all or only a somewhat vague dragging sensation in the lower abdomen or groin. Varicocele may interfere with optimal sperm production by increasing scrotal and testicular temperatures. Surgery under spinal anesthesia is relatively simple, involving an incision in the scrotum and tying off and removal of the varicose veins.

In one study of 504 subfertile men who underwent surgical correction of varicocele and were followed up for at least one year afterward, semen quality improved in 71 percent and more than half of the wives became pregnant. The higher the sperm count prior to operation, the better the results. In 56 percent of the men with very low sperm counts to begin with, the use after surgery of human chorionic gonadotropin, a hormone found in pregnancy urine, improved results and increased the subsequent pregnancy rate.

Some recent work suggests that clomiphene citrate, a drug that has been used to help infertile women ovulate (sometimes to the point of multiple births), may be helpful in increasing male fertility in some cases. At Duke University School of Medicine, Durham, North Carolina, Drs. D. F. Paulson and Jeff Wacksman employed the drug for 22 low-fertility men. The men received clomiphene for 25 days each month for up to 6 months. In all but 3, the sperm count rose, with several pregnancies resulting.

Sometimes, when a man is subfertile, pregnancy may result when sexual activity is made more appropriate than it may have been before. Frequent intercourse does not insure greater likelihood of conception, because too much of it may deplete the quantity of sperm. Timing of intercourse to take advantage of the wife's fertile period, with coitus avoided for four days prior to this period so the man can deliver the best sperm at this optimal time for her, sometimes is helpful.

This optimal time is around ovulation, when an egg is released from the ovary. Generally, this occurs about two weeks before the menstrual cycle begins. Usually, body temperature drops several tenths of a degree just before ovulation and rises even more sharply about 24 hours thereafter. Some women have still other clues to rely on. At the time of ovulation, they experience a peculiar, sudden cramp followed by a heavy feeling in the lower abdomen that may last several hours. They may also notice an unusual amount of mucous secretion at this time.

A new coital technique may be helpful when a man has poor quality of semen associated with high semen volume, Drs. Richard D. Amelar and Lawrence Dubin of New York University School of Medicine have reported. It's based on the finding that the first portion of the ejaculate of some subfertile men is superior in sperm concentration and motility to the remainder of the ejaculate. The technique involves withdrawal of the penis from the vagina after deposition of the better first portion of the ejaculate during the fertile period of the wife's cycle. In the first 33 cases, after barren marriages of many years, the technique led to wives becoming pregnant within one to six months.

When a man has a low volume of semen with otherwise normal semen quality, there may not be enough semen to make proper contact for insemination. In such cases, artificial insemination with the husband's sperm has often worked.

Sterilization

Voluntary sterilization has become a contraceptive phenomenon. In 1973, a national survey showed that nearly one in four married couples using contraception relied on sterilization. This figure may now have grown to one in three. Since 1973, more than a million sterilizations have been performed annually in the United States.

The balance between male and female sterilizations has shifted as the surgical method for women has become safer and easier. In 1970, only 20 percent of the 924,000 sterilizations were obtained by women. Five years later, the proportion for women had risen to 51 percent.

FOR WOMEN.   Female sterilization once required major abdominal surgery, general anesthesia, and several days of hospitalization. Today the procedure has been greatly simplified.

A new technique—sometimes called "Band-Aid" sterilization—may be done during an overnight hospital admission or even on an outpatient basis. It makes use of laparoscopy, previously employed for problems of female fertility and for diagnosis in other conditions.

The laparoscope is a fine optical instrument with "cold light" that can be inserted easily through a minute incision to explore abdominal organs. For sterilization, a tiny incision is made below the navel and the laparoscope is inserted. A second incision, which may be only one-eighth inch long, is made. A second instrument, combining a tiny forceps and a cauterizing device, is inserted into the second incision.

Carbon dioxide gas is introduced into the abdominal cavity and later is removed through a valve in the laparoscope. The gas helps to push away the intestines, permitting better access to the fallopian tubes (each about four and a half inches long), which connect the ovaries to the uterus.

While looking through the eyepiece of the laparoscope, the surgeon cauterizes each tube and cuts out a tiny piece of each. The entire procedure takes fifteen to twenty minutes. Both incisions are small enough to be covered with Band-Aids.

Complications are rare. An occasional hemorrhage usually can be handled through the laparoscope.

After sterilization, a woman will continue to have normal menstrual periods until her menopause, which will occur just as it would if she had not had the operation. Each month her ovaries will produce an egg but the eggs will be blocked where the tubes have been cut. There, the egg will disintegrate and be absorbed back into the body. There is no change in sex hormone production or in sexual characteristics or satisfaction.

FOR MEN: VASECTOMY.   A relatively simple operation in the hands of an expert such as a urologist, who specializes in genitourinary tract surgery, vasectomy can be carried out in the doctor's office or the outpatient department of a hospital or in a vasectomy clinic.

In the procedure, the vas deferens, or sperm duct, which carries sperms from the testicles to the area of the prostate, where they are mixed with other fluids prior to ejaculation, is cut on each side.

A local anesthetic can be used. To reach the vas deferens, a small incision is made on each side of the scrotum. Through the incision, each tube is cut. Many urologists remove a small section to make the separation more certain. Each cut end is blocked off. This can be done by tying with surgical thread, knotting the tube itself, or cauterization. The sperm then cannot move through the duct to be ejaculated and, with no place to go, they dissolve and are absorbed.

Vasectomy takes from fifteen to thirty minutes. A scrotal suspensory is applied and the patient goes home. He may be advised to remain inactive for the rest of the day, after which he can resume usual activities, including intercourse.

Right after surgery, many sperms remain in the duct system. So a supplementary contraceptive method must be used until medical examination indicates that all sperms have been ejaculated. This may take four to six weeks.

Vasectomy should have no effects on sexual potency unless there are psychological complications, which may stem from misunderstanding of the nature of the operation.

The male hormone, testosterone, involved in virility, libido, sexual potency, and orgasm, is produced in the testes and absorbed directly into the bloodstream at a site distant from where the operation is performed. The hormone and its functions are not affected by vasectomy.

Vasectomy results only in interruption of the transport of sperms. The testes continue to form sperms, which, as noted, will be absorbed. The constituents of semen come from the prostate and seminal vesicles, and secretions from these organs continue unchanged after vasectomy. The gross appearance and quantity of the semen will be essentially unchanged; the only alteration will be the absence of sperms.

Some men may be emotionally upset by vasectomy. It appears that because virility is mistakenly equated with ability to father a child, sterility is confused with impotence. Most urologists agree that with adequate understanding and counseling before operation, psychological effects are nil or at most minimal.

Venereal Diseases

For some years, public health authorities have been warning that venereal diseases may be getting out of control. By conservative estimate, every minute at least four Americans are being infected. In one recent year, some 2.3 million cases of gonorrhea were treated; syphilis, although on the decline a decade ago, has about-faced, with as many as 81,000 cases reported treated in a year.

But the number of cases treated is no accurate reflection of actual incidence of either gonorrhea or syphilis. According to recent estimates, more than half a million people in this country are suffering from undetected syphilis and in urgent need of medical attention. And as gonorrhea has increased, so have the numbers of untreated women acting as unknowing reservoirs. At some family planning clinics, for example, 10 percent of all women tested have asymptomatic gonorrhea.

VD may once have been confined largely to the three "P's"— the poor, prostitutes, and promiscuous men. But today it is common in the upper strata of society.

"Today, we find nice college girls with salpingitis" (inflammation of the fallopian tubes), says Dr. Edwin J. DeCosta of Northwestern University. "Study after study indicates that 5 to 10 percent of young women have gonorrhea, even pregnant young women, even pretty young women, from nice families—even married women with grown children."

According to Dr. James McKenzie-Pollack, former director of the American Social Health Organization's VD division, "Even pillars of society, just returning from conventions and business trips, present themselves in increasing numbers each year in doctors' offices. Their harried and secretive attitude reveals their problem. The visit ends with a 'never again' promise—until the next year."

THE "BAD COLD" FALLACY. One factor involved in the increased VD rate has been penicillin, which has lulled many into complacency. For the first time, with the antibiotic, syphilis and gonorrhea could be cured. Gonorrhea, in some circles, even acquired a reputation for being little worse than a bad cold. Clearly, this is untrue. Both syphilis and gonorrhea have serious effects.

Syphilis in particular can be a deadly disease if untreated. Since 1900 in the United States alone, it has taken the lives of 1 million adults and 3 million babies.

Caused by a spiral-shaped organism, *Treponema pallidum,* syphilis has a dangerously deceptive element: initial symptoms disappear without treatment, but the organism remains in the body and after ten years or more causes lasting damage to blood vessels, brain, heart, eyes, and other organs.

In the primary stage, a sore develops, usually on the genitals, three to six weeks after contact with an infected individual. The sore will resolve on its own, but if untreated the disease next manifests itself, about three to six weeks later, with a rash that may appear anywhere on the body, fever (sometimes), sore throat (sometimes), or other nonspecific symptoms. With or without treatment, these symptoms also will disappear. If still untreated, the disease next goes underground for many years, progressively attacking various organs but indicating its presence only by a positive blood test. Finally, when damage has been done to vital organs, the patient usually seeks help. Treatment at this stage can arrest further damage but cannot completely erase already-inflicted ravages.

Because the disease can affect virtually every organ, the great physician Sir William Osler observed that "To know syphilis is to know medicine." For example, neurosyphilis (of brain and spinal cord) can manifest itself as insanity, stroke, shooting pains throughout the body, or joint deformities. Syphilis affecting the arteries can cause congestive heart failure or even heart attack.

Gonorrhea, caused by an organism called the gonococcus, manifests itself in men first by a whitish penile discharge, with or without burning on urination, beginning three to seven days after exposure. In women, there may be a whitish vaginal discharge and burning on urination, but often the symptoms may be mild or even entirely absent.

In men, untreated gonorrhea may affect the prostate or epididymis, causing severe discomfort and, in some cases, infertility. In women, infection may affect the fallopian tubes, sometimes with spillover into the abdominal cavity, causing fever, severe abdominal pain, and peritonitis. Women run a high risk of infertility from repeated gonorrhea episodes because the fallopian tubes may become chronically infected and scarred. And both gonorrhea and syphilis can be passed from mother to unborn child.

Thus, any idea that either disease is to be taken lightly is dangerous. So, too, is casual treatment. While curable when adequately treated, VD organisms can become increasingly resistant with half-baked treatment—and such resistance has become a factor in the increasing incidence.

Also contributing to the high incidence: new attitudes toward sex and lessened fear of pregnancy because of modern contraceptive methods.

Modern travel is another factor in spreading VD. One example: the case of a California prostitute and her far-roaming clients. Public health authorities began a roundup effort after one of her customers sought treatment for syphilis. When the woman was located and treated for syphilis, she had a detailed diary of her customers—names and "home bases" of 310 sexual partners during the time when she could have acquired and spread syphilis. Texas accounted for 50; California was next with 24; 20 were from Arizona, 16 from Tennessee, 15 from Alabama, 13 each from Arkansas and Oklahoma, 12 from Minnesota, and 10 each from Florida and Missouri. Fewer than 10 each were from the 24 other states, and there was one each from Canada and Mexico.

Some investigators blame oral contraceptives not only for encouraging promiscuity among nonprostitutes but also for increasing the risk possibility. Unlike mechanical devices and vaginal foams and jellies, the Pill presents no barrier to the gonococcus. Moreover, it creates an alkaline environment in the vagina that encourages gonococcal growth. Older contraceptives such as the diaphragm and jelly, foams and powders, produced an acid environment that provided some protection against infection.

AN UNRECOGNIZED AND UNTREATED VENEREAL DISEASE. Although gonorrhea has long been considered the most common venereal disease in the United States, some recent studies suggest that an even more common cause may be the same organism, *Chlamydia trachomatis,* that, when it invades the eyes, causes trachoma.

In one study among young men, 92 percent of infection was found to be unrelated to gonorrhea. The infection was commonly caused by *Chlamydia*.

What often happens in the case of chlamydial urethritis, according to Dr. King K. Holmes of the University of Washington, Seattle, is that a physician may simply reassure a patient that it is nongonococcal, or may treat with antibiotics and, since it is not gonococcal, make no attempt to find and treat the patient's sexual contacts, so allowing a reservoir of infection to persist in women who may have no symptoms.

Once thought to be viruses, *Chlamydia* organisms more recently have been found to have some characteristics similar to those of bacteria and are now considered to be "intermediate agents." They respond to antibacterial drugs, of which the most effective appear to be tetracycline and sulfa compounds.

Only recently have complex testing procedures for identifying *Chlamydia* been developed, and they still are not available to most physicians. But Dr. Holmes and his associates have been treating nongonococcal urethritis patients with two grams of tetracycline hydrochloride a day for seven days and finding it effective for 80 percent of those among them with chlamydial infection. They have recommended that all nongonococcal patients and their sex partners, many of whom are likely to have *Chlamydia,* be treated with tetracycline.

OTHER VENEREAL DISEASES.   These are less common and include chancroid, granuloma inguinale, and lymphogranuloma venereum.

Chancroid, also known as soft chancre, is an acute localized disease caused by bacteria that produce ulcers in the genital area. After two to five days (sometimes longer) of incubation, the disease begins with the appearance of blisters and small, raised red pimples that soon form into tender, painful ulcers, between half and three-quarter inch in size, that bleed easily. Untreated, they last for months. They can be treated effectively with sulfa drugs or antibiotics, and continuous cleaning with soap and water speeds recovery.

Granuloma inguinale is a mildly contagious, slow-growing venereal disease of the skin and sometimes of the lymph nodes, usually localized in the genital or anal areas. It develops 8 to 12 weeks after contact, appearing as pimples, blisters, or nodules that turn into red ulcers with pus discharge and, in time, with sour, pungent odor. Without treatment, the ulceration can persist for years. The disease can be cured by treatment with effective antibiotics.

Lymphogranuloma venereum, after an incubation period of three days to three weeks, produces a small blister or pimple in the genital area which heals quickly. But lymph nodes in the groin later swell up. Symptoms may include fever, chills, headache, abdominal pain, nausea and vomiting, joint aches, skin rashes, and sometimes hemorrhoids. In the severe form, the penis or vulva may become greatly enlarged.

The disease is caused by a large virus and there is no specific treatment. But good results have been obtained with sulfa drugs and suitable antibiotics.

AVOIDING VD.   The best means of preventing VD spread as of now is the condom.

And an overlooked means of VD control—soap and water—is now being emphasized by some public health authorities. They argue, with some reason, that if sexual partners washed genital areas after contact, the infection risk would be materially reduced by the removal of some germs by the mechanical action of washing and the killing of others by the soapy fluid.

The fact is that VD is not 100 percent infectious; on the average, for every five persons who have intercourse with a person with syphilis, only one is likely to be infected; for gonorrhea, the figure is one in three. This suggests that infection likelihood might be further reduced by washing after intercourse (and preferably before as well).

5
The Middle Years and Beyond

The "Mid-Life Crisis"

At some point about the age of 40—give or take as much as half a dozen years or even more—men commonly enter an uncertain stage which has been variously called the "mid-life crisis," the "dangerous age," and "adolescence in reverse."

It's a time when depression, more often a complaint of women, increases sharply in the male; a time when a "changing partners" syndrome is more likely to develop, with a high risk for divorce; a time when career dislocations are not uncommon and some men may chuck jobs and start all over again; a time when a few just "give up" on virtually everything and worry themselves into bad health and premature old age.

The symptoms of the time can be mild or severe; they can be good as well as bad. If some men start drinking heavily, others go in the opposite direction; if some leave home and family for girls young enough to be their daughters, others may for the first time start trying to make a long-shaky marriage work.

Because the mid-life crisis can sometimes be as disturbing as change of life can be for some women, it has been called the "male menopause" and "male climacteric." But few serious investigators use such terms, which imply that the sex glands are involved and there are hormonal changes like those that end a woman's cycle of fertility.

Although men do experience hormonal changes, they are not nearly as discrete and relatively abrupt as those in women but rather occur over many years, even beginning in the 20's. And while men do have a climacteric in the opinion of many investigators, it doesn't take place until years, even as many as 20 years, after its occurrence in women. What happens in a middle-aged man is rather, in the view of many, a pseudoclimacteric—more psychologically and culturally than biologically induced.

ARRIVING AT THE CRISIS. Writing not long ago in an American Medical Association publication, Don A. Schanche described the process this way: "It is as if during the first 40 years a man has been unrolling a fresh parchment scroll that bears the narrative of what he was and what he was striving to become as worker, thinker, father, husband, lover, doer, everything. All that he has achieved or failed to achieve is there—even his most implausible fantasies, like imagining himself as President, or Marilyn Monroe's lover, or winner of the Nobel Prize.

"Gradually, he reaches the midpoint of the story, where some event in the narrative gently or abruptly forces him to see what and where he really is. At about the same time, he discerns that the edges of his life's parchment scroll are crinkling and beginning to yellow with age."

At that point, he has arrived at the mid-life crisis.

The triggering event for it can be something as seemingly inconsequential as no longer being able to beat his son in tennis. Or losing a job. Or losing a promotion to a younger man. Or getting the promotion and fearing that he no longer has the physical resources to do it justice.

Suddenly, he finds himself increasingly conscious of such things as youth and age, of objectives (even fantasied) and actual achievements.

He becomes conscious, too, as not before, of physical changes. These are not sudden. They've been going on, always go on, gradually, subtly. He's not as vigorous as he was at 20 even if he has tried to remain so. Effort makes him huff and puff more. His hearing may not be fully as sharp as it was, and he may be beginning to notice presbyopia and a bit of difficulty with close work and reading. Possibly, there is some urinary difficulty, a beginning indication of prostate enlargement.

What the physical changes amount to is loss of some reserve capacity. Plenty remains. The situation, physically, is far from being as desolate as it may seem. But there are now intimations of aging and mortality. And these, of course, play a role in the mid-life crisis.

STAGES IN AN ADULT MALE'S LIFE.   At Yale University a group of scientists, headed by psychologist Daniel J. Levinson, have been studying the crisis and the events leading up to and succeeding it.

Their subjects, volunteers between 35 and 45 when the study began, are divided between four occupational groups: industrial blue- and white-collar workers, business executives, teaching and research scientists, and writers.

And in these diverse groups, which the Yale group believe include a fairly typical variety of personality types and life-styles, they have been finding a kind of life progression, a series of developmental stages, that the men generally share in common.

Stage 1: "Getting into the Adult World."   This begins in the early 20's when a man, breaking away from home, becomes independent in terms of such things as job, friends, sexual relationships. But at this point he has no real inner commitment to his way of life. Over the next several years, he is influenced toward an adult commitment. Very commonly, the influence is exerted by what the researchers call a "mentor." He is an older friend—an executive, a foreman, or anyone who, in effect, takes the young man under his wing, acts as a kind of big brother, teaches, criticizes, encourages.

Stage 2: "Settling Down."   This stage, entered into with the commitment, commonly comes in the early 30's. Despite differences in circumstances, the Yale researchers have been finding, the men in the diverse groups entered the "settling-down" stage at approximately the same time. In some cases, it was a matter of continuing in jobs already held, taking on responsibilities for home and family, and establishing and maintaining a position in the community. In other cases, it meant major changes such as a new job, a move to another location, or a new wife.

Stage 3: "Becoming One's Own Man" (BOOM).   This, a transitional period and one that may involve some explosive capabilities to match the BOOM acronym, usually begins in the late 30's and extends for several years. "Settling down" has brought with it some constraints and dependencies. Now a man begins to be annoyed somewhat by both. He may experience feelings of being oppressed by his work, his boss, his wife. She may take a great deal of satisfaction in their life-style—their home, children, growing security. He's not so sure about the security or the basis for it. He may have gnawing doubts about whether this is the way to live, whether this is what life is all about. His wife has something of a maternal aura about her—and, in fact, he may have earlier sought and been grateful for her "mothering." Now, even if one part of him still welcomes it, another part feels oppressed by it and by a kind of "little boy" feeling it may arouse in him. At this point, sexual fantasies, all about young, nonmaternal women, are common. Some men just have the fantasies; others have affairs. Often, too, at this time, a man's mentor palls on him and he may reject him, wanting to stand on his own.

Somewhere between the age of 39 and 42, most men, the Yale research indicates, feel a desperate need to be affirmed by society. The affirmation they picture is a promotion, a new job, or some other success, such as winning a major award or writing a best-seller.

There are, of course, two alternative possibilities: that the affirmation will come or will not. If it doesn't, a man then has to deal with a sense of failure and the question of what next. If the affirmation does come, the happening may bring far less satisfaction than what he dreamed it would. Either way, it's at that point that the BOOM period ends and the next stage begins.

Stage 4: "The Mid-Life Crisis." This is the stage, at some point about 40, that a man faces what Dr. Levinson calls a "sense of disparity." It's common whether he has had no affirmation of worth or has had the dreamed-for promotion, best-seller, or whatever. Either way, he faces a sense of disparity, as Levinson puts it, "between what he is, what he's done so far, what appears to be his, what he's like, and what he's going to contribute." Even if, for example, he has won the Pulitzer Prize for a book, he realizes that there is still a question of whether he is a great writer. There is still some disparity.

According to the Yale research, some businessmen may escape the crisis for a while. Executives often have a sense of being something like runners, accumulating track records. They work toward reaching specific subgoals by certain times—getting a vice-presidency by 40, for example. As long as they keep up with their set timetable, they are reassured enough to avoid considering such questions as whether it's worth it. They may have only a minimal crisis at age 40 but a much more severe one at 50.

Anything more than the mildest mid-life crisis is rough. Sooner or later, however, a man moves on to the next stage.

Stage 5: "Restabilization and the End of the Mid-Life Decade." This stage, so named by the Yale group, involves, in effect, a settling with reality. For some men, it means making radical changes in life; for others, only minor changes or none. The Yale study suggests that most men go on with the same marriage, job, and way of life, at once becoming reconciled to most aspects that are not particularly happy or fulfilling for them while increasingly putting emphasis on those that are.

An overall conclusion from the study is that while all men experience some degree of mid-life crisis and are at least a little changed by it, for many and even possibly for most the change is for the better. Tough as the reappraisal that occurs during the crisis may be, it often leads to new values and new growth.

The Male Climacteric

Controversy over whether there is any such thing as a male climacteric—a kind of man's equivalent of woman's menopause—has been going on for many years and still goes on.

Many medical men doubt its existence. Many others are convinced it is very real.

The climacteric for a woman begins the end of her fertility. From puberty until the late 40's or early 50's, a woman maintains high levels of female hormones. Then at menopause the manufacture of these hormones drops very suddenly.

Nothing so dramatic happens in a man. His testosterone levels, which increase rapidly for about half a dozen years after puberty, usually peaking at about 20, begin to fall off after that—but so slowly that he is not aware of what is happening.

At some point, however, he may become aware of change. The point may come in the 50's or 60's or even later, or sometimes earlier. But it is not inevitable, no foregone conclusion. It may not occur at any age. According to Dr. Herbert S. Kupperman, endocrinologist and associate professor of medicine at New York University Medical Center, who has had considerable experience with it, about 20 percent of men between 48 to 58 experience the climacteric and 30 to 35 percent of those between the ages of 58 and 68.

THE SYMPTOMS.   As testosterone levels drop, they may approach the area they were in at puberty. That can mean a decline in libido and sexual capacity as well as in muscular strength and aggressiveness.

The ability to have an erection or an ejaculation may begin to diminish. When an erection occurs, it may not be maintained for an adequate period of time.

Associated with the sexual manifestations may be a variety of symptoms, some of them similar to those in the female menopause, although usually not as severe or predominant.

With declining testosterone production, the hypothalamus, or lower brain, responds by sending messages to the pituitary gland in the brain, urging it to stimulate the testicles to increase the hormone output. But the testicles fail to respond. Whereupon, as one invesigator puts it, "the hypothalamus explodes with chemical and electrical activity trying to get the sex glands working again. But all that happens is that this part of the brain fatigues itself and runs amok, you might say."

There may then be repercussions throughout the body—hot flashes, sweating attacks, sudden body temperature changes, anxiety, depression, nightmares and sleeping difficulties, increasing irritability.

TESTS FOR THE TRUE CLIMACTERIC.   One possible reason for the confusion and controversy even within medical circles about the existence of the male climacteric is its noninevitability. Another is that symptoms such as those that may occur with a climacteric may have other possible causes. Psychological causes, yes. But physical ones, too—for example, diabetes, gout, a pituitary gland tumor.

The true climacteric, Dr. Kupperman argues, involves a cessation of testicular function accompanied by the varied symptoms. If the symptoms occur without evidence of change in testicular function, they are not due to the climacteric.

Evidence of testicular change in the climacteric is to be found in two measurements—one showing diminished production of testosterone; the other, no less important, showing increased levels of gonadotropins, hormones produced by the pituitary gland trying to increase output of testosterone by the testes. If a man has gout, diabetes, or a pituitary tumor that is responsible for low testosterone levels, the levels of gonadotropins would be low, too.

A confirmatory test also can be used. It involves injecting gonadotropins and then measuring sex hormone levels. If it's the climacteric that's the problem, the gonadotropins will produce little or no change in the sex hormone levels.

TREATMENT. Women today can avoid such menopausal problems as hot flashes and sweating spells through hormone-replacement therapy. Can similar treatment, using testosterone, be helpful for men in the climacteric?

Some physicians think not. They worry that the dosage of testosterone may have to be constantly increased to be effective and that that could be hard on the cardiovascular system, possibly shortening life. They prefer to try to ease a man's adjustments to the climacteric in other ways.

Says Dr. Peter H. Forsham, an endocrinologist and director of the Metabolic Research Center at the University of California in San Francisco: "The most important thing is to reverse the psychology from one of despair over what has been lost to one of enthusiasm over the powers that are left for enjoyment and accomplishment."

Other physicians believe that testosterone can be helpful when used cautiously. The hormone is available in various forms and can be given by injection every two to three weeks or can be implanted in pellet form, often effective for about six months.

Side effects sometimes occur. Some men develop breast tenderness. When the prostate is unusually sensitive, difficulty in urination may occur. In some cases, there may be priapism or persistent erection unrelated to sexual desire. Occasionally, there may be acne eruptions. Or, in some men, fluid may be retained, leading to an increase in blood pressure, which may require reducing the hormone dose and use of a diuretic to increase fluid elimination.

Use of hormone therapy can be definitely contraindicated in men who have had prostatic cancer, marked high blood pressure, significant edema (tissue swellings with fluid), or congestive heart failure.

When testosterone is used, careful checks every four to six months —with examination of the prostate and tests of blood fat levels and glucose tolerance (as a guard against developing diabetes)—are considered by many physicians to be essential.

When a man responds well to testosterone, improvement usually becomes evident within about six weeks.

Mental Ability and Middle and Old Age

It has been a common assumption that human intellectual functioning hits a peak at about age 17 and then declines for the rest of our lives. That this is a myth has been evidenced by many recent studies.

At the University of Southern California, Los Angeles, Dr. Walter Cunningham administered a U.S. Army intellectual capability test to 36 men, all of whom had taken the same test as teen-agers 20 years before. Comparing the results of both sets of tests, Cunningham found that verbal abilities had increased significantly. Considering that such abilities are the best indicator of academic success, Cunningham concludes that a man might be a better student in middle age than during high school or college years. "There are," he notes, "interesting implications here in regard to adult education. The old adage about not being able to teach old dogs new tricks may be wrong."

Another study following subjects from childhood into their 40's has shown no decline in intellectual functioning. Still another, following college students who were tested at the time of World War II and are now in their 50's, similarly has shown no decline.

Dr. Lissy F. Jarvik, professor of psychiatry at the University of California at Los Angeles, who is on the advisory board of the New Center for Aging at Wadsworth Veterans Administration Hospital, has been studying intellectual functioning in an aging population for several years. She has found that generally there is no decline in knowledge or reasoning ability—not only into the 30's and 40's but into the 60's and 70's as well.

Jarvik has been particularly concerned with a study of 136 pairs of identical twins who were first examined when they were more than 60 years of age. Complete life histories were taken, medical examinations given, and a series of psychological and psychiatric tests administered. As the twins were followed into their 70's and 80's, they generally showed none of the intellectual decline expected. It did take them longer to perform intellectual functions. But when speed was not a factor, there was a great deal of intellectual stability.

A critical loss of intellectual functioning did occur in some. Since identical twins were the subjects, the genetic factor could be ruled out. The loss appeared to be due to arteriosclerotic changes in the brain.

The most common complaint of older men is that memory is no longer as good as it once was. Yet Dr. Jarvik reports studies showing that when learning is studied under laboratory conditions, there is equally proficient learning between young and old people, and memory is also often equal.

Much of what is considered loss of memory may be due to inadequate learning in the first place, possibly caused by some factor such as hearing difficulty, impaired vision, inattention, or learning taking place too fast.

In addition, mental deterioration—or more accurately, what is misdiagnosed as mental deterioration—is often a symptom of depression and can often be restored by treatment for depression.

There is, as Jarvik emphasizes, a stereotype of older people and loss of memory. When an older person puts something somewhere and can't find it later, it is often said that this is "because of age." However, when a young person does the same thing, some other excuse is given; the loss of memory is ignored.

People often point to the striking accomplishments of youth: Mozart composing his first symphony at age 8, Alexander the Great making his major conquests in his early 20's, Albert Einstein publishing his first work on the theory of relativity when he was 26. But it's also fact that Cervantes completed *Don Quixote* when he was nearing 70; Goethe finished *Faust* at 82; Verdi began *Otello* at 72 and composed his *Requiem Mass* at 87; Milton did not begin his greatest poems until he was 50 and blind; Sophocles was an octogenarian when he wrote *Oedipus Tyrannus;* Isocrates wrote his *Panathenaicus* when he was 94; Titian and Michelangelo had long lives, productive throughout; Plato philosophized with his last breath; Beecham conducted orchestras without need for scores after he was well over 80; Leopold Stokowski continued to conduct and Artur Rubinstein to perform brilliant piano performances in the 90's; at 90, P. G. Wodehouse published a new "Jeeves" novel, approximately his ninetieth book.

When the National Institute of Mental Health, in a human aging study, followed a group of men as they moved from an average age of 71 to an average age of 81 years, not only did retests at the end of the ten years reveal performances remaining to a considerable extent close to what they had been at the beginning of the study. What stood out, too, was the "remarkably high quality" of mental functioning and the "residual capabilities" despite fairly advanced age.

The study indicates that the aged may be getting less credit than they deserve for the extent of their intellectual, perceptual, and personality strengths and capabilities, including their capabilities for acquiring new knowledge, concepts, and skills.

On some intellectual tasks there may even be increased capability with age. Stored information continually increases with the passage of years. If, for example, as a college graduate, you knew 20,000 words, by age 65 you are likely to know 40,000.

On the other hand, with age the store of knowledge and experience is often searched more slowly. The young do better under time pressure than do the aged. A boxer, because he must respond quickly, may be "old" at 30. A golfer, however, because he need not hit the ball until ready, can use experience advantageously and do well in the late years.

Older people may do best when they have opportunity to make maximum use of their experience on a self-paced basis, which is why writing, for example, is a skill that often flourishes in late life. Occupational research has shown that, if given a choice, a man as he ages will move from a job subjecting him to time pressure into another that is self-paced.

Creative Ability and Age

The notion that creativity as well as ability to learn new skills diminishes rapidly with age is, unfortunately, common. It has given rise to a view that a business organization can expect creative impetus only if it acquires "new" young minds.

Refuting this are the results coming from creativity development programs set up in major U.S. business organizations by Jack W. Taylor, director of executive development, Planning Dynamics, Inc., Pittsburgh.

The programs have been demonstrating that, if anything, the older man has the best of it when it comes to creative accomplishments and productivity. At later ages, there is less waste of and greater conservation and use of vital energy; activity has greater direction and control and therefore efficiency; older people are inured to work; they have the experience to avoid fads and pitfalls that often trap the young; they have tenacity, willpower and persistence needed for creative achievement; they bring better continuity of attention, interest, and motivation to their work.

"Contrast all this," says Taylor, "with the all-too-observable tendency of so many youngsters toward short attention spans . . . preoccupation with status, personal advancement, politicosocial relations, etc., rather than self-fulfillment . . . proclivity for 'reinventing the wheel,' not knowing what has already been tried . . . grasshopperish pursuits (as of conquests rather than concepts, for example) . . . desire, as C. F. Kettering once expressed it, to 'revolutionize the world without having to bother with the necessity of first building a working model' . . . and the like. And the contrast becomes sharp indeed."

In the creativity development programs set up in industry by Taylor, there were pretests of the creative ability of participants, comprehensive training in the principles and techniques of creative thinking, testing to measure the results of the training, and continuing follow-up evaluation of participants' subsequent creative contributions.

Analyzing the results over a period of nearly 20 years, Taylor found that the greatest positive response, as indicated by performance in posttraining versus pretraining tests, was made by older men. Average improvement for those under age 30 was 62 percent; for those over 40 it was 140 percent. Moreover, the highest level of posttraining scores was achieved by the over-40 group. The under-40 men had average scores at the 78th percentile; the average for those over 40 was at the 92nd percentile.

Most convincing of all, in the practical application phases, 80 percent of all the most workable and worthwhile new ideas later came from those over 40.

Physical Changes with Aging

There are, of course, realities of altered physiology with time. Some changes may be obvious: a little lessening of height, rounding of the nape of the neck, thinning and graying of hair, appearance of wrinkles and brown, so-called liver spots.

Although some body functions do not change with age, there is generally a gradual decrease starting at age 25 to 30 and continuing.

The rate varies with different functions, in many cases, considerably. Thus, the kidneys' maximum excretion ability is generally halved between ages 30 and 90, but the speed of conduction of nerve impulses falls off by only 15 percent in that time.

Age does produce some alteration in the nervous system's functioning as coordinator of the interactions of muscles, glands, and blood; and this could account for a gradual decline in muscular strength, which peaks by or before age 30. Commonly, baseball and football players, boxers, and track athletes never perform as well again after 30 as before.

Some investigators have found that a decrease in the heart's blood output begins at about age 20, but the aged heart is not necessarily a diseased organ.

There are digestive system changes. Some older people experience a decreased flow of saliva, leading to dryness of the mouth. There is often some decline in the amount of gastric juice secreted and in the acid and pepsin content of the secretion, and there may be some reduction in stomach motility and intestinal muscle contractions, with a greater proneness to constipation.

With advancing age, lung capacity may be reduced. Both obesity and weakening of muscles that lift the rib cage for breathing may be factors in the reduction.

Between youth and age, about 15 percent of bone may be lost. The loss is usually somewhat greater for men than for women and for whites than for blacks.

Tooth loss and gum disease are often marked in the aged, and there may be stiffening of joints and difficulty in particular in bending the hip and knee joints.

Sensory changes take place. Aging may bring some reduction in the senses of touch, pain, taste, and odor. Hearing may be affected. With changes in the lenses of the eyes that may occur with aging, accommodation may be slowed, tolerance for glare diminished, and there may be some shrinkage of visual field and delayed adaptation to darkness.

Stress imposes demands which the body meets by hormonal and other changes. Afterward, body functioning shifts back to normal for routine demands. With increasing age, the rate of recovery from stress—the shift back to normal—is slower.

But if there are negative changes with age, there are also positive ones.

While there may be some loss of visual acuity, for example, ability to comprehend what is seen improves with experience, which, of course, grows with time.

Investigators have found that the number of duodenal ulcer cases actually decreases with advanced age. They have also found that while high blood pressure tends to shorten life expectancy at any age, elevated pressures of equivalent levels have far less adverse significance at older ages than at younger ages.

The same is true of obesity, abnormal glucose tolerance tests (for diabetes), and electrocardiographic abnormalities—all less ominous in older than in younger people.

Even cancer has a less fulminating course as a rule in older people than in younger. The likelihood of survival after a heart attack is much better the later the age at which it occurs. "If one has to be afflicted with cancer or a coronary attack," as one medical journal article pointed out recently, "it is better to have it happen at the age of 70 than at 40, and not simply because one has already lived a long life."

THE VARIABILITY OF CHANGE. Individual differences in rates of aging can be marked. And different organ systems in the same person can age at markedly different rates. While one 70-year-old may have a heart output no better than that of an 80-year-old, another may have an output equal to that of a 40-year-old. But the 70-year-old with the 40-year-old heart may have kidney function like that of an 80-year-old.

Is such individual variability significant? It is for investigators, since it may contain clues to causes and underlying mechanisms. And it should be to individuals and physicians, since, as a Public Health Service publication has pointed out, "It means that the elderly patient must be carefully assessed and dealt with as an individual and not as a member of any age group, since groupings based on chronological age are much less homogeneous in the old than in the young."

CHANGING THE CHANGES. Can changes with age be controlled, held in check, or at least slowed?

There's evidence that many can be. You may have noticed that the current generation of older people generally looks younger than the generation at the turn of the century. "Many of our 65-year-olds today," says Professor Walter M. Beattie, Jr., of Syracuse University, "are more like their 50-year-old counterparts [of 75 years ago] due to improved nutrition, health care, and environmental sanitation. Whistler's mother, who epitomizes 'old age,' was 44 years old when she sat for that famous painting."

Recent scientific reports concerned with alterability of changes in aging indicate that

· Muscle strength and tone can be regained by men aged 60 to 90 with an exercise program of six to eight weeks.

· Some of the fatigue, irritability, insomnia—and even confusion —can be reversed in elderly patients through improvement in diet.

· Tooth loss and gum disease are not inevitable; preventive techniques can effectively minimize the destructive processes.

· Loss of bone density because of loss of bone calcium, a common problem in the aged, may not be age-dictated but rather the result of many years of faulty diet and hormone imbalance, earlier correctable, with some increasing possibility of being correctable later.

· Hearing loss, too, is not purely a matter of age, and there are indications that it often may be related to artery hardening, possibly to the toll of long exposure to noise, and in some cases thinning of the ear bone structures needed for good hearing. Some investigators are now hopefully studying the effects of various substances, including fluoride, in preventing such thinning of bone structure.

The Unusual Agers

From some "exotic" areas of the world reports have come from time to time of people leading active, productive, even disease-free lives at age 100 and beyond.

A serious scientific study of people in three such areas was carried out not long ago by Dr. Alexander Leaf of Harvard Medical School. The three areas: Vilcabamba, a tiny village in the Andean mountain terrain of Ecuador; Abkhazia, a district in the U.S.S.R. Caucasus Mountains; and Hunza, a province in the Karakoram Mountains, part of Pakistani-controlled Kashmir.

In Vilcabamba, the 1971 census recorded 9 people aged 100 or more in the population of 819—a rate of 1,100 centenarians per 100,000 population as against the U.S. rate of 3 per 100,000. In the Caucasus Mountains, the rate has been reported as 35 to 65 per

100,000. For Hunza, no figures are available but there is evidence that the longevity rate is high.

Leaf found the aged wrinkled but vigorous and remarkably free of disease. Photographs were obtained of a 95-year-old man in Hunza, in the field, binding hay for fodder; of a 95-year-old in Abkhazia chopping logs; of a 98-year-old in the Caucasus spinning sheep wool as his daily responsibility.

In 1969, a team of Ecuadorean physicians studied some of the aged in Vilcabamba, checking hearts, lungs, blood pressures, and carrying out various laboratory tests. They found a 100-year-old businessman, entirely free of symptoms, with normal heart and lungs and a blood pressure of only 125/70; a 120-year-old farmer with blood pressure of 135/60, also in normal health; another 120-year-old farmer, also normal.

Leaf's mission was to pick out if possible any factors common to exceptional longevity and old age free of debility.

Heredity? Generally, if favorable, it provides some advantage, but a modest one. Studies based on life insurance records in the United States have shown that children of long-lived parents have a life expectancy at age 20 that probably does not exceed three years more than that of others of the same age whose parents were short-lived. And Leaf found that while in Vilcabamba and Hunza the elderly seemed related to one another, that wasn't true in the Caucasus, where the centenarians included Russians, Georgians, Armenians, Turks, and others.

Diet was checked. It was almost exclusively vegetarian in Vilcabamba, largely so in Hunza, not so among the Caucasus group, who consumed animal products almost daily, although animal fat intake runs only about half that in the United States. Two dietary factors were uniform for all three areas: low intake of animal fats and moderate caloric intake, under 2000 a day, often 1800 or less, some 600 less than current U.S. National Research Council recommendations.

Physical activity, too, was checked. In all three areas, the level was striking. All are mountainous, and Leaf found that "an incredible amount" of physical exertion was required just to attend to the daily business of living.

Somewhat to his surprise, Leaf found psychological factors to be highly significant. In all three places, social status is largely age-dependent; the older the person, the greater the regard for him by both contemporaries and the young. There is no such thing as retirement; elders go right on working, participating in the economic and social life. Their activity may diminish somewhat in vigor, but they remain active, and in all three places the elderly have a sense of purpose and usefulness.

Vices? In all three areas, the elderly are not without them, though they tend to be moderate. They drink, smoke, maintain into old age an interest in the opposite sex; if a spouse dies, remarriage even at ages up to 100 is common.

Dr. Leaf returned with what he calls a "new perspective" on the aging process. "The tendency in medicine," he reported, "has been to equate arteriosclerosis and vascular [blood vessel] degeneration with aging. I now know that one can view the disease process as separate and apart from the aging process, that disease is not an essential part of the aging process itself. That these two are separable means that medicine can do something to eliminate the one and, if not to extend the other, at least make old age more enjoyable."

Current Research and the Span of Life and Vigor

If some hopeful investigators are right, there is for the distant future a good possibility of a human life span of 200 years or more —and, for the nearer future, before the end of the twentieth century, no small possibility of a span of 100 years containing a longer period of active, vigorous life.

Research is taking a considerable variety of approaches, with investigations into the influence on aging of such factors as the free-radical phenomenon, cross-linking, autoimmunity, diet, copying error, and temperature regulation.

FREE RADICALS. These are molecule fragments, produced by radiation and other forces, which are highly reactive, seeking to recombine and find new molecular homes. Free molecules, for example, turn butter rancid and to neutralize their effects and help preserve foods, antioxidant chemicals are used.

Free radicals are present in the body and could play a role in aging. At the University of Nebraska, Dr. Denham Harman has found them involved in forming a fibrous protein called amyloid that appears in increasing amounts in blood vessels of the brain with age, and also in areas of cell degeneration in brain tissue.

Harman has been feeding laboratory mice regularly on anti-oxidants, such as vitamin E and BHT (often used in breakfast foods as a preservative). In some mouse strains, average life-span has been increased as much as 50 percent.

CROSS-LINKING.   In common with such materials as leather and rubber, human skin and blood vessel walls lose elasticity with time, the result of a cross-linking process. In each case, the original elasticity is provided by long fibers of collagen, a basic body-building material. With aging, chemical cross-links develop between the fibers, reducing the elasticity.

Actually, the cross-linking process is always going on, but most of the time body enzymes break apart the linkages as fast as they form. A certain percentage, however, develop in a way that enzymes fail to split. And a cross-linking theory of aging holds that as such linkages increase with time, normal cell functioning may deteriorate.

Investigators working on this theory are hopeful of finding enzymes able to split cross-linkages unaffected by natural body enzymes. They see soil bacteria as a possible source. The reasoning is that the bacteria contain suitable enzymes, otherwise the earth might be covered with undecomposed animal bodies.

AUTOIMMUNITY.   The body's immune system is designed to provide protection against disease. The system provides antibodies to combat foreign invaders—not only disease-producing bacteria and other organisms but errant body cells capable of producing malignancy.

However, many studies suggest that a number of diseases—including arthritis and multiple sclerosis—result when the immune system misguidedly produces antibodies that attack the body's own tissues. Such diseases are called antoimmune, and one theory holds that aging as well may be the result of the mistaken immune system onslaught.

Certain drugs are now commonly used to give transplanted organs a chance to "take"; they suppress the immune system. In one study with animals, one such drug, Imuran, fed in late adulthood, extended the life-span by about 10 percent.

DIET.   In some of the pioneering experiments in aging research in the 1930's, Dr. Clive McCay of Cornell University found that hungry rats are longer-lived rats. He fed rats a diet sharply reduced in calories and found that some lived as long as 1450 days while rats on conventional diets seldom lived beyond 965 days.

More recently, Dr. Roy Walford, of UCLA School of Medicine, has shown that cutting food intake of mice not only lengthens life but reduces susceptibility to cancer. Some of his low-calorie mice have lived to double normal life-span and have had a markedly lower incidence of cancer than normally fed mice.

Other investigations have shown that underfeeding also increases longevity of bees, chickens, rotifers, silkworms, and other animals.

But it appears that for diet to increase life-span, food intake must be limited enough to retard growth and must be kept limited throughout life, which is not likely to make it attractive to humans.

COPYING ERROR.   Every body cell has stored within its nucleus a set of blueprints for its operations. The information is coded into the DNA molecules that also govern heredity. Cell subunits are instructed on when and how to make enzymes, hormones, and other essential materials. Some investigators believe that over a long period errors may develop in the DNA system, leading to faulty material production, which is then mirrored by aging.

The errors, or mutations, may be triggered by chemicals and radiation. When animals are subjected to undue exposure to x-rays or radioactivity, they suddenly look older and develop the usual fatal diseases earlier.

Interestingly, Dr. Denham Harman first fed mice a drug sometimes used for radiation sickness and found they lived longer. Later, he fed mice compounds that appear to be somewhat similar chemically, compounds like BHT, the antioxidant, and found that these extended mouse life by 50 percent. So a possibility is that radiation and other influences set loose free radicals which produce errors in the DNA system.

Some researchers believe that even in the presence of mutations in the DNA system, original blueprints may still be present in suppressed form; and if so, there is the possibility of finding a way not only to eliminate the causes of mutation but also to reactivate the original valid instructions and thus turn back the years.

TEMPERATURE REGULATION.   Evidence that body temperature has an influence on the aging process has been accumulating. Dr. Walford has doubled the life-span of some fish by lowering water temperature by five to six degrees centigrade. At the Rockefeller Institute, fruit flies live twice as long as usual when kept at 19 degrees C instead of the normal 25.

At the University of Southern California, Dr. Bernard Strehler has, by cooling, kept alive and well some mice to the advanced age of eight years, though they ordinarily live only two or three. Strehler believes that the principle that lower body temperature favors longevity may apply to man. There is some thought, in fact, that long-lived people may be so because they have slightly lower-than-average body temperatures, and that a thorough investigation of this possibility is called for.

OTHER THEORIES. Also under study as a possible factor behind at least some symptoms of aging is the body's complex system of hormones. Although ability to produce many hormones generally does not decline with age, the action of the hormones does become less efficient.

Among the latest studies are some suggesting that a hormone produced by the thymus gland, a long-mysterious organ behind the upper part of the breastbone extending into the neck, may be related to aging. The hormone, thymosin, only recently purified, has been found by Dr. Allan Goldstein and other investigators at the University of Texas Medical Branch, Galveston, to decline with age. A significant fall in thymosin levels in the blood of normal people between the ages of 25 and 45 has been noted. Moreover, thymosin blood levels in people with specific immunodeficiency disorders are lower than those in normal people. Goldstein and his co-workers hope to find a way to increase immunological response to disease by manipulating the amounts of thymosin in the blood.

There is some rationale for all of the theories and the research going into proving or disproving them. Some can be expected to be invalid. One or more may hold up and lead eventually to useful measures that can be applied to extending life and making later years more vigorous.

Practical Measures for Now

Based upon what's known now, can anything much be done on a practical basis to possibly extend your span of life and vigor?

Some measures are obviously useful. Early detection and control of certain forerunners of serious disease—such as high blood pressure, a major factor in coronary heart disease, heart attacks, strokes, and kidney damage; elevated blood fat levels, another major factor in the same; excessive weight, also linked to such diseases and to many others as well—makes sense.

Another: along with moderation in diet for weight control, use of a varied, balanced diet as a practical means of helping to assure an optimal intake of essential nutrients, the known and the still-unknown—optimal in the sense of no excesses, no deficiencies.

Still another: Minimizing not necessarily so much stress itself as potentially harmful reactions to stress, such as long-continued tension and anxiety—achievable through use of any of the methods of relaxation mentioned earlier that you like best, and not neglecting physical activity as a healthy means of dissipating tension and anxiety.

Exercise or physical activity is important in other ways: as a means of aiding in body weight control as well as tension and anxiety, and as a means of helping to ward off some of the characteristics of many of the elderly that have nothing to do with aging. As Dr. Fred Schwartz, chairman of an American Medical Association Committee on Aging, has put it: "Many so-called infirmities of age stem directly from lack of conditioning. Great numbers of individuals, after leaving high school or college, settle down to a routine of breadwinning that uses only a small portion of their muscle or physical equipment. In these circumstances, it is easy to understand why physical horizons have become cramped and why hands shake and why the gait becomes uncertain and tottery."

And another matter deserves emphasis: That life-span can be influenced by social and psychological factors is indicated by a 13-year study at Duke University by Dr. Erdman B. Palmore. Palmore's investigation suggests that when such factors are taken into account, the accuracy of longevity predictions can be improved by about a third over that of predictions based only on actuarial tables.

Palmore studied 270 volunteers, aged 60 to 94, each undergoing a series of tests designed to reveal social, mental, and physical factors most influential in adjustment to aging. From hundreds of answers supplied during two days of testing, 38 variables were chosen for correlation with a "longevity quotient (LQ)". LQ is the actual number of years an individual survived after the study divided by the expected number of years given by actuarial tables based on age and sex alone. An LQ of 1.0 means that an individual lived exactly as long as expected actuarially.

Of the 38 different variables, which included intelligence, education, hobbies, and community and leisure activity, 4 proved to be most important. One was work satisfaction. The second was happiness rating, designed to show attitudes toward life in general. The third was a physical functioning rating gauging how well an individual functions despite any physical limitations. The fourth was use of tobacco.

Surprisingly, the work satisfaction and happiness ratings turned out to be the most important in determining longevity. If an individual's work satisfaction was high, his life-span was predicted to be longer, and the prediction usually proved to be true.

As an example, an 81-year-old man in the study had an actuarial life expectancy of another 5.6 years. His health was average but his work satisfaction rating was the highest possible. According to prediction based on Palmore's variables, he was expected to survive 9.5 years, though he actually lived another 11.6 years, more than double the actuarial prediction and reasonably close to that of the Palmore method.

Generally, among all taking part in the study, those who professed satisfaction with their work (whether paid employment or other activity) and displayed an optimistic attitude lived longer than those who were unhappy with their work and pessimistic.

That the mind can affect the body has been recognized for some time. The Duke study offers further evidence of a relationship between mental and physical states and even between mental state and longevity.

It also underscores the importance of social influences on the mental state of older people. To a great extent, the elderly have been, in effect, detached from modern society.

"If a person is forced to retire, if he feels useless and his income drops, then his health, his interest in taking care of himself and his urge to live longer may also suffer," says Dr. Palmore. "His decline may have nothing whatever to do with his chronological age or genetic makeup."

It appears that those who live longest and most vigorously are those who, despite the inhibitions of society, refuse to give in. The decision to have an active mental, physical, and social life is really the important decision.

6

The Prostate

All This from the Prostate?

Among human health problems, prostate troubles—with emphasis on the plural—occupy a somewhat unique position. Only men, of course, are affected—but prostate disorders are among the commonest afflictions of the male, and almost every man, if he lives long enough, can expect to experience one or more. The older the man, the more likely some trouble—but young men are by no means exempt.

The disorders take many forms, sometimes confusing. Different though they may be in nature, all can produce similar symptoms: painful, difficult, too frequent or incomplete urination. But they needn't invariably lead to such discomforts and may sometimes produce no urinary symptoms at all, or just mild urinary discomforts but some low back pain, or none of these but chills and fever seemingly having nothing to do with the gland. They can be involved in sexual problems, such as premature ejaculation and impotence—as cause or consequence.

And, beyond all this, they have been indicted as possible triggers for, on occasion, a wide variety of problems—ranging from neuritis and sciatica to headache and irritability, from nausea and flatulence to palpitation and insomnia.

Even many years ago, one perceptive urologist—in fact, the man who founded the classic medical publication in the field, the *Journal of Urology*—was urging examination of the prostate and seminal vesicles "in any painful condition between the diaphragm [in the chest] and the toes."

Still Something of a Mystery Organ

As the kidneys process blood, the waste is passed along down twin pipes, the ureters, to the bladder—and, from there in due course, down a single tube, the urethra, which carries urine out of the body.

The prostate, normally about the size of a chestnut and weighing about two thirds of an ounce, is wrapped around the urethra and the base of the bladder.

For a long time, its only function was thought to be producing a lubricating fluid to transport sperms during intercourse.

Sperms take a circuitous path. They don't travel just the few inches from testicles where they are produced to penis from which they are expelled. Instead, a tube, the vas deferens, one for each testicle, carries them to the seminal vesicles, a pair of small saclike structures above the prostate, which feed and vitalize the sperms with fructose, a sugar of the kind found in fruit. From the vesicles they move along to the prostate. And at the time of ejaculation, the muscles of the prostate squeeze the gland to discharge a fluid that helps to transport and nourish the sperms.

But is that the prostate's only job? Present-day investigators think not. They're convinced that much more goes on in the gland, including the production of possibly important enzymes and hormones, which still remain to be identified in terms of both chemistry and function.

The Acute Prostate Infections

Unless the gland becomes infected, a man under age 50 isn't likely to have prostate trouble. Prior to antibiotics the commonest cause of such infection—prostatitis—was gonorrhea. Today, other types of bacteria, including *E. coli,* a normal resident of the gut, manage to get into the urethra, as do other organisms such as *Trichomonas,* which are protozoans rather than bacteria, getting there from an infected vagina, and finding a happy home and a lot of nourishment in the prostate.

Whichever microbe does the infecting, the symptoms of acute prostatitis are much the same. Urination becomes difficult to get started and painful once it does start. Urgency (sudden need to urinate) and frequency (with embarrassingly frequent trips to the john) are common. The urine may be discolored by pus or sometimes blood. And there can be low back pain, chills, and fever.

Confronted with a man with acute prostatitis—and it's nothing to fool with on your own—a urologist will take urine samples and send them to a lab for culturing and orgnism identification. Once identified so a suitable antibacterial or other antimicrobial agent can be used by injection or mouth or both, the infection is likely to be overcome.

The Chronic—and Now Treatable—Infections

Chronic infection of the prostate most commonly is caused by the *E. coli* bacteria, which may get into the prostate during intercourse.

The symptoms can be varied. There are varying degrees of low back or perineal pain, with frequency and difficulty of urination and burning on urination. There may be persistent morning drip or urethral discharge. Some patients may have predominantly sexual symptoms, such as loss of libido, impotence, or premature, painful or bloody ejaculations.

Until recently, no antibacterial agents could penetrate deeply into the prostate. Acute superficial infections responded well enough. But chronic deeper infections were beyond elimination. The prostate often served as a focus for continued reinfection of the urinary tract. And the best that could be done was to try to clear the urinary tract and confine infection to the prostate. Which meant repeated recurrences.

Now a new medication—a combination of two drugs, trimethoprim and sulfamethoxazole, available under the trade names of Septra and Bactrim—is often effective. The usual dosage is two tablets twice a day for ten days to two weeks. Cure is obtained in many cases, and the cure rates go higher with longer periods of treatment (six weeks or longer).

Noninfectious Prostatitis (Prostatosis)

Its victims are among the most persistent of doctor-shoppers, in and out of clinics and physicians' offices for years, often users of quack remedies.

Their problem: all the same symptoms of acute prostatitis, very definitely an inflamed prostate gland, but no discernible infecting organisms. Because of that, it's called by such names as noninfectious prostatitis and prostatosis. In fact, some urologists believe that there could be some as yet unidentified virus or microbe involved.

The problem is treatable—even if not ideally so (which it cannot be until the cause is established). In some cases, the antibiotic tetracycline relieves symptoms, although the relief is often short-lived. Sitting in a hot tub is a distinct help. So, too, massage of the prostate periodically. Many patients improve with the massage—perhaps, some physicians think, because along with the inflammation the gland becomes "congested" and the mechanical emptying of the fluid by massage brings the relief.

"Priests' Disease"—But Not for Priests Alone

Many of the common urinary difficulties of prostate trouble can arise in the absence of any infection and may be the result of what many urologists consider a possible form of prostatosis and call congestive prostatitis. Some term it "priests' disease." The idea is that the gland may become congested as a consequence of a change in sex habits or abstinence from sex.

On a day when there is no sexual arousal, the prostate secretes up to as much as one third or a little more of a teaspoon of prostatic fluid which moves into the urethra and out with urine. With sexual arousal, the secretion may be at least quadrupled and even multiplied by a factor of 10. Unless there is orgasmic ejaculation, the fluid may be too much for ordinary disposal and may congest the prostate and possibly lead to inflammation.

It's possible that this picture is the correct one. But there are urologists who wonder about it, finding it curious that nature, which has made the body so adaptable in other ways, should fall down here. It seems to them strange that, for one thing, the prostate could be unable to adjust secretion to need and that, for another, the gland couldn't handle with equanimity even a considerable increase in fluid within its structure.

If sexual arousal without fulfillment may be involved, it also seems possible that the problem may lie with either abnormally large prostate secretions or abnormally slow gland drainage.

Many men find relief in prostatic massage.

The Strangely Remote Symptoms

How can disorder of the prostate be responsible for a remarkable array of symptoms that seemingly have nothing to do with the gland?

This is just a partial list reported over the years by numerous investigators:

Neuritis including sciatica; muscular pain; backache; abdominal pain; nausea; flatulence; constipation; rectal pain; headache; irritability; palpitation; insomnia; apathy; depression; testicular pain. The list even includes instances of arthritis, bursitis, eye lesions, neuroses, and heart problems.

The "how," it has been suggested, lies in nervous reflexes that can be set up by overdistention of the prostate. And for some years a school of urologists has been advocating a "therapeutic test." Massage the prostate and the seminal vesicles as well, and if these relatively simple maneuvers are followed by relief of symptoms, however remote from the prostate area, then it could well be that those symptoms were referred from the prostate and vesicles.

The Big Bugaboo: Benignly Enlarged Prostate

In medical terminology, it's *benign prostatic hypertrophy (BPH)*, which simply means that there is enlargement of the prostate gland without evidence of cancer.

Not quite accurate, though. "The 'benign enlargement,' " emphasizes Dr. John K. Lattimer, professor and chairman of the Department of Urology, Columbia University College of Physicians and Surgeons, "is really an overgrowth of urethral glands which lie inside your prostate. As these enlarge, the prostate is pushed outward, away from the urethra. This is an important point, because in most operations referred to as removal of an 'enlarged prostate,' the prostate capsule is left behind and only the mass of overgrown urethral glands is removed from inside your prostate."

The prostate is made up of three lobes—one middle and two lateral (one on each side of the middle). Even large overgrowths of the laterals lead to just slight interference with urine flow. But a very small overgrowth of the middle lobe will be directly in the way and can slow the stream considerably.

If you've been noticing what might be some indications of BPH, you are certainly not alone. At least half of American men have the trouble sooner or later. Even by age 40, enlargement is present in about 10 percent, and by age 80 the proportion reaches 80 percent.

Why enlargement is so common and increases with age remains unknown. Theoretically, instead of enlargement with time, just the opposite should be true, because shrinkage or atrophy of such structures is expected with aging.

"We do know, however," Dr. Lattimer observes, "that enlarged prostates are not caused by sexual excesses, masturbation, or gonorrhea, as is popularly supposed! In fact, weekly intercourse seems to keep the prostate in good condition, even though it does not prevent enlargement. Remember the three stages of sexual activity in men: triweekly, try weekly, and try weakly (but do try)."

SYMPTOMS. BPH produces many of the same symptoms as prostatitis. The most common, and one of the earliest to develop, is a need to get up in the middle of the night to void. Urination then may start slowly and proceed feebly, with some discomfort.

Says Dr. David F. Paulson, director of urological research at Duke University: "Patients who have BPH will often complain of difficulty in starting their urine stream, some dribbling, some straining, a weak stream—down here in North Carolina they talk about the inability 'to knock the bark off the tree anymore'—and occasionally repeated voidings with inability to feel they've emptied their bladder."

With growing enlargement, there will be increasing need for frequent urination during the day, and in more severe cases pain in the lower back and perineal area will be felt. There may also be a decrease in the desire and ability to carry out sexual activity and some discomfort with erection.

In some cases, at some point, there may be a sudden shutoff of ability to urinate at all, requiring relief by passage of a tube into the bladder to remove the urine.

As Dr. Lattimer warns, during the weeks, months, or even a year or so of increasing inconvenient symptoms that a man may try to ignore, the obstruction to normal urine flow can build up some dangerous complications.

"The muscles of your bladder wall," Lattimer notes, "must be contracted with effort to force urine through the ever-narrowing urethra. These muscles become enlarged from the extra exercise, just as any other muscle would. This thickens the bladder wall and reduces your bladder's capacity. Occasionally the increased muscular effort forces weak spots on the wall of the bladder to become pockets called diverticula. These can become focal points for chronic bladder infection.

"The enlarging mass of glandular tissue within your prostate may push the bladder wall into the bladder, carrying the urethral opening high enough above the 'water line' to prevent complete emptying of your bladder. This residual urine not only is an irritant and potential source of infection but partially fills your bladder and further reduces the amount of new urine it can receive from your kidneys. The back pressure that is built up by a heavy muscular bladder wall, an enlarging and obstructing mass and residual urine may lead to hydronephrosis—a condition in which the kidney pelves, which collect urine from the kidney, and the ureters, which carry it to the bladder, are distended by fluid pressure. If this lasts very long the kidneys themselves are damaged and cannot filter waste products from the blood. Uremic poisoning results, which may lead to lethargy, coma, even death."

BPH: Cancer Forerunner

Does benign enlargement of the prostate increase the risk of developing prostate cancer? There have been concern and speculation that it does. Reassurring news comes from New York State Department of Health investigators who followed for more than ten years 838 men with enlargement and 802 others, matched for age, who had no enlargement. Twenty-four of those with enlargement and 26 of the others subsequently developed prostate cancer. Thus, prostate enlargement, the study indicates, does not mean increased risk of malignancy.

Surgery for BPH

Several well-developed surgical procedures are now available for treating BPH.

When enlargement is only moderate, it may be operated on through the penis with an instrument called a resectoscope, and the operation is called a *transurethral resection*. After anesthesia is induced, the urological surgeon inserts a tube through the urethra and, in turn, through the tube he inserts a fine knife or other cutting instrument to cut away the swollen tissue and remove it through the tube. Some surgeons freeze and kill the tissue with a liquid-nitrogen cryosurgical probe, instead. The tissue then sloughs off after several months. In either case, recovery is usually uneventful and the operation a success. Commonly, the patient is out of bed within a few days and home within ten days, able to void normally and with complete control in a short time.

When enlargement is greater and the transurethral approach is not feasible, one of the other procedures can be used.

SUPRAPUBIC PROSTATECTOMY. This is performed through an incision in the abdomen below the navel. The bladder is opened, and by inserting a finger through the opening and into the bladder outlet forward into the urethra, to where the urethra is surrounded by the prostate, the surgeon can work through the urethral lining and, with his fingertip, remove prostate tissue from its capsule. The operation takes about an hour, and only moderate pain, which can be relieved by medication, is felt afterward. Catheters and drains are left in place for about ten days until there has been sufficient healing to permit normal urination. The hospital stay is about two weeks.

RETROPUBIC PROSTATECTOMY. This, too, is carried out through an abdominal incision but the bladder is not opened. The thick fibrous capsule of the prostate is opened so prostate tissue can be removed with scissors or finger. A catheter to the bladder is left in place for about ten days during healing. Pain after operation is moderate, and after removal of the catheter, the patient may go home from hospital. After about a month of convalescence, normal activities may be resumed.

PERINEAL PROSTATECTOMY. In this procedure, the incision is between the legs in the perineal area, forward of the rectum and close to the gland. Except for the incision, the operation is carried out in the same way as retropubic prostatectomy.

SUCCESS RATE. In the vast majority of cases, prostatectomy is curative. With advances in both surgery and anesthesia, even sick, weak, and very elderly men do well.

A complication that may develop, sometimes several weeks after surgery, is bleeding. This can be stopped, when it occurs, by irrigation through a catheter.

The chances that a prostate, once removed, will grow back are less than 5 out of 100.

With successful prostate surgery, length of life is not affected nor is there usually any interference with sexual activity. In fact, because of the improvement in general health, better sleep, and increased strength, you may well feel more like doing things, including sexual intercourse, you felt too tired or worried to attempt before.

There will be one difference. The sensation of ejaculation will remain the same but the amount of semen coming out will be tiny. Most of the semen will be ejaculated backward into the bladder after any prostate operation and can be seen in the urine during the first urination after intercourse.

Experimental Nonsurgical Treatment for BPH

As it stands now, surgery remains the definitive method of overcoming the discomforts and possibly serious later consequences of benign prostatic hypertrophy. Nonsurgical methods, however, are under study.

One newer experimental drug, medrogestone, has shown some early promise in first small-scale trails. At Duke University, Dr. David F. Paulson did a double-blind study of 40 patients. (Double-blind means that the patients received the active drug some of the time and placebo, or a look-alike but inert preparation, at other times, with neither patients nor physician knowing which was being used when until the end of the study.)

All the patients felt better whether on the drug or the placebo. (The placebo effect, resulting to some extent from increased hope with a new "treatment" and to some extent, too, from increased medical attention, can be powerful.) But the recorded outflow of urine improved only on the drug.

Dr. Paulson has reported being unable to say yet whether the drug could be an alternative to prostatectomy. For one thing, it has had occasional cardiovascular side effects. Also, it may make men impotent who are of borderline potency—a problem many older men have—although those who are frankly potent don't seem bothered by it. Several men in the study refused further medication because they no longer got erections. The erections returned after discontinuation of the drug.

"The question," Dr. Paulson has observed, "is whether you can leave patients on medrogestone for a while, get some reduction in prostate size, then take them off and let them become potent again."

HELP FROM ZINC? Zinc is one of a group of what are called *trace metals* (found in the human body in only tiny amounts), as little understood for the most part now as were vitamins 75 years ago, yet vital. Iodine is one; copper, another; chromium, still another; and there are more.

Their combined weight in the body amounts to no more than an ounce. Yet they play essential roles. Without the speck of iodine present, the thyroid gland could not produce thyroid hormones, which would leave us cretins, mentally and physically under-developed.

Only recently has zinc come in for study. It's present to some extent in all body tissues—red and white blood cells, bone, kidney, liver, muscle, heart, spleen, and brain. The prostate gland, however, has one of the highest concentrations measured—about 530 micrograms (millionths of a gram) of zinc per gram of dry gland weight.

For a decade, the possible role of zinc in prostatic disorders has been under study by Dr. Irving M. Bush and researchers from the Cook County Hospital, Chicago Medical School, Hektoen Institution for Medical Research and Mount Sinai Medical Center, Chicago.

In their work, the Chicago scientists found that blood levels of zinc are generally reliable indicators of prostate zinc concentrations. And, overall, they found that 7 percent of men have definitely low zinc levels while 30 percent more have borderline levels.

Curiously, in men with prostatosis, contrary to the general rule, blood zinc levels may be normal but prostate and semen levels are low, Bush and his colleagues have reported.

And when they tried giving oral zinc sulfate in doses ranging from 50 to 660 milligrams a day for 2 to 16 weeks, they found that in 70 percent of the first 40 patients, all symptoms of prostatosis were relieved. In a subsequent study, they found that even lower doses—as little as 50 to 150 milligrams of zinc per day—achieved the same results in the same percentage of more than 200 men.

The Chicago researchers then went on to check into a possible role for zinc in BPH. It turned out that men with enlarged prostates have normal blood zinc levels; and when given zinc, their prostate or semen zinc levels do not markedly increase. Yet, in a trial with a group of men with BPH given 150 milligrams of zinc sulfate per day for 2 months and then 50 to 100 milligrams a day thereafter, symptoms were reduced in all cases, and in slightly better than 70 percent there was some actual shrinkage of the prostate.

TREATING THE CHOLESTEROL INFLUENCE.   For several years, some mystery has surrounded a drug called candicidin and its reported effects on BPH.

The drug is an antifungal agent. It is widely used for the topical treatment of a vaginal fungal infection in women. Yet, for reasons unknown, candicidin has been showing beneficial effects on BPH in a number of studies.

In one, 92 patients with BPH were treated with 300 milligrams of oral candicidin daily for a minimal period of 5 months. Of the 92 men, 87 normally would have required surgery. After candicidin therapy, 64 patients, or 73 percent, were able to avoid surgery for as long as 18 months without harmful effects. In addition to feeling better, most of the men showed objectively measurable improvement, including marked reduction in residual urine in the bladder. Those who did not respond to the drug and required surgery showed no adverse effects.

In another study, 43 BPH patients received the drug for periods longer than 3 months. Nearly 90 percent showed partial to complete remission of symptoms and improvement in urinary flow rate and urine retention. Over one third showed a decrease in prostate size. The only undesirable effect noted was occasional stomach upset.

In still another study, although there was no change in prostate size, better than 75 percent of the men had improvement in such symptoms as dribbling, hesitancy, and frequency of urination.

Now, coming after these studies, what appears to be a striking new insight into BPH itself as well as the role of candicidin has been provided by research by Dr. Carl P. Schaffner of Rutgers University and other investigators.

Using highly refined analytical techniques, they have been able to show that gland enlargement is associated with cholesterol accumulation—and the greater the enlargement, the greater the overall content of cholesterol.

In related studies on both laboratory rats and hamsters, Schaffner has shown that cholesterol production in the prostate is regulated by the amount of the hormone testosterone present. Castrated animals produce no testosterone so there was little cholesterol produced and the prostate remained small.

Schaffner's findings indicate that the human prostate produces cholesterol just as the liver and intestinal tract do. But where the liver has a regulatory control that shuts off cholesterol production when a certain level in the body is reached, the prostate has no such regulatory control and continues to manufacture cholesterol regardless of a man's sexual activity. A large amount of cholesterol accumulates, and the accumulation may increase with age and declining sexual activity, which may cause further retention of prostate cholesterol that would otherwise be lost in ejaculation.

Schaffner's studies also show that the drug candicidin, in addition to its antifungal activity, has a cholesterol-lowering ability. Administered as an oral capsule, it binds with cholesterol to form a complex which passes out of the body through excretion.

The drug has not been approved for use in the United States for prostate conditions. But Schaffner has reported that it is currently under study at New York Medical College, Mount Sinai School of Medicine, and the College of Medicine and Dentistry of New Jersey, where urologists, working with it experimentally, have achieved an overall 78 percent elimination of the need for surgery by using it to remove accumulated cholesterol.

Cancer of the Prostate

Unlike benign enlargement, cancer of the prostate is a malignant growth of the prostate itself rather than the urethral glands in the prostate. It, too, produces urinary difficulties.

Most enlargements are benign, yet autopsy findings indicate that 20 percent of men past the age of 50 will have prostatic cancer, with the risk climbing with age, so that by 70 half the men in this country have the beginnings of the malignancy. The disease is found after death in many men over 50 in whom it existed in hidden form because prostate cancer grows slowly.

After age 65, it is the commonest malignancy in men, occurring much more often than cancer of the stomach, the lung, or even the skin.

Although prostate cancer grows slowly at first, once it starts to spread, it tends to spread widely throughout the body.

The best chance for cure comes with early detection while the cancer is still a tiny nodule on the surface of the gland. Usually, the nodule forms on the part of gland closest to the rectal wall, where it can be detected by a simple finger rectal examination, done as part of an annual physical examination in the doctor's office. Unfortunately, all prostatologists agree that far too few men over 40 have an annual physical examination which includes a rectal examination of the prostate. Failure to examine the prostate is perhaps the greatest omission in physical examinations.

TREATMENT.   When prostate cancer is found at very early stages, it may in many cases be removed by transurethral resection through the penis in much the same manner as the procedure is performed for benign prostate enlargement.

At more advanced stages, still when the malignancy is confined to the gland, a more radical procedure may be used to remove the entire prostate—contents and capsule. This may be done through an incision in the perineal area, between the anus and scrotum. Because this requires cutting through nerves and muscular tissue surrounding the capsule, impotence follows. For erection, nervous impulses go from the brain to nerves actuating muscles around the uppermost part of the urethra which are involved in the process of creating tumescence or swelling in the penis for erection. Without the intact nerves and muscles, there can be no erection.

In some cases, when the malignancy either is still confined to the gland or has extended locally outside it, radical radiation treatment may be the treatment of choice.

One technique of high-energy radical radiation treatment, developed by Dr. Malcolm A. Bagshaw of Stanford University Hospital in California, uses a beam from a 4.8 million volt linear accelerator, although other sources of high-energy radiation, such as the cobalt-60 unit, can be employed. Usually for about five days a week for a period of about seven weeks, the sharply defined beam is concentrated briefly on the prostate and immediately surrounding tissue, with a little directed higher up in the pelvis to catch any cancer cells that may have advanced upward.

Among hundreds of patients treated by the method, 72 percent of those with cancer limited to the prostate have survived at least five years, and 44 percent at least ten years. Of those with disease extending beyond the prostate capsule, the corresponding survival rates are 51 and 38 percent.

When the cancer is further advanced, with metastases or spread beyond the reach of surgery or radiation, hormonal manipulation may be used. Prostate cancer is sensitive to sex hormones. Testosterone promotes its growth while the female hormones, estrogens, tend to inhibit growth.

The hormonal manipulation can be by either castration or use of estrogen. About 80 percent of men are more comfortable as a result, and some experience objective improvement in the cancer.

Men in whom the cancer has spread to liver or lung may not respond well to hormone manipulation. For them and for others who do respond but then go into relapse, chemotherapy (use of anticancer drugs) may be indicated. Recent studies by the National Prostate Cancer Project indicate the value, in terms of both subjective and objective improvement, of the drugs 5-fluorouracil and cyclophosphamide, even though they are not curative.

Currently, intensive research is under way with at least nine new drugs that may be useful, perhaps more useful than present ones, for prostate cancer.

7
Heart, Circulation, and Lungs

Heart

On Not Being Fooled by a Chest Pain

Commonly, the first thought of any man experiencing chest pain is that the heart is the problem. It may be. But chest pain much like that from heart trouble (see below) can stem from many conditions which have nothing to do with the heart itself.

One that can be mistaken for heart disease is irritability of the esophagus, called cardiospasm. It can cause chest pain similar to the anginal chest pain of real coronary heart disease, often spreading upward to shoulders and arms. But it is usually briefer than real angina, appears during rest, and is often relieved by walking about.

A local chest or shoulder girdle problem can produce pain on exertion, especially when chest muscles are used. But angina is more likely to be triggered when leg muscles are used.

It's possible to mistake gallbladder disease, mild rib inflammation, or arthritis in the joints between rib and spine for heart disease. Bursitis, especially of the left shoulder, can act like coronary heart disease. So can neuralgia from spinal arthritis, particularly in the neck or cervical region. In one study, 35 of 151 patients who thought they had heart disease had the neuralgia, with chest pain, numbness, tingling, and weakness stemming from irritation of

147

nerves in the neck area of the spine, most commonly as the result of poor posture or acute neck strain from a fall or other injury.

Air swallowing (page 188) is a common cause of anginalike pain that may spread to neck, shoulders, arms, and be accompanied by trembling, sweating, weakness, breathlessness, and pallor.

Chest pain can come from hiatus hernia (page 192); from pleurisy, an inflammation of the lining of the lungs; from shingles, when nerves are irritated by a viral infection; from food poisoning; from sleeping with arms or shoulders in unnatural position; and from an unsuspected broken rib incurred during coughing.

The Real Thing: CHD, Anginal Chest Pain, Heart Attack

The chest pain of coronary heart disease (CHD), which also can cause heart attack, is termed *angina pectoris* (angina meaning choking or suffocating pain, pectoris referring to the chest).

The situation in coronary heart disease is not unlike what occurs if you happen to have a car with a fuel line corroding inside, becoming encrusted with rust deposits that reduce its bore. Enough fuel may flow through the line from tank to engine for slow or moderate speed on a level road. But speed up or climb a hill and the fuel flow is inadequate and the motor sputters. So may the heart in coronary heart disease, in which fatty deposits clog the interior of the arteries feeding the heart muscle, producing angina.

Angina is NOT like a heart attack in which blood flow to part of the heart muscle is suddenly restricted severely or cut off completely, damaging the part of the heart deprived of nourishment. Angina represents protest rather than attack.

It usually appears during exertion—shoveling snow, climbing stairs, running for a train, playing tennis. As a rule, it's felt as a constricting sensation in the midchest which often shoots out to left arm and fingertips. But there are variations. Occasionally, the pain occurs between the shoulder blades, in the left hand or wrist, in the left arm or shoulder, in the pit of the abdomen, in the jaws and teeth, and/or in portions of the right arm with no chest pain at all.

Commonly, an attack of angina makes the victim stop whatever he is doing immediately; it's painful, also frightening, producing a sense of foreboding.

An attack usually lasts only a few minutes and is quickly relieved by rest. If the pain lasts longer than 15 minutes, it's not likely to be from angina.

HEART ATTACK VS. ANGINA. The hallmark of a heart attack is chest pain that may range from a slight feeling of pressure to a sensation of the chest being crushed in a vise.

An angina victim who experiences a heart attack may assume at first that he is having another angina bout. But this time, stopping activity doesn't help. Typically, pain of a heart attack lasts for several hours and doesn't subside until a narcotic such as morphine is administered.

Along with the pain, almost always there is a feeling of great anxiety, a sense of death being near. Commonly, the face turns ashen gray, a cold sweat develops, and often there are retching, belching, and vomiting—which is why a heart attack sometimes is confused with stomach upset. Shortness of breath is frequent. Palpitations—sensations that the heart is beating abnormally fast and hard—may occur.

GUIDELINES. Several may help distinguish the chest pain of heart attack from angina and from chest pains with nothing to do with the heart:

A heart attack is less probable when chest pain is below the nipple and to the left; when pain is localized completely to the left; when pain is sharp rather than a dull pressure or squeezing sensation; when pain comes and goes; when it lessens when you lie down. If it lasts only 1 to 5 minutes, it is probably angina, not a heart attack.

Because first hours and even minutes can be critical in dealing with a heart attack, if pain lasts more than 15 minutes and, even before that, if you have the slightest suspicion of a heart attack, get yourself or ask someone to get you to the nearest hospital or call the rescue squad. And immediately on arrival in the emergency room, tell personnel there that you may be having a heart attack and insist on being taken to the coronary care unit.

How to Know If You Are at Increased Risk

Why do some men, especially relatively young ones, develop CHD and others do not?

Recently, studying more than 1,300 Army men with CHD and

comparing them with other healthy men, National Academy of Sciences–National Research Council investigators found that those who developed the disease had high blood pressures, greater weight, heavier frame, and tended to be shorter in height. More so than others, they tended to come from the Middle Atlantic States, to be of higher socioeconomic status, to have some graduate education and to be of officer rank, and also to be of Jewish origin and have blood group A. There seemed to be significantly lesser risk among men from rural areas and those whose earlier jobs had involved much physical activity.

In another study, this one in Israel, University of Tel Aviv Medical School researchers picked 10,000 men, aged 40 and over, all then free of angina and with no heart attack history. Over a 5-year period, during which the group was followed, some developed angina. Among factors significantly associated with the development: high blood pressure, high cholesterol level, diabetes, lack of physical activity, anxiety, peptic ulcers, serious psychosocial problems.

Data from scores of studies indicate that many factors seem to enter into development of CHD, with the most prominent including high blood pressure, excessive blood fat levels, smoking, heredity (history of CHD in the family), excessive weight, too little exercise and physical activity, tension and stress, diabetes.

Any one risk factor tends to increase the likelihood of CHD. Two or more are often present in the same person. Men with three, four, or more make up an especially high risk group. It is unlikely that all risk factors would be present in any one person, but if they should be, he would have 25 or more times the likelihood of getting a heart attack than the average man.

Preventive Measures: Do They Really Work?

One of the best indications that combating risk factors—in this case, three such factors—comes from a 5-year study that began in 1972 in a county (North Karelia) in eastern Finland that for years has recorded one of the world's most morbid statistics: more people dying there from heart disease than proportionally anywhere else in the world.

After concerned community leaders petitioned the national government for help, a state-financed program began with assistance from the World Health Organization, aimed particularly at three major risk factors.

Laws were passed forbidding smoking in public buildings and on public transportation, and many private offices voluntarily joined the campaign. Prior to the project, 54 percent of men smoked; 44 percent still do.

Reducing blood fat was difficult because the diet in the county of North Karelia is traditionally based on fatty foods using local products. Dairies, a key source of fat, promoted low-fat and eventually nonfat milk. People liked to spread thick butter on bread; they were asked to use margarine. Grilled sausages were a popular food, especially after a steaming sauna. But the local product contained large amounts of fat. After experiments, sausages were made with a 25 percent mushroom content and, being delicious, sold well. Fresh vegetables were rarely seen on the dinner table. Families were urged to buy vegetables.

Blood pressures were taken at frequent intervals and drug treatment to reduce excessive pressure given as needed. The number of men receiving treatment more than tripled.

End result: The heart attack rate for men which, until 1972, had been increasing over a 30-year period, dropped 40 percent.

The Eating Factor

How much good can it do to modify diet in order to cut fat and cholesterol intake?

In a recently reported 10-year study, investigators of the Atherosclerosis Research Group, Montclair, New Jersey, put 100 men, aged 30 to 50, all with coronary heart disease and all with a history of heart attack, on a low-fat diet and matched them with a group of comparable men not under dietary management.

Over the 10-year period, the diet-managed men experienced significant reductions in blood fat levels compared with the others and ended up with a 17 percent greater survival rate.

Can already-present artery-clogging be reversed by a low-fat diet? Some hope that it can be comes from animal studies at the University of Chicago. There Drs. Draga Vesselinovitch and Robert W. Wissler fed monkeys high-cholesterol diets for 18 months, then sacrificed some of the animals and, upon autopsy, found extensive artery disease.

They then divided the remaining monkeys into two groups, one remaining on the same original diet, the other going on a low-fat diet. Later, upon sacrifice, the animals on the low-fat diet had markedly fewer fatty deposits on artery linings than did the others, suggesting to the investigators that "to some degree, even advanced stages of the disease can be reversed if sufficiently low blood cholesterol levels are sustained for a long period of time."

But is it really what you eat—or how much you eat—that counts most in holding cholesterol and blood fat levels down? An answer comes from an investigation in Tecumseh, Michigan, of more than 4,000 adults by University of Michigan Medical School researchers.

For each of the participants, tallies were made of consumption of 110 different food items; of average consumption of foods high in fat, starch, sugar, and alcohol; and of total daily caloric intake.

It turned out that the cholesterol and blood fat levels showed no striking correlation with kind of diet but did with body fat. It's overnutrition, the investigators believe—too much caloric intake leading to weight gain and body fat accumulation—that is more important in raising blood levels than the proportions of fat, starch, sugar, or alcohol in the diet.

The Exercise Factor

Does exercise really reduce your chances of suffering a heart attack?

A lot of people today are running, jogging, or otherwise ambulating in gyms, on athletic fields, in parks and along roads to keep fit, lose weight, for a sense of well-being—and, very often, beyond that with the idea that such activity will prevent or benefit coronary heart disease.

But whether exercise actually does help against heart disease is no simple question to answer. Many studies have been made—with contradictory results.

For example, seven years ago came results of an international cooperative study in which research teams checked 12,770 men of ages 40 through 49 in the United States, Japan, and five European countries. The findings: no evidence of difference in CHD risk between sedentary and active men, suggesting to the researchers that "if physical inactivity is indeed a risk factor, it is of much smaller magnitude than hypertension, cigarette smoking, and elevated serum cholesterol."

More recently, a 5-year English study covered 18,403 government workers aged 40 to 64. Those who exhibited evidence of heart disease were evaluated separately from the others. It turned out that over the term of the study active members of the group with evidence of disease experienced a slightly higher rate of fatal heart disease than did the less active. In the group without previous evidence of disease, the reverse was true. The more active men had a slightly lower death rate than the less active. In neither group, however, was the difference significant enough to be outside the limits of chance.

On the other hand, many studies support the value of activity. A famed British study found that conductors of London double-decker buses, who spent much time running up and down stairs, had a markedly lower incidence of heart attacks than the drivers, who sat at their jobs. An American study found that heart attacks, when they occurred, were fatal for 49 percent of the least active men, for 25 percent of the moderately active, and only 17 percent of the most active men. A British study turned up much the same findings on fatal versus nonfatal outcomes.

A 22-year study of San Francisco longshoremen found vigorous activity to be the significant factor. Compared with workers with light or moderately strenuous jobs, those doing the heaviest work had a lower incidence of heart disease and only one-third the rate of sudden deaths from heart attacks.

In Palo Alto, California, where Stanford University has a Heart Disease Prevention Program, investigators studied men, aged 35 to 59, who averaged 15 miles of running a week. Blood fat levels in these men were more like those of young women least vulnerable to heart disease than those of men of comparable age leading sedentary lives.

In one of the latest studies, researchers looked into why New Mexico has the lowest heart attack death rate among men of any state in the union. They found that in New Mexico there is a stepwise decrease in death rate according to altitude, with the rate 28 percent lower among men living above 7,000 feet than among those living at 3,000–4,000 feet. There seemed to be no other difference beyond altitude between the men overall. The likely explanation, the investigators suggest: in thin mountain air, any activity, even the most routine, involves greater exercise than when performed at lower altitudes.

Smoking

Various studies have shown the detrimental influence of cigarette smoking. In one, covering 187,783 men, the CHD death rate was more than twice as high for smokers of a pack or more daily as for nonsmokers; and the greater the number of cigarettes smoked and the number of years of smoking, the higher the death rate.

The government's famed long-term study in Framingham, Massachusetts, covering some 5,000 people in that community has shown a heart attack risk nearly double in heavy cigarette smokers, a threefold excess of sudden deaths among smokers compared with nonsmokers, and five times greater sudden-death risk in heavy smokers.

A study of men who already had coronary heart disease showed that those who continued to smoke a pack or more daily died 16 years sooner, on the average, than the nonsmokers.

Water and the Heart

A role for soft water in heart attacks and strokes has been suggested by numerous studies. In one, for example, in Monroe County, Florida, after the local water supply was switched from soft rain to hard well water, heart attack and stroke deaths were halved over a 4-year period.

Exactly how soft water may increase risk is not established, but two possibilities have been proposed: that soft water in some way may directly affect the heart muscle or that it may favor high blood pressure, which often is more prevalent in soft-water areas.

Although hard drinking water in itself may not assure reduced risk, some investigators suggest that if you live in a hard-water area and are softening your water, you may do well to leave at least one tap producing hard water for drinking purposes.

High Blood Pressure

High blood pressure, or hypertension, known to affect upward of 23 million Americans, is recognized now as a major factor in heart attacks, strokes, and kidney failure as well.

Even when it produces no overt symptoms—a common phenomenon—elevated pressure can have a disastrous effect on arteries
in various areas of the body over a prolonged period. The constant
high pressure tends to thicken arteries and make them arteriosclerotic. The heart muscle then has to pump harder, becomes
enlarged to do so, and manages for a time. Eventually, it may lose
pumping efficiency. Impaired blood circulation then may lead to
congestive heart failure—with fluid accumulation in body organs,
including legs and lungs. Heart pain, or angina, may appear; so
may a heart attack.

Increased pressure over an extended period may also damage the
kidneys, leading to kidney failure, or may harm brain blood vessels,
leading to stroke.

The first conclusive evidence of the value of treating hypertension came from studies in the late 1960's and early 1970's by a
Veterans Administration Cooperative Study Group. Even in men
with relatively moderate hypertension, treatment reduced the risk
of serious complications over a 5-year period from 55 to 18 percent.
The incidence of stroke was reduced fourfold, and heart failure
and kidney deterioration did not occur over the 5 years.

Hypertension today can be controlled effectively—in some men,
by diet emphasizing weight reduction and reduced salt intake; in
others, by drugs. Treatment efficacy has begun to lead to a change
in attitude among insurance companies, which until recently either
refused policies to hypertensives or provided them at stiff extra
premium cost. A study by one company, Aetna Life and Casualty,
shows that treated hypertensives, as compared with untreated,
have a 50 to 100 percent lower death rate in every disease category.

Type A Behavior

A pattern of behavior has been linked in recent years to CHD
by Drs. Meyer Friedman and Ray H. Rosenman of San Francisco
and other investigators.

Called type A, it is characterized by excessive ambition, drive,
and competitiveness and by a strong sense of time urgency. In
contrast, type B individuals are not necessarily passive, unproduc-
tive, or unsuccessful but they are not excessively driven or excessively competitive and are relatively free of a sense of time urgency.

According to an 8½-year Friedman-Rosenman study, type A

individuals are more than twice as prone to CHD, five times as prone to a second heart attack, and twice as prone to fatal heart attacks.

Additional facts were determined in a more recent study by University of Western Ontario, Canada, researchers of managers from 12 companies, of whom some 60 percent were type A. The type A people were found to have markedly higher blood pressure and higher cholesterol and blood fat levels; a greater percentage were cigarette smokers; they were also less interested in and participated less in physical activities.

The Canadian investigators determined that where an average man at age 45 has a 4.4 percent probability of developing CHD in the next 6 years, type A individuals have a 6.3 percent probability, or about a 50 percent greater risk.

For a fuller discussion of type A behavior and breaking out of it, see page 19.

If You Have a Heart Attack

For more and more reasons now, your best chance for survival is to get to a hospital as quickly as possible after a heart attack starts or after you have even a slight suspicion that you're experiencing one.

For one thing, the major danger in the first minutes and hours is an abnormal rhythm triggered by the attack. It can progress rapidly to the point of causing death. In a hospital, heart rhythm can be monitored and kept or rapidly returned to normal by drugs and other measures. Oxygen and anticlotting agents can be administered to help.

A new procedure, shown in studies in more than 20 medical centers to halve the mortality associated with moderately severe heart attacks, is called *external pressure circulatory assist (EPCA)*. It involves encasing the legs in special bootlike equipment and applying pressure to the large blood vessel bed in the legs. The pressure is synchronized so it is exerted between heartbeats and increases the flow of vital blood through the coronary arteries feeding the heart muscle.

Other new assistance techniques are being developed rapidly based on new insights into what actually happens during a heart attack. It once was thought that damage to the heart muscle produced by the attack occurred all at once. Now it appears that that isn't necessarily so, that damage may be small to begin with but may increase progressively in the hours after an attack. And promising measures that seem capable of immediately stopping progression of damage are being evaluated.

After a Heart Attack: Early Activity

Once it was customary to keep heart attack patients in bed for extended periods. Now, with good reason, the tendency is to abbreviate the bed rest period and encourage early activity when a patient has no complications.

Typically, in a recent study, 154 patients free of complications on the first or second day after an attack were assigned to two groups. One group stayed in bed for the traditional period of 3 or more weeks. The other group were placed on a program of progressive activity. Hospital stay for the latter group was 21.3 days compared with 32.8 for the others. There were no significant differences in attack recurrences, heart failure, or anginal attacks. But over a period of 6 to 20 months, the strict-bed-rest group had greater disability than did the active group.

Coronary Artery Bypass Surgery

Since the mid-1960's, a surgical technique of bypassing obstructing blocks in coronary arteries has come into increasing use, especially for men with severe angina. It involves application of a length of vein from elsewhere in the body. Commonly, the saphenous vein from a leg is employed. It can be removed from the leg (it commonly is in varicose vein operations), and other veins in the leg can take over its functions.

A section of the vein is then attached at one end to the aorta, the main trunkline artery coming out of the heart, and at the other end to a point in the coronary artery beyond where it is obstructed. Several such bypasses of blocked coronary arteries may be performed for an individual patient.

When is bypass surgery needed and likely to be more effective than medical management with drugs to improve the outlook for survival? There has been some controversy between cardiologists and heart surgeons, which is not likely to be resolved completely until the results of many long-term studies are in.

But experiences to date suggest that certain patients may do best with surgery. Patients who benefit most appear to be those with blocking of at least two of the main coronary arteries or of the left main coronary artery alone, which between them may account for about half of all patients with angina.

One study at the University of Alabama Medical Center followed 85 patients who underwent operation because of at least 50 percent closing off of their left main coronary arteries. Eighty-seven percent were alive after two years, contrasted with 62 percent among comparable patients treated medically. None of the medicated patients was ever completely free of angina; about 60 percent of the bypass group were pain-free after operation. Further experience at Alabama indicates equally good results at two years with bypasses for patients with two or more main arteries involved.

At the VA Hospital, Oteen, North Carolina, of more than 100 patients with at least 50 percent blockage of the left main coronary artery, 2-year mortality for those medically treated was 38 percent, for the surgically treated, 17 percent.

At the VA Hospital, Houston, a study following up for a mean of 34 months two groups of comparable men, 56 of whom had surgery while 60 received medication, found that most patients in both groups improved, but more of the surgically treated were entirely free of symptoms (68 percent versus 8 percent), and exercise tolerance improved by more than twice as much in the surgically treated.

One of the largest studies has been carried out at The Hospital of the Good Samaritan and University of Southern California, Los Angeles, with 1,532 patients operated on since 1969. Previous studies have shown that over a 5-year period, a person with single-artery disease faces a 2 to 4 percent risk of death per year; with two-artery disease, the risk is 7 to 8 percent; with three-artery disease, 10 to 12 percent. Patients undergoing surgery and followed for 5 years had an average yearly death rate of 1, 3, and 3.9 percent, respectively. There was some risk of death during surgery—0.6, 2.2, and 4.4 percent, respectively, for single-, double-, and triple-artery obstruction—at the time these patients were operated on.

Improved operative techniques now are reducing the operative risk.

Stroke

On Your Chances

Your risk of having a stroke before you are 70 is 1 in 20. But recent medical advances allow you to do something to lessen your chances and, if a stroke should occur, increase your chances of returning to a productive life afterward.

More than 200,000 Americans have been killed each year by strokes, sometimes also called cerebrovascular accidents, which are commonly caused by a fatty deposit or clot in an artery supplying blood to the brain.

Catching the TIA's

As late as the 1950's, treatment and prevention of stroke was almost nonexistent. It wasn't generally understood then that before a full-scale disabling or fatal stroke, many people experience warning episodes, sometimes called "little strokes" but more accurately known now as *TIA's* or *transient ischemic attacks,* indicating temporary interruption of blood flow to the brain and producing fleeting symptoms such as a period of slurred speech, loss of vision in one eye, or weakness in an arm or leg. If left untreated, at least one third of TIA's go on within 3 to 5 years to completed strokes in which brain function may be permanently impaired.

Increasingly now, surgeons can restore adequate circulation to people who suffer one of these ominous early episodes and prevent serious subsequent strokes.

Often, the problem lies in a blockage in the internal carotid artery in the neck. The artery is accessible. An x-ray procedure, using an injected dye, can reveal the problem, and the diseased section can be opened and the deposits reamed out with relative ease.

Until recently, when the blockage occurred higher up, in an artery in the brain itself, surgery couldn't help. But recent development of microsurgical techniques now enables surgeons to help in such cases by constructing a bypass around the obstruction.

In a new operation, the superficial temporal artery, a branch of the external carotid artery that runs from the temple across the forehead, is exposed by a scalp incision and cut just above the eyebrow. One end is sutured and left in place; the disconnection involves no danger, since the scalp receives adequate blood from other vessels. A half-dollar-size piece of bone is then removed from the side of the skull above the ear, exposing the middle cerebral artery, an extension of the internal carotid. The free end of the severed forehead artery is then run into the hole, and with the help of a microscope, the surgeon attaches it to the middle cerebral artery, thus bypassing the blocked brain vessel.

Other measures may be used in addition to or in place of surgery. Anticoagulant and other "blood-thinning" drugs are often helpful for several reasons. Abnormally thick blood favors a "clot" stroke. The drugs may minimize that risk.

Other factors enter the picture. They include high blood pressure, excessive blood fat levels, diabetes, obesity, cigarette smoking.

A stroke prevention program at the University of Pennsylvania Hospital, Philadelphia, has demonstrated that major strokes can largely be prevented by attention to these factors as well as any narrowing of arteries leading to or in the brain.

In patients entering the program after their first TIA, any such factors present are identified and treated with diet, medication, avoidance of cigarettes where smoking is involved, and surgery where necessary. During a 5-year follow-up period less than 7 percent of patients went on to develop a major stroke, and 82 percent were free of any further TIA's.

A Major Preventive

High blood pressure is a major risk factor in TIA's and strokes. Studies have shown decisively that treatment of high blood pressure, even of mild degree, will drastically reduce the likelihood of a stroke. Typically, in a period of 5 years, when mild high blood pressure was treated effectively, the incidence of stroke was reduced by 75 percent.

Unfortunately, high blood pressure goes untreated in many men who skip periodic physical examinations and only seek medical help when they have some obvious trouble. Hypertension, however, can be present for long periods without producing any obvious symptoms.

It's possible to minimize the likelihood of your developing hypertension. If you were in good health at age 25, you should weigh for the rest of your life what you weighed then. That ideal weight materially diminishes the risk of pressure elevation. So does a reduction of salt intake in the diet. The healthy man needs only 0.25 gram of salt a day; the average American consumes close to 10 grams, 40 times as much. You should know, too, that every time you inhale a cigarette, blood pressure goes up.

Lungs

Lung Cancer

The most common malignancy in men, lung cancer may well be the most preventable of cancers. Its most likely victims: men over 45 who are heavy smokers, work in dirty or dusty jobs, and live in large cities. Lives lost: 70,000 people a year, 4 men to every woman.

Air pollution from incomplete burning of heating systems, smoke from industry, car exhaust fumes, dust, even asbestos from asphalt roads, are related to the increased incidence of cancer of the lungs, which is higher in large industrial communities. Those who breathe both cigarette smoke and polluted air into the lungs have greatly increased risk.

SMOKING—BUT WITH REDUCED RISK. The association between smoking and lung cancer has been established by many studies. One of the largest involved a follow-up of more than one million people for a 4-year period. It determined that the risk of dying from lung cancer for men aged 35 to 84 who smoke less than a pack a day is 6 times as great, and for men smoking two or more packs 16 times as great, as for nonsmokers.

Inhaling is a significant factor. Every smoker gets some smoke into his lungs, but purposeful inhalation multiplies the amount. Men who think they do not inhale or inhale only slightly have 8 times the risk and men who inhale deeply have 14 times the risk of lung cancer as nonsmokers. The earlier smoking starts, the greater the risk. Men who begin before age 15 have nearly 5 times as much risk as those who start after 25.

Lung cancer victims and normal people differ markedly in cigarette smoking habits, according to a recent study by Dr. W. H. Anderson of the University of Louisville of 933 subjects, 47 of whom had lung cancer.

With special equipment used to establish "puff profiles," the study found that the lung cancer group consumed more than twice as much tar during their smoking lifetimes, spent an average of 1 minute and 12 seconds longer with each cigarette, smoked more cigarettes before breakfast. Total daily smoking time for lung cancer patients, at 2 hours and 28 minutes, was about twice as long as for the others.

Short of eliminating smoking altogether, Dr. Anderson suggests, it may be possible to decrease the risk by smoking cigarettes with relatively high nicotine but low tar content, smoking no more than one pack a day, and not allowing one cigarette to last longer than about 3½ minutes so as to minimize overall smoking exposure and tar consumption.

ON INHALING CIGAR SMOKE. Cigarette smokers who switch to cigars and then inhale are not better off and in fact may even be worse off, although they—and some physicians who have advised the switch and given no further thought to it—may not realize it.

Cigar smokers who never were habitual cigarette smokers usually don't inhale, but "reformed" cigarette smokers often carry the inhaling habit over. Dr. Allen L. Goldman, chief of the pulmonary disease section of the University of South Florida College of Medicine, compared cigarette smokers and inhaling cigar smokers, measuring in both a well-known ill effect of cigarette smoking: reduction in the oxygen-carrying capacity of the blood. It was twice as great in the inhaling cigar smokers. Anyone who smokes cigars, Goldman urges, should be specifically warned against inhaling.

SYMPTOMS. The first symptoms of lung cancer are not dramatic and rarely send anyone to a physician. Many people pay little attention to a bit of chest pain, beginning mild cough, a little wheezing, foul breath. An older man, especially a smoker, expects some shortness of breath.

In time, the cough intensifies, becomes hacking; the shortness of breath becomes more acute; wheezing increases; fever may appear; chest pain, dull or stabbing, becomes more pronounced. With further progression of the disease, fatigue, weight loss, hoarseness, and night sweats appear. Except in a small number of cases, coughing up of blood is a late sign. Repeated episodes of pneumonia or bronchitis sometimes may be early indications.

Diagnosis is made through the history of symptoms, sputum samples, x-ray studies, bronchoscopy (visual inspection of air passages through a lighted instrument), and biopsy or removal of a sample of tissue for microscopic study.

TREATMENT. Lung cancer has been difficult to treat. When possible, it has usually required removal of a whole lung or part of a lung. Irradiation and drug treatment (chemotherapy) have been used when the growth has spread beyond the lung. The outlook has been grim: only 5 to 10 percent of patients alive at the end of 5 years.

Recent developments, however, are beginning to make the outlook at least a little more favorable. For example, one type of lung cancer—oat-cell or undifferentiated small-cell carcinoma—has been rapidly fatal in more than 95 percent of cases. A new method of treatment involves simultaneous use of three anticancer agents—Cytoxan, adriamycin, and vincristine—and radiation to the tumor in the chest and also to the brain where the cancer commonly spreads. Radiation is used for 3 weeks, the drug therapy for 3 months, then all treatment is stopped.

Of the first 27 patients to receive the treatment, reports Dr. Ralph E. Johnson of the National Cancer Institute, 26 experienced complete disappearance of their cancers, with 21 remaining free of disease for periods of up to 16 months at the time of the report.

Another promising development has been reported by Dr. Jules E. Harris and a medical team at the University of Ottawa, Canada. Even in early lung cancer, surgery has not produced gratifying results. At one major cancer institution, only half of patients with quite early tumor have lived 2 years after surgery.

In the Ottawa study, 41 early lung cancer patients received surgery and were divided into four groups. Twelve received no further treatment; 8 received chemotherapy (high doses of methotrexate followed by doses of citrovorum factor as an antidote); 11

received immunotherapy; and 10 received a combination of chemotherapy and immunotherapy.

The immunotherapy used consisted of a vaccine specially prepared by Dr. Ariel C. Hollinshead at George Washington University, Washington, D.C. After receiving from Ottawa specimens of surgically removed tumors, Dr. Hollinshead developed a specific vaccine for each patient.

In the controlled comparative study, the 21 patients who, after surgery, received immunotherapy with or without chemotherapy were found to stand a 100 percent chance of being alive 36 months later, compared with a 46 percent chance for those who had surgery alone or with chemotherapy. No patient receiving both immunotherapy and chemotherapy suffered a recurrence of lung cancer.

Chronic Bronchitis and Emphysema

Not lung cancer but emphysema ranks as the major single cause of disability of pulmonary origin in the United States today. Emphysema causes more than 20,000 deaths annually. It disables 1 of every 14 wage earners over the age of 45. In recent years, almost 500,000 new victims a year have come under medical care.

Are emphysema and chronic bronchitis different diseases? When lung tissue is studied microscopically, a distinction can be made. But during life the distinction is hazy because the two problems so often coexist. For this reason, they are often described together under the name of *chronic obstructive lung disease (COLD)* or *chronic obstructive pulmonary emphysema (COPE)*. The word "obstructive" in both names refers to changes in the air passages (the bronchi and bronchioles) that conduct air to the lung areas where oxygen is exchanged for carbon dioxide.

The bronchi and bronchioles, which serve as a first line of defense against infection, have special cells that destroy invading organisms. They also have cells that produce mucus to trap foreign material. The mucus is washed up to the throat where it is swallowed or eliminated through the mouth and nose. Cigarette smoke impairs these mechanisms and particularly hampers proper elimination of mucus from bronchi and bronchioles. As a result, chronic infection sets in, destroying or weakening and narrowing the bronchioles. Retained mucus acts to narrow the air passages, too, making cough less efficient and leading to further mucous retention and narrowing of bronchioles.

Because of the obstruction and distortion of lung architecture, greater force is needed to expel air. This puts abnormal strain on the walls of the alveoli, the little chambers in the lungs where oxygen and carbon dioxide are exchanged. The abnormally high, prolonged pressure overdistends and finally disrupts the alveoli. Moreover, the high pressure in the lungs tends to compress blood routes, further impairing oxygen-carbon dioxide exchange. In emphysema, the patient must produce positive pressure to force air through the narrowed and compressed bronchi and bronchioles; in effect, he must squeeze air from his chest.

The stage of mucus collection and chronic inflammation is called chronic bronchitis; the stage in which alveoli are affected is called emphysema.

SYMPTOMS. To begin with, there may be persistent cough and repeated respiratory infections, sometimes complicated by pneumonia. Gradually infections become more severe and disabling for longer periods. Shortness of breath and wheezing will sooner or later become evident, progressively limiting activity. These indications may take as few as 5 or as many as 30 years to develop. Later, heart failure may develop because of the strain on the heart which must pump blood through the vessels of the diseased lungs.

TREATMENT. Although damage to lung tissue cannot be reversed, men with chronic obstructive lung disease can be helped.

Drugs can be used to loosen and thin secretions, helping to keep the bronchioles open. Colds and minor respiratory infections may be treated vigorously to try to avoid serious lung infection, and in some instances antibiotic treatment may be needed continuously.

In some cases, periodic treatment with machines that push air into the lungs (intermittent positive-pressure breathing, or IPPB) to help open collapsed areas in order to drain mucus collections or prevent their formation is valuable.

Exercises may be prescribed for developing muscles ordinarily not used for breathing so as to help increase breathing effectiveness.

NEW AIDS. For very severe emphysema, with breathing difficulty even while eating, talking or at rest, lung drainage may be helpful. A tube is introduced into the trachea or windpipe through the mouth, and a special suction tube is inserted through the first tube to remove obstructing secretions. Some patients have benefited from a few such drainage procedures and then have required no more for extended periods, but others are not helped unless lung drainage is done daily.

For the latter, now, self-drainage can be made possible by an operative procedure, *tracheal fenestration,* which creates an entrance to the trachea through an opening in the neck just above the breastbone. The opening, which is skin-lined, airtight and leakproof, and does not interfere with speech, allows a patient himself to insert the tubes. Drs. M. C. Gluck and E. E. Rockey of New York Medical College report experience with a group of patients who, within days to weeks after the operation, were able to carry out their own drainage and experienced significant improvement—to the point of returning to work.

Another major development: special outpatient programs for emphysema patients. Commonly, the lot of the man with severe emphysema has been repeated emergency hospitalizations for severe episodes of respiratory failure. In most general hospitals, now, emphysemics can expect excellent crisis care. They are far more likely to be discharged alive than a decade ago, thanks to sophisticated emergency techniques. But too often they are admitted again to the same hospitals a month or six months later. What has been lacking is comprehensive rehabilitation treatment outside the hospital to help patients improve their lot, minimize need for hospitalizations, and interfere with progression of the disease.

It's into this gap that special outpatient programs are stepping. More and more are appearing. Among the pioneers have been the New York University Institute of Rehabilitation, Gompers Rehabilitation Center in Phoenix, Ralph K. Davies Medical Center in San Francisco, Mountaineer Breathing Clinic in Beckley, West Virginia, Gunderson Clinic in LaCrosse, Wisconsin, the Rehabilitation Institute of Chicago, the Albert Steiner Memorial Emphysema Clinic at St. Joseph's Infirmary in Atlanta, and the Velda Rose Outpatient Respiratory Care Program in Mesa, Arizona.

The programs differ somewhat in detail but have much in common. They provide complete examinations, intensive tests of lung function, clear-cut information for patients and spouses, lectures, physical training sessions, breathing instructions, graded programs of exercises and activities (including walking, swimming, bicycling), group sessions, instructions for spouses on methods of helping loosen secretions by tapping of chest, side and back.

At Velda Rose, for example, more than 95 percent of patients have experienced improved senses of well-being; 83 percent have shown significantly increased physical capacity and endurance. Patients previously unable to walk more than a few steps without gasping now walk several miles. Hospital admissions for emergency care have dropped 75 percent.

Asthma

Asthma, from the Greek for "panting," is a chronic disease involving obstruction of air flow in the smaller air passages. It can occur not only in childhood but in young adulthood and in middle age. Commonly, its victims have an inherited allergic constitution.

In half or more, allergy to molds, pollens, animal danders, lint, insecticides, foods, or drugs may be present. In other cases, there is sensitivity to the bacteria responsible for respiratory infections. In still others, nervous tension is a factor.

Episodes appear periodically, varying markedly in frequency, duration, and intensity. Typically, an attack is characterized by wheezing and breathing difficulty, with the victim having to sit upright and lean forward in order to try to use all of his breathing muscles. His chest feels tight, his neck veins stand out, he sweats.

Treatment is complex. It often begins with efforts to determine the cause or causes of allergy so they may be avoided if possible.

Bacterial vaccines may be used, although there is some question about their preventive value. Sometimes densensitization—administration of first small, then increasingly larger doses of a culprit allergen to build resistance—may be helpful.

Drugs to relieve symptoms include bronchodilators such as epinephrine and aminophylline, which enlarge air passages. Other drugs that thin secretions and help in coughing up obstructing mucus may be prescribed. Acute flare-ups of infective asthma are treated with antibiotics.

Chronic asthma if not properly treated can lead to emphysema.

Not infrequently, an asthmatic may be able to help himself by studying his attacks. Did he do something to bring one on? Was he exposed to a new place, an animal, a new food? Was he in a garden? Was it windy? His analysis of what may be contributing to his attacks may not result in self-cure but may well reduce the number and severity of attacks.

Lung Abscess

An abscess in a lung can produce symptoms much like those of pneumonia—chills, fever, chest pain, purulent sputum. In an abscess, however, there are repeated chills, whereas in pneumonia they usually occur only at the beginning.

An abscess may develop because of airway obstruction due to pneumonia, malignancy, a foreign body, or foreign material that may get into the lung during regurgitation.

Antibiotic treatment is usually effective. In the relatively uncommon instances when antibiotics fail, surgery may be needed to establish drainage or, even less commonly, to remove the affected section of lung.

Empyema

Involving a collection of pus in the fluid between the membrane layers encasing a lung, empyema may be caused by pneumonia, tuberculosis or other respiratory disease. It is characterized by chest pain on one side, coughing, fever, breathing difficulty, malaise. Bacteria are involved, never viruses. Treatment includes antibiotics and often drainage with a needle or tube to eliminate the pus collection.

Pleurisy

An inflammation of the membrane (pleura) investing the lungs, pleurisy can produce sharp, sticking chest pain, worse on inhaling, plus fever, cough, chills, rapid shallow breathing. It may be caused by pneumonia, influenza, lung abscess, or other lung disease.

The membrane encasing each lung consists of two close-fitting layers with lubricating fluid between. The pleurisy is called "dry" when the fluid remains unchanged, "wet" if the fluid increases. In dry pleurisy, the two membrane layers may become swollen and congested, rubbing against each other as the lungs inflate and deflate, causing pain. Wet pleurisy is less likely to produce pain but the fluid may compress the lungs and interfere with breathing. If the excess fluid becomes infected and pus forms, the condition is called empyema, or purulent pleurisy.

Effective treatment includes antibiotics, heat applications, rest, and, if the pain should become extremely severe on breathing, strapping of the chest to limit its movement.

Pneumonia

Pneumonia is an acute inflammation or infection of the lungs due to bacteria, viruses, or other organisms, or chemical irritants. Symptoms may include a shaking chill followed by fever up to 105°, headache, chest pain, breathing difficulty, production of pinkish sputum that becomes rusty.

In *lobar pneumonia,* a segment or entire lobe is affected. When both lungs are involved, the pneumonia is called bilateral, or double. Antibiotics and sulfa drugs have greatly reduced the seriousness of lobar pneumonia.

Bronchial pneumonia, or *bronchopneumonia,* which is more common than lobar, is less dramatic. The infection is localized in or around the bronchi, and symptoms are milder, temperature lower, and no crisis occurs as in lobar pneumonia. If the infection is bacterial, penicillin or another antibiotic can be used effectively. If viral in origin, antibiotics are not effective, and the disease runs its course, with supportive treatment provided to ease symptoms.

Primary atypical pneumonia, which is most common in young adults, can be due to viruses or to organisms known as mycoplasma. Symptoms are much like those of a common cold, including headache, fever, dry cough, generalized aches, and fatigue. Antibiotics are used.

Other types of pneumonia include *chemical,* from inhalation of toxic gases; *aspiration,* from accidental inhalation of food or liquid; *traumatic,* from a blow or injury to the chest that interferes with normal breathing; and *lipid,* from inhalation of oily materials. Treatment for these forms of pneumonia may include antibiotics.

Occupational Lung Disorders (Pneumoconioses)

These disorders, caused by inhalation of dust particles, are of several types.

Silicosis, from inhalation of silica dust, is the most common of industrial lung diseases, occurring particularly among miners of coal, lead, copper, silver, gold, talc, mica, and bauxite, and among others including metal grinders, stonecutters, and sandblasters. It may lead to tuberculosis.

Anthracosis, or black lung, from the inhalation of coal dust, causes the lungs of miners to turn dark or black.

Siderosis, from inhalation of iron particles, is usually a benign problem requiring no treatment.

Asbestosis, from inhalation of asbestos fibers, once was limited to people working in asbestos factories. But use of the material in automobile brakes has spread the fibers about in the air and there is some concern that they may have some part, not yet clearly established, in many lung disorders.

In varying degrees, the pneumoconioses may produce shortness of breath, wheezing, coughing (with or without phlegm), and eventually pneumonia, tuberculosis, and cancer of the lung.

Damage to lungs, once inflicted, cannot be reversed. Use of bronchodilating, or airway-expanding, drugs can provide relief. A victim does best to change jobs, removing himself, even with some economic difficulty, from a hazardous occupation in order to prevent further progression of disease.

Tuberculosis

This infectious, communicable disease most often attacks the lungs but the causative organism, the tubercle bacillus, can invade other parts of the body as well, including bone, kidneys, bladder, and genitalia. The source is often the sputum of an infected person, which, even when dried, may harbor live organisms for months. The organism can be spread by droplets and be carried by air and on eating utensils, in unpasteurized milk, and in other dairy products from tuberculous cattle.

In early stages, there may be no symptoms or, in some cases, fever and weight loss. Listlessness and vague chest pains may go unnoticed because they may not be severe enough to demand attention. The symptoms commonly associated with TB—cough, purulent sputum, night sweats, bleeding from the lungs—do not occur in the earliest stages of the disease.

As TB progresses, severe cough develops, sputum becomes yellowish and often streaked with blood, chest pain is present and aggravated by breathing effort.

TB of bones and joints in the legs leads to joint pain and swelling, and limp. Disease in the arms causes joint swelling, tenderness, and limitation of movement. In the spine, TB may produce painful muscle spasm, limitation of movement, followed by curvature of the spine and abscess formation.

Among the drugs used effectively to treat TB are INH (isoniazid), PAS (para-aminosalicylic acid), ethambutol, and rifampin. Treatment often must continue for 18 to 24 months.

8
The Eating Man

The suspected link between diet and health has produced plenty of aphorisms over the centuries: "We are what we eat"; "An apple a day keeps the doctor away"; and Jonathan Swift's "The best doctors in the world are Doctor Diet, Doctor Quiet and Doctor Merryman," among them.

But only recently has this fanciful foodlore been translated into specifics. Although scientific controversy still abounds in many areas of nutrition, public confusion is rampant, and quacks flourish, it's clear enough overall—and with some sets of specifics as well—that much of what's wrong with medical patients is caused by something they either ate or didn't eat; that what we put into the gut each day does more than stoke the body furnace, playing no small part in health or the development of both minor and major disorders.

The body's immune system (its defense), the blood, the fluids bathing the tissues, and most tissues themselves are dynamic systems whose functions can be markedly altered by the nutrients available to the body.

Diseases, far from being caused, purely and simply, by outside factors, have complex histories determined by interplay between the body's internal milieu and stresses imposed by its outer environment.

This seems to hold not only for the once-prime problems, the diseases of infectious origin, but also for the modern plagues—artery hardening, diabetes, heart disease, stroke, cancer—which account for almost two thirds of all U.S. deaths now. It also seems to hold for many chronic debilitating diseases.

Among the most frequently implicated dietary factors for the major killers are obesity; overconsumption of animal fats, sugar, and salt; and underconsumption of crude dietary fiber.

Lately coming into the picture, too: recognition of the importance, often previously unsuspected, of a lengthening list of nutrients.

Obesity

Obesity is probably the most common and one of the most serious nutritional problems among Americans. Among men, over 30 percent of all between 50 and 59, for example, are 20 percent overweight—and fully 60 percent are over 10 percent overweight. About one third of the total population is overweight to a degree known to diminish life expectancy.

Excess body weight is associated with increased blood cholesterol, blood pressure, and blood sugar levels and, because of these effects, is an important risk factor for heart disease. Reduction of weight helps significantly in high blood pressure and diabetes, thereby reducing the risk of heart disease and stroke.

One example: In men 35 to 55 years old, a recent study reveals, each 10 percent reduction in weight would result in about a 20 percent decrease in incidence of coronary disease. Conversely, each 10 percent increase in weight would result in a 30 percent increase in coronary disease.

CAUSES. By far the most common is the obvious one—eating more than is needed. Usually, the basal metabolic rate in the obese is normal, no different from that of others, so the problem isn't organic but rather eating to satisfy appetite rather than hunger.

In some cases, other causes may operate. Hypothyroidism can be involved. Too much insulin secretion, leading to the low blood sugar state of hypoglycemia, can produce increased hunger and so increased food intake. Other causes include lack of enough physical activity to burn up excess calories and use of food to relieve nervous tension or to substitute for the lack of sexual or other pleasures.

WHAT SHOULD WEIGHT BE?   A good way, in the opinion of some experts, to determine obesity is to measure the thickness of a skin-fold between shoulder and elbow (the triceps) between two fingers. For young boys, it should be 12 millimeters or a little less than half an inch; for men, 23 millimeters, or about an inch. (Figures for girls and women: 14 millimeters or a bit more than half an inch, and 30 millimeters or just over 1¼ inches, respectively).

You can also refer to a table of ideal body weight for men:

Height	Small Frame	Average	Large Frame
5′ 2″	112	124	141
5′ 3″	115	127	144
5′ 4″	118	130	148
5′ 5″	121	133	152
5′ 6″	124	137	156
5′ 7″	128	141	161
5′ 8″	132	145	166
5′ 9″	136	149	170
5′10″	140	153	174
5′11″	144	158	179
6′	148	162	184
6′ 1″	152	166	189
6′ 2″	156	171	194
6′ 3″	160	176	199
6′ 4″	164	181	204

Note: The weights shown are with shoes and indoor clothes. For nude weight: deduct 5 to 7 pounds.

Ideal weight provides another useful guide: Per pound of that weight, ideal daily food intake is nine calories.

GIMMICKS.   Dieting is the number-one national pastime in this country. At any one time, some 20 million people are on some reducing diet or other.

"Magic" dietary regimens are as numerous as they are almost incredibly bizarre and even self-defeating and health-impairing.

There are magic-pair diets: lamb chops and grapefruit; eggs and spinach; bananas and skim milk. Crash diet formulas include grapefruit and coffee and nothing else for days on end; or celery and virtually nothing else; or cottage cheese and little more.

There are high-protein diets which, with intake limited to steak, eggs, and other high-protein foods, are purported to reduce, but any single-category diet can be dangerous because it omits other necessary food groups with their nutrients.

There is an "eat-fat" diet supposed somehow to put fats you eat to work melting away fat deposits in the body. There is a low-carbohydrate diet, restricting intake of "carbohydrate units" but allowing eating of just about anything else. But restricting carbohydrates severely may upset both digestion and body fluid balance, and the high concentration of fats may have harmful effects on the arteries.

When they are not outrightly dangerous, such diets are self-defeating. They may appear to be initially successful in removing weight, but the loss usually is the result of loss of water rather than body fat or the result of a reduced appetite and thus lower caloric intake due to radical changes in eating practices. Because they differ markedly from normal eating patterns, such diets can't be tolerated for long periods—and weight is quickly regained once customary eating is resumed.

You can forget, too, such gimmicks as massage and saunas. No amount of massage can remove an ounce of weight. And while you can sweat off some weight, it's water and quickly returns.

Drugs are generally not advisable. Those in use are commonly amphetamines or related compounds, which at best are short-term crutches that soon lose any effectiveness and at worst may produce sleeping problems, elevated blood pressure, and other disturbances.

"Sly" and effective loss. Except for the relatively few people who have an organic problem that needs correction, the only really useful way to lose weight and keep it lost is with a "sly" or quite mild change of eating habits.

If you usually have a couple of eggs and two or three slices of toast for breakfast, you're not going to suffer much if you leave off one egg or one slice of toast. And if you put a couple of spoonfuls of sugar in your coffee, omitting half a spoonful isn't an insufferable hardship.

Many other mild changes are possible: starting dinner with salad so you eat a bit, or maybe a lot, less bread and butter before the entree; using a little more fish and a little less meat to cut calories; eating lean corned beef in place of hamburger; and occasionally or often substituting cottage for cheddar cheese.

Such changes don't produce 2 to 4 pound losses in a week, which are undesirable anyway. But they do, over a period of months, produce substantial losses without discomfort, and still more losses if coupled with a little extra exercise such as a walk of a mile or so daily. In the process, there is no likelihood of deficiencies of one or more vitamins, minerals, or other nutrients. And the new eating habits, because they're reasonable and easily tolerable, keep weight off permanently.

BEHAVIOR MODIFICATION. For some people who may have special difficulties in altering obesity-promoting eating habits, behavior modification techniques may be useful.

In one of the first studies of behavior modification applied to obesity, carried out at the University of Pennsylvania, Philadelphia, a group of obese patients were asked to keep a daily record of their eating activities to establish how much they ate, speed of eating, and circumstances associated with eating. They were also asked to confine any eating, including snacking, to one place rather than, as many obese do, eat in various places at different times of the day.

Additionally, they were to make eating a pure experience, involving no other activity such as reading, watching TV, or arguing with other family members. Finally, they were to count each mouthful of food during a meal and deliberately put utensils back on the plate after every third mouthful until that mouthful was thoroughly chewed and swallowed.

More than half of the people in the group (53 percent) lost more than 20 pounds, and 13 percent lost more than 40 over a period of months.

In a later study at Stanford University, a somewhat modified approach was used. Dieters participated in a weekly group-therapy session and in addition kept a diary in which they entered daily what, when, and where they ate, with whom, and their emotional state while eating. The objective: again to make eating less an automatic reflex action and more a conscious effort. Half the group lost 20 or more pounds in 16 to 20 weeks and have kept the weight off for at least a year.

Fats

In an average person, fats account for about 15 percent of body weight, and this does not represent excess weight but is normal and useful. Fats play many useful roles and are essential in every cell for cell-operating mechanisms.

If there is any such thing as an ideal amount of fat in the diet, nobody knows exactly what it is. According to animal studies, the healthiest diets contain something between 20 and 30 percent fat. But in the United States and in many Western countries, the diet for some decades has had a fat content hovering around 40 percent.

Too much? So many authorities believe—in terms of the possible role of fats in some cancers as well as of certain types of fats in heart disease.

Steak, hamburger, ice cream, butter, cream, all of animal origin, when substituted for foods of vegetable origin in the diet, appear involved in increasing risk of ill health. Yet, today, "eating well" is commonly identified with eating foods of animal origin.

In addition to increasing blood fat levels and risk of coronary heart disease, high levels of meat consumption and of use of meat by-products are associated with high rates of colonic cancer. More studies are needed to understand the association, but it is possible that diet may alter body handling of potential cancer-producing agents (carcinogens) or alter the body's immune mechanism for defending against malignant changes.

The arrangements of carbon, hydrogen, and oxygen atoms in fats go to make up glycerol, a form of alcohol, combined with fatty acids. The fatty acids—and the fats they form—can be classified as saturated or unsaturated. The saturated contain all the hydrogen they can hold; they're saturated with hydrogen. The unsaturated are able, under certain conditions, to take on more hydrogen.

All the common unsaturated fatty acids are liquid at room temperature, but through a process called hydrogenation, hydrogen can be added, saturating and solidifying them.

Research has indicated that unsaturated fats (also called poly-unsaturates) are less likely than saturated to be used in injurious ways by the body. The theory is that the normal blood concentration of cholesterol is increased by saturated fats, which are found mainly in animal fats, such as in meat, butter, and eggs. Alternately, the unsaturated, found in large amounts in vegetable oils, such as corn oil and safflower oil, are supposed to help reduce the amount of cholesterol in the blood.

Some investigators believe that eating certain foods rich in cholesterol itself—egg yolks, for example—also increases blood cholesterol. And cholesterol is considered to be a major factor in atherosclerosis, in which fatty deposits form in arteries and can impede blood flow, leading to heart attacks and strokes.

Although the case is not closed, many physicians believe it's prudent to moderate the intake of fat and cholesterol.

Sugar

For centuries, only apothecaries sold sugar, measuring out the granules by the ounce. It was expensive, in short supply. In Elizabethan times, total consumption for all of England was only about 88 tons a year.

Less than a century ago, with Latin America going in for sugar-cane cultivation and with the development of refining processes, table sugar production began to soar. Currently, we consume individually something on the order of 140 to 150 pounds of sugar a year, more than 2 pounds a week.

It's in almost every prepared food we buy and in almost every snack we consume. The growth of the fast-food industry has markedly increased consumption of sugar in hidden quantities; we don't know what we're eating in many precooked foods.

Excess sugar consumption clearly leads to dental caries. Many studies now show that it increases risk of adult-onset diabetes, which, in turn, increases the risk of premature death. There is some evidence that high sugar consumption tends to raise blood pressure, and it also may be associated with obesity and the risks of that problem.

Recently, nutritionists have been trying to provide practical advice for a sugar-loving public on how to manage well with less. Among the suggestions:

If you must have a sweet dessert, try fruit with a little liqueur. Instead of cakes, try fruit and cheese or crackers and cheese. For baking, have your wife use half the sugar recommended in some recipes and train yourself and family to like things that taste less sweet. The retraining may not be as tough as you might think.

Toasting bread helps to break down carbohydrates and gives the bread a sweeter flavor.

Salt

The American diet includes a high level of salt. Increased salt intake is very strongly correlated with increased blood pressure, which, in turn, is highly correlated with death from heart disease and stroke. While there are effective drugs for lowering high blood pressure, none is curative; they may be used daily. Reduced salt intake may have preventive value against hypertension; and in fact, salt restriction was one of the first useful methods, prior to antihypertensive drugs, to treat elevated pressure, although that fact wasn't recognized to begin with.

In the 1940's, when a rice-fruit diet was being used with some good results in hypertension, one investigator, Dr. Lewis K. Dahl of Brookhaven National Laboratory, wondered what ingredient in the diet lowered pressure. In four years of studies, he determined that there was no special ingredient at all but rather the very low salt content. That was double-checked in trials when salt was added to the diet and there was no longer any beneficial effect on hypertension.

Dahl then began to consider that if a low salt intake could lower blood pressure, a high salt intake might possibly be a cause of hypertension. He was soon noting—and continued to note over many subsequent years—that of the many new hypertensive patients he saw, not one was on a low salt intake.

Adding salt to food is an ancient custom. But the appetite for salt, Dahl has pointed out, is acquired, and some people acquire an enormous appetite, which is no reflection of body needs.

Because large amounts of salt are consumed almost uniformly by Americans and others as well from childhood to old age, establishing how much of an influence salt intake is in an individual is difficult.

So Dahl worked with rats—32,000 of them over a 20-year period. Thousands developed hypertension in response to chronic salt feeding. As the work progressed, Dahl noticed that rat response ranged all the way from no effect of salt to gradually increasing blood pressures to rapid, sharp elevations. Even after high salt consumption for most of their lives, about one fourth of the animals had no elevation of pressure at all. The remaining three fourths developed elevations of varying degrees, with 2 to 3 percent dying of hypertension after just a few months on salt.

Since this suggested hereditary influences, Dahl mated rats at either end of the response range, and after a few generations had two colonies. In one, the rats of the resistant strain showed little harmful effect from high salt intake; in the other, of the sensitive strain, even moderate amounts of salt in the diet led to marked pressure elevation, and with high salt intake death occurred in a few months.

If the same thing applies to man, as well it may, Dahl suggests, at one extreme there should be people with such strong genetic predisposition that only a little in the way of a stimulus such as salt intake can lead to hypertension; at the other extreme there should be those so weakly predisposed by heredity that they could fail to become hypertensive even after long and intense exposure. But most people would fall in between, having only a modest predisposition and liable or not to develop elevated pressure depending upon the severity and duration of an inciting factor such as salt intake.

In fact, many studies have shown the influence of heredity in human high blood pressure. For one thing, the pressures of identical twins with exactly the same inheritance have been found to resemble each other much more than those of nonidentical twins. And among people diagnosed as being hypertensive at a mean age of $36\frac{1}{2}$ years, 44 percent of the parents had been hypertensive, whereas in another group of subjects of the same age and free of hypertension, only 14 percent of the parents were hypertensive.

Especially where there is a family history of blood pressure elevation, Dahl advises, salt intake should be limited.

Fiber

The marked decrease in fiber in the modern diet is discussed later in terms of the relationship of low fiber intake to such problems as constipation, diverticular disease, hiatus hernia, irritable colon, and cancer of the colon (page 211).

There appear to be other repercussions as well.

The decrease in fiber consumption may be directly related to the simultaneous increase in the consumption of sugars and fats. The basic pattern of Western dietary change has been a switch from bulky foods of low caloric density and more fiber (which is not digested and absorbed) to refined foods with relatively high caloric density, such as the "pure" calories from sugars and fats. Because low-bulk, low-fiber diets are easier to chew and swallow, give less satisfaction per calorie eaten, with more required to "fill the stomach," and are pleasing to the palate, this diet pattern may easily lead to overconsumption and hence to overweight.

Fabricated Foods

The American diet has become increasingly a fabricated diet, consisting of more and more food items that have been taken apart and put together in new form. Fabricated foods today are an annual $18 billion industry in the United States.

According to some estimates, at least 75 percent of the food consumed in North America has been factory-processed in one way or another.

A considerable amount of attention has been focused only recently in the fact that some 1800 chemicals have been added to the cans, bottles, boxes, and packages to be found on supermarket shelves. Dangerous? Quite possibly, most are not. But nobody can be certain at this point about all of those that may be, and with the best will in the world, scientific determinations of safety are not overnight matters.

What is also beginning to receive attention is that if consuming certain food additives may be unhealthy, no less so and possibly even more so is the consumption of undernourishing and nonnourishing food.

A U.S. Ten State Survey and a Nutrition Canada Survey have shown that many people are not getting enough vitamins and minerals in their diets, largely because substantial amounts are lost during food processing.

When Dr. P. A. Lachance and associates at Rutgers University, concerned about loss of nutrients in reheated convenience foods, checked commercially frozen chicken pot pies, using vitamin C as a ready indicator of nutrient levels, they could find none of the vitamin at all in the pies even though they were full of vegetables.

They then added known amounts of the vitamin to the thawed pies, refroze them, and two days later reheated them to serving temperature; on reanalysis, 25 percent of the added vitamin had disappeared.

But if processing removes nutrients, why can't efforts be made to restore them? In fact, there are such efforts, but some very critical problems lie with knowing, indeed, all the nutrients that are actually removed so that all can be restored.

For example, it's an old story that the milling of grain removes nutrients. For many years, U.S. government regulations have permitted manufacturers to identify flour as "enriched" if thiamine, niacin, riboflavin, and iron are added. But with recent evidence that many American diets today are deficient not only in the three vitamins and the one mineral but in other important vitamins and minerals—vitamins A, B_6, and folic acid, and calcium, magnesium, and zinc among them—the Food and Nutrition Board of the National Research Council is urging a change in enrichment with an increase in both the number of nutrients and the foods to which they are added.

Nor is this necessarily all the nutrient restoration that may be really needed in engineered foods. The importance of zinc, for example, has been recognized only very recently. The importance of a number of other nutrients, especially "trace" minerals, is only beginning to be understood. It is likely that other essential nutrients naturally present in foods remain to be recognized.

What can you, as an individual, do to protect your health by ensuring that you receive the best possible nutritive value from the food you eat?

These suggestions have been offered by Dr. Ross Hume Hall, professor and past chairman of the Department of Biochemistry at McMaster University in Hamilton, Ontario, and author of *Food for Nought, The Decline in Nutrition* (Harper & Row, 1974):

1. As much as possible, avoid canned, bottled, or packaged food in favor of fresh fruits and vegetables and home-prepared foods. Because some nutrients may be lost during cooking, eat at least some—even as many as possible—fruits and vegetables raw.

2. If you must eat fabricated foods, check ingredients on the labels. Avoid those with the longest lists of additives. Beware, too, of those with excessive amounts of sugar and salt, and don't be

fooled by labels that refer to invert sugar, dextrose, or corn syrup, which are all sugar.

3. In choosing bakery products and breakfast cereals, select those made of whole grain, which provides maximum dietary fiber.

4. Where possible, avoid precooked and frozen products such as chicken pies, vegetable mixes, TV dinners, canned stews, and warm-up dishes, all of which may be deficient in vitamins and minerals. And avoid fabricated snack foods, which tend to be high in fat and salt, and add only empty calories; eat fresh fruit, raw vegetables or nuts instead.

5. And even with eating well-balanced meals as much as possible, including fresh fruit and vegetables and whole grain products, you may find it wise insurance to take a carefully balanced and complete mineral and vitamin supplement.

Trace Elements and the Growing
Knowledge of Their Importance

Total up the weights of all the trace elements in the human body and the combined figure comes only to about an ounce or less.

It has been a long wait for techniques precise enough to identify the tiny quantities of many elements—now detectable to a few parts mineral to a billion parts body tissue—and to provide some understanding of their role.

Currently, it appears that the vital trace elements function through the cells, either as part of enzymes that catalyze metabolic activities or as triggers for activating enzymes.

More than 60 trace elements have been found to date in living organisms, from bacteria to man. Some are well established as vital to man; others are suspected of being so on the basis of strong evidence; still others, among the known and the still unknown, may well be vital.

Copper is essential, a part of many enzymes, involved in normal development of bone and muscle and in the functioning of the central nervous system, also working with iron to form hemoglobin, the red blood cell pigment that carries oxygen.

Some investigators now believe that chromium, zinc, and, in special instances, copper may be deficient in the American diet. Healthy adults eating a well-rounded diet are not likely to develop copper deficiency, but people with kidney disease or celiac disease sometimes have low copper levels in their blood. One unpleasant consequence of copper—and also of zinc—deficiency can be taste distortion.

Zinc today is under increasingly intensive study. The mineral is necessary for growth, for sexual maturation, and as a component of many vital enzymes. It has come into increasing use recently as a therapeutic agent.

Zinc has been used successfully to speed the healing of wounds; in adult dwarfs it has led to some gains in height, along with normal sexual maturation that was previously lacking, and improved learning ability. That zinc depletion can cause mental changes—poor memory, depression, disorientation—and that these can be overcome by zinc supplementation has been shown in recent work at the Baylor College of Medicine.

Chromium in tiny amounts is indispensable, with some evidence indicating it may be essential if diabetes and heart attacks, and the atherosclerotic, artery-choking disease that produces the attacks, are to be avoided.

After a meal, as glucose from food reaches the bloodstream, insulin is secreted by the pancreas to take the excess of glucose out of the blood and store it. Recent studies indicate that fully effective glucose handling requires the presence of both insulin and chromium, and that if chromium is deficient the rate at which glucose is removed from the blood is halved.

Other studies, notably those of Dr. Henry A. Schroeder of Dartmouth Medical School's Trace Element Laboratory in Brattleboro, Vermont, indicate that chromium deficiency is common, particularly in people on Western diets. It appears that virtually all children are born with a healthy reserve of chromium, but the reserve declines with age.

Dr. Schroeder has offered an explanation for this. When you eat sugar—and also starches that are split in the gut into sugars and absorbed as such—blood sugar rises. In response, more insulin enters the blood and simultaneously chromium blood levels increase as the metal is mobilized from body stores to help the insulin handle the increased blood sugar content. After performing its function, the chromium in the blood reaches the kidneys, where about 20 percent of it is excreted in urine.

If the sugar and starch in the diet contain adequate amounts of chromium, enough is absorbed to make up for the urinary loss. But if the sugar or starch contains little chromium, a net loss results, and body reserves are depleted.

And the fact is that the sugar and the starch most common in Western diets are very low in chromium. While raw sugar contains 36 micrograms per 150 grams, refined white sugar has only 3 to 4. Schroeder has calculated that if you consume 150 grams, or a little more than 5 ounces, of refined sugar a day (the average American consumes 208 from all sources, including even bread, which contains up to 8 percent sugar), there will be a net loss of about 8.75 milligrams of chromium in the urine in a year—more than the body's total content—unless the chromium is replaced from other sources.

And other than sugar, the major source of carbohydrates in our diet is refined white flour. Whole wheat contains 175 micrograms of chromium per 100 grams, but refined white flour contains only 23. So white flour may cause depletion of body chromium just as does white sugar.

In many animal studies, Schroeder has found that groups getting adequate chromium in the diet lived longer and at death showed no fatty deposits in the major artery, the aorta, whereas groups receiving inadequate chromium had abnormally high blood sugar and cholesterol levels and numerous fatty deposits in the aorta.

Schroeder also notes that although the role of fats and cholesterol in artery disease has been heavily emphasized, it is also true "that practically everybody with clinical atherosclerosis of moderate severity has a mild form of diabetes, and the long known fact that people with moderate and severe diabetes have especially severe atherosclerosis, from which most of them die, links the two disorders of fat metabolism and sugar metabolism together and demands a search for a single causal factor basic to both." Chromium depletion could be such a factor.

Among other important trace elements are iron, iodine, cobalt, and fluorine. Iron, of course, is needed for hemoglobin formation, and its inadequacy leads to anemia. Iodine is required by the thyroid gland for hormone production. Cobalt's principal function is as an essential component of vitamin B_{12}. Fluorine is an important aid in preventing dental decay and, along with calcium and vitamin D, also stimulates bone formation; there is some evidence that it is helpful in preventing osteoporosis, the thinning of bone in older people that leads to proneness to fractures.

Although no human role has yet been definitively established for a number of trace elements, they have proved essential in animals and are believed likely to be for man.

Selenium is believed to protect membranes and other fragile structures from oxygen damage, much as vitamin E does.

Manganese deficiency in rodents leads to growth retardation, seizures, and impaired lactation. The mineral is believed to be part of a number of enzyme systems and to be required for normal bone formation, nervous system functioning, and reproduction.

Nickel deficiency in experimental animals has led to abnormal liver changes, poor growth, and changes in hair coat.

Vanadium deficiency in animals has led to increased blood fat levels, altered bone development, and impaired reproductive performance.

Silicon is necessary for proper bone calcification in animals. Tin, from animal evidence, may be important in the structure of proteins and various body reactions.

Complete Nutrition: Simple Guidelines

Nurition is clearly complex—which should serve as warning against fads that put emphasis on this or that particular nutrient as if it were something special.

No nutrient is preeminent. All nutrients, in fact, are interrelated and, together, jointly constructive. Moreover, if one is deficient, supplying it in adequate amounts will be effective—but excesses can be harmful. Increase calcium intake to abnormally high levels, for example, and you may induce zinc-deficiency symptoms. Increase molybdenum levels excessively and there may be an effect on copper. An excess of phosphorus in the diet can limit iron absorption. In short, an excess of some one nutrient can interfere with the activity of one or more other nutrients.

The simplest and probably most effective way to assure complete nutrition, guarding against both deficiencies and excesses, is to rely on a *balanced* and *varied* diet supplied by the seven major food groups.

The groups:

1. Milk or milk products
2. Meat, fish, poultry, eggs, nuts, dried beans, and peas

3. Green, yellow, and leafy vegetables
4. Citrus fruits, tomatoes, raw cabbage, and salad greens
5. Noncitrus fruits, potatoes, and other vegetables not included in group 3
6. Bread, cereals, and pasta
7. Butter, margarine, or vegetable oil

Milk or milk products include cottage cheese, yogurt, cheeses, and ice cream, and contribute calcium, vitamins B_2, B_{12}, and A, many minerals (but not iron), and protein. Low-fat milk can be substituted for whole milk.

Meat, fish, poultry, and the other foods in group 2 contain large quantities of protein. Fish and poultry have less fat than most meats. Eggs contain virtually all vitamins and minerals but large amounts of cholesterol. Liver is rich in iron and vitamin A but also in cholesterol.

Green, yellow, and leafy vegetables—excellent sources of minerals and A, B, and E vitamins—include spinach, kale, Swiss chard, watercress, collard, mustard and turnip (the greens), and carrots, pumpkin, squash of various types, and yams (the yellow).

Citrus fruits, tomatoes, raw cabbage, and salad greens contribute vitamin C. Lettuce, cabbage, and salad greens provide somewhat less of the vitamin than do tomatoes, oranges, grapefruit, tangerines, and other citrus fruits.

Potatoes and other vegetables and fruits that include broccoli, Brussels sprouts, green peppers, cauliflower, berries, cherries, melons, and peaches contribute vitamin C, minerals, some protein, and energy.

Bread, cereals, and pasta provide proteins, iron, and B vitamins as well as carbohydrates. They help fill energy requirements. Enriched flour and cornmeal offer vitamins B_1 and B_2, niacin, and iron. And whole-grain flour, bread and brown rice contain other B vitamins, minerals, and desirable dietary fiber.

Butter, fortified margarine, and vegetable oil provide vitamin A as well as calories.

If you get at least one food from each of the seven groups each day, you will be eating a well-balanced diet. And if you make varied choices from each group, the likelihood of getting everything needed—all nutrients—in adequate and well-proportioned amounts, without excesses of any, will be markedly increased.

9
Gut Matters

Gut Rumblings—and What to Do About Excessive Gas

All bowels rumble, and long ago the father of medicine, Hippocrates, used the sound-descriptive, onomatopoeic term *borborygmus* for the noises. They arise from contractions of the intestinal wall and movement of gas and liquids.

Normally, they're soft and gurgling, and wax and wane with the contractions. When they're otherwise, they can point to various disorders which an astute physician, who hasn't forgotten how, can diagnose with a little careful listening through a stethoscope applied to the abdomen.

For example, loud, high-pitched noises similar to those made by water splashing in a container may indicate a peptic ulcer blocking the opening from the stomach into the small intestine. Explosive, staccato pops can mean an obstruction in the colon or large bowel.

With a lot of gas in the gut, the noises will be rushing, crackling, louder, and more turbulent than normal. Gas distress—what the estimable Benjamin Franklin called "whirlwinds in the bowels"— is by far the most common gastrointestinal complaint, the cause of bloating and, commonly, of symptoms that can be alarmingly similar to those of organic diseases.

Excessive gas can trigger pain in the lower left chest that may sometimes radiate to the left side of the neck, shoulder or arm, much as does angina pectoris, the chest pain associated with coronary heart disease. It can produce discomfort similar to that of gallbladder disease.

WHERE IT COMES FROM. Gas in the gut is normal and inevitable. Some air is swallowed with food and drink. Belching can follow but only when you're in upright position or lying on your left side. In these positions, gas is near the upper opening of the stomach and belching can take place when the circular or sphincter muscle at the opening relaxes.

Unbelched air descends the gut, reaching the upper part of the large bowel in 6 to 15 minutes. It may be expelled in as little as half an hour and, quite normally, half a quart is expelled per day, either as part of defecation or independently.

Some people are aerophagics—literally, "air eaters." Unknowingly, they swallow large amounts of air because they eat too fast, chew gum, are emotionally upset, do a lot of sighing. Carbonated drinks, often taken to foster a burp, can actually increase air swallowing.

A certain amount of gas also diffuses into the gut from the bloodstream. And some—not as much as many people suppose, but up to about 30 percent—comes from bacterial fermentation and food ingredients.

Because individual reactions to foods are marked, no one food can be pointed to as an excessive gas producer for all people all of the time. But many gas sufferers are aware that for them some foods "don't set well." In one recent study with 500 patients, the most commonly named "worst gas producer" was onions, followed by raw apples, radishes, baked beans, cucumbers, milk, melon, cauliflower, chocolate, coffee, lettuce, peanuts, and eggs, in that order.

REMEDIES. If you're a chronic gas sufferer, a trial of eliminating some foods, such as those just mentioned, could be worthwhile. Also: souffles, beaten omelettes, cake, fresh bread, and meringues, which contain more gas than other foods; and malted milk, effervescent drinks, and whipped egg white, which contribute more gas than fluid to the stomach.

To cut down air swallowing:

Check for any tendency you have to sigh a lot under stress—and stop it. Each sigh means a swallow of air.

Don't rush your eating; don't eat when upset; and practice exhaling just before swallowing. And rather than wash down food, drink liquids at the end of a meal, not sipping or gulping, but drinking slowly and tilting cup or glass enough to keep your upper lip submerged.

Avoid gum chewing if that's a habit, all carbonated drinks, and any deliberate swallowing of air to produce a belch (which only makes matters worse, since you're likely to swallow more air than you bring up).

OTHER REMEDIES. If you're stuck with a bout of gassy pain and distention, you may get relief by applying a hot water bottle or heating pad, massage, or taking a pint-sized lukewarm tap-water enema.

Alternatively, you can often hasten gas elimination by taking the "telephoning teen-ager" position—lying stomach down on a bed, legs bent at knees at 90-degree angle, arms bent at elbows and turned toward each other and stretched out ahead and supporting the head.

Another position useful for stubborn flatulence: a headstand to reverse the gravitational field and roll back any fecal obstruction to allow gas to move on. Make it a brief headstand and, if you like, prop feet against a wall or support body in a corner while standing on your head. Return immediately to a comfortable reclining position and take advantage of the proximity of the gas to the rectum to expel it.

Medications? Simethicone-containing preparations are available, the simethicone being a silicone material that may help by encouraging release of entrapped gas.

But we've lost some old remedies that, in the opinion of some leading gastroenterologists, were more effective than any in common use today. One was asafetida, a gum resinous substance, excellent for removing gases from the gut when taken in pill form but no longer available in this country.

Plain charcoal is often helpful but not always easy to find. Still, with a little trying, your pharmacist can get it for you in tablet form.

Also helpful: buttermilk, used by every society since New Testament days. You can try a quart a day—or, if buttermilk is anathema to you, commercial *Lactobacillus* preparations (available in drugstores under such trade names as Bacid, DoFUS, and Lactinex) are the next best.

The Real Heartburn Story—and Coping with It

Few afflictions cause more periodic discomfort for more people than esophageal reflux, better known as heartburn. About half the population suffer from it at various times and 20 percent have it as a chronic problem. It helps to account for a considerable proportion of drug commercial bombardment on TV and the huge sale of antacids and other preparations.

Vastly misunderstood and mistreated, heartburn is a burning sensation deep in the chest, similar to what might be expected if you swallowed a hot coal or hot poker. Along with the burning, there is an oppressive tightening sensation. The discomfort can extend from the lower end of the breastbone up to the throat, following the course of the esophagus or gullet.

Gas? That's commonly present and commonly there are efforts, often successful, to belch. But if some TV commercials make it seem that gas is the primary cause of heartburn, it isn't.

Heartburn involves a reflux, or abnormal return, of material, including acid, from the stomach into the esophagus. Out of place there, the acid produces a painful reaction.

It used to be thought that reflux was caused by a hiatus hernia (see later). But investigators have been finding that not all people with a hiatus hernia have heartburn, and some with severe heartburn have no hiatus hernia.

So a hiatus hernia, if sometimes a factor, usually isn't critical. The problem really lies with an area about an inch long at the lower end of the esophagus where it meets the stomach. Called the lower esophageal sphincter (LES), the area acts like a valve, opening to allow food to pass on into the stomach, then closing behind.

Recent studies have shown that heartburn occurs when LES pressure is below normal, so the sphincter doesn't close tightly enough and there is less of a barrier against reflux.

Given that situation, the size of a meal is one important factor in producing heartburn, since overfilling the stomach may create pressures sufficient to overcome a weak LES. Lying down within two hours after a meal, when the stomach still may be full, doesn't help; it removes the downward pull of gravity on stomach contents so they may pop through the LES more readily.

The dietary approach to heartburn has until recently been more a matter of folklore than scientific insight, with prohibitions against so-called spicy (a poorly defined adjective) foods and roughage. Late studies actually measuring LES pressure have shown that alcohol and certain foods—notably chocolate and fat—reduce sphincter pressure. Smoking, it should be added, does the same.

Additionally, it's natural for the abdomen to distend after a meal; this, in fact, reduces pressures within the abdomen and in doing so reduces the likelihood of reflux. But a tight belt or clothing can get in the way of the distention and promote heartburn.

Obesity also tends to increase pressures within the abdomen, and weight loss is often helpful.

If you're a chronic heartburn victim, a little attention to any of the preceding factors could solve your problem.

If not, antacids? They help. Recent evidence suggests that in addition to neutralizing acid, they may also increase the LES pressure. Liquid antacids are considerably more effective than tablets even if not as convenient. If you need an antacid, the best time to take it is one hour after meals. And don't consider milk an antacid, since it actually increases acid secretion in the stomach and, in addition, its fat content may reduce LES pressure.

A promising development for severe heartburn cases that don't yield to other measures is the finding that a drug, bethanechol, has a marked LES-pressure-increasing effect and often provides relief. You need a prescription to get it.

On Being Friends with a Hiatus Hernia

The diaphragm, a dome-shaped muscle, separates the chest from the abdomen and has several openings through which pass blood vessels, nerves, and also the esophagus on its way to join the stomach. When the normal opening, or hiatus, for the esophagus is enlarged, part of the stomach may be pushed up, out of place, into the chest, either intermittently or constantly, by the pressure within the abdomen.

This is a hiatus hernia, also known as a diaphragmatic hernia. Troublesome? Not at all in many, even most cases. A hiatus hernia is sometimes discovered during routine chest x-ray in a person who has never experienced any discomfort.

But in some cases, the hernia can be a considerable nuisance and even an anxiety-provoking masquerader. It can cause backup or reflux of stomach acid into the esophagus with pain ranging from mild heartburn to a deep-seated ache behind the lower end of the breastbone. Often the pain may radiate to the left shoulder, simulating a heart attack—but, unlike a heart condition, the pain does not worsen with effort. Hiatus hernia symptoms also may sometimes be confused with those of peptic ulcer or gallbladder problems.

Typically, pain starts up immediately after meals, especially when bending or lying down. A sneeze, cough, or straining at stool may aggravate it. Sleep may be interrupted by the pain. Bleeding may sometimes be seen in vomit and in stools.

What causes the enlarged hiatus? In a few cases, it may be present at birth; in a few others, it may result from injury to the diaphragm, sometimes in connection with a rib fracture.

But such relatively rare causes don't explain the high incidence in the Western world and, as investigators have found recently, the rarity elsewhere, such as in Africa, among populations not yet exposed to Western ways of eating. And one theory is that hiatus hernia commonly is the end result of inadequate fiber in Western diets.

Basis for the theory: Fiber-depleted diets are a major cause of constipation and the exaggerated bowel contractions needed to propel through the bowel the small hard fecal content associated with low-residue stools and the straining at stool that goes with constipation. Straining raises pressures within the abdomen. Such pressures may then exert force upward, enough over a period of years to push up the stomach, widening the gap in the diaphragm.

How do you get along with a hiatus hernia?

Any one or a combination of several measures often can help. Elevate the head of your bed 6 to 8 inches on blocks; that lets gravity work in your favor during the night. Try more and smaller meals, with the last no closer than two hours before bedtime. Try putting some fiber back into your diet (page 180). Avoid tight belts and other tight items of clothing because they raise abdominal pressure. Do any bending at the knee, not the waist, to avoid upping abdominal pressure. It may also help to avoid or cut down on carbonated drinks, coffee, tea, smoking. Antacids? They may be of some use.

Surgery? Only as a last resort in the relatively rare case of hiatus hernia that does not respond to simpler measures.

Surgical techniques vary somewhat in detail, but all are directed at returning the stomach to its normal position below the diaphragm and repairing the hernia. The operation produces moderate discomfort for a few days and requires about 10 days of hospitalization. It eliminates symptoms permanently in most cases, but 10 to 20 percent experience recurrences.

The Constipated Gut

Constipation is not just a common problem; it's very good business. The difficult or infrequent passage of stools supports a huge commerce in laxatives, cathartics, and other "bowel openers" which are not without hazards and do nothing to correct the basic problem.

Constipation can arise from organic causes such as a debilitating infection, a thyroid or adrenal gland disorder, or intestinal obstruction. But these are rare causes.

One more common cause: failure to respond to the urge to evacuate. Sometimes, especially when traveling, it may be impossible to respond promptly. If this persists, it can lead to constipation, and a good way, then, to relieve it, along with eating properly and drinking plenty of fluids, is to engage in regular physical activity. After a particularly inactive period such as riding in a car, boat, plane, or train all day, a good long walk when you reach your destination is in order.

The most common cause by far: faulty diet.

Centuries ago, Hippocrates admonished Athenians that it was essential that they pass large bulky motions after every meal (not currently recommended) and that to ensure this they had to eat abundantly of whole-meal bread, vegetables, and fruits.

Hippocrates was intuitively right about the needed contents of the diet. Recent scientific studies clearly demonstrate that the dietary fiber in such foods both increases the size of stools and shortens transit time—the time needed for material to move through and out of the gastrointestinal tract.

Investigators have found that stool weights of rural Africans on high-fiber diets range up to 350 grams—three times those for Western whites. And using dyes to help trace the progress of individual meals, researchers also have shown transit times among rural Africans to be as little as one-third those for whites.

Not only have repeated studies shown that on a diet low in fiber bulk is significantly reduced and transit time significantly lengthened. They have also demonstrated marked increases in bulk and shortening of transit time in whites given fiber in the diet.

If you're a chronic constipation sufferer, try adding, better than any medication, a little fiber to your diet. It doesn't have to be a huge amount (see page 180).

The "Irritable," "Nervous," "Spastic" Gut—or Is It Not So Much Irritable as Irritated?

The names for this common disorder are numerous—among them, irritable colon, spastic colon, and mucous colitis (the latter being erroneous since colitis implies inflammation and the irritable or spastic colon is not inflamed).

The symptoms: extremely variable.

There may be abdominal distention; sharp, knifelike or deep dull pain; cramps that may mimic those of appendicitis when they occur on the right side (but they sometimes may occur on the left).

Commonly, victims suffer from constipation and sometimes constipation alternating with diarrhea. Excess mucus appears in the stool. Many victims complain of lack of appetite in the morning, nausea, heartburn, or excessive belching and, not uncommonly, weakness, palpitation, headaches, sleeping trouble, faintness, and excessive perspiration.

Cause? Many theories have been propounded. Most popular: that emotional stress or anxiety is a prime factor. And victims do often turn out to be tense, anxious, given to emotional ups and downs, many with a history of overwork, inadequate sleep, hurried and irregular meals, and abuse of laxatives.

Colonic activities are under nervous system control. Some nerve impulses stimulate activity; others inhibit it; a fine balance between the two types allows gastrointestinal contents to pass smoothly.

In the irritable colon, the balance is disturbed. Constipation occurs when regular colonic contractions are inhibited; diarrhea, when the contractions are excessive. Abdominal discomfort and pain result from spasm of the colon and gas distention of the bowel.

Treatment has included mild sedatives, tranquilizers, drugs such as belladonna tincture and atropine (which may relieve symptoms but often only in doses that also produce dry mouth and vision disturbances). Patients whose symptoms seem exacerbated by very hot or very cold drinks, coffee, alcohol, and tobacco have been urged to avoid these. Bland diets have been advocated.

While some victims have been helped by one or more such measures, on the whole treatment results have been less than outstanding.

A new element of hope has recently entered the picture. In England, researchers interested in the role of dietary fiber in many aspects of gut functioning have proposed that in irritable colon, it is not the colon that is somehow abnormal and irritable but rather that the colon is being irritated and the lack of dietary fiber is the irritant. One investigator in London has reported excellent results in treating many irritable colon patients with a high-fiber diet and nothing else. His work has been confirmed in the United States by Dr. J. L. Piepmeyer, a U.S. Naval Reserve medical officer at Beaufort, North Carolina, Naval Hospital, who has reported that 88 percent of patients with irritable colon have responded within three weeks to the use of 8 to 10 teaspoons of bran a day. (The bran used, miller's bran, is the part of the cereal removed in the process of commercial milling. It is usually to be found in health food stores although some supermarkets may stock it.)

On Indigestion—"Acid" and Otherwise

It's variously called dyspepsia, upset stomach, nervous indigestion, acute indigestion, or just plain indigestion—and few if any of us escape an occasional experience.

It can sometimes produce midriff discomfort, sometimes upper abdominal pain and distention, gas, belching, nausea, heartburn, singly or in combination.

Possible triggers include gallbladder or liver disease, kidney stone, peptic ulcer, appendicitis, intestinal obstruction, food poisoning, milk or other food intolerance, or a nutritional deficiency state.

But by far the most common causes are eating too rapidly or too much, inadequate chewing, eating during emotional upsets, and swallowing a lot of air. Other causes include excessive smoking, eating foods with high fat content, and sometimes eating foods such as cucumbers, beans, radishes, cabbage, turnips, onions, or such seasonings as garlic, chili, and pepper.

Inadequately chewed food prods the stomach into secreting more acid to aid in digesting it. This, combined with excessive air that

may be swallowed with hurried chewing and swallowing, can ir-
ritate the stomach lining.

Most indigestion symptoms stem from altered stomach activity.
Normally, stomach motility or food-churning activity is stimulated
when the stomach is only moderately full and distended with food.
With overeating and marked distention, the activity is inhibited,
leading to sensations of fullness and nausea.

Foods high in fat or fried in fat also tend to slow stomach activity
and prolong the time before the stomach passes its contents along
to the small intestine. An excess of fatty food can have the same
effect as overeating.

Fear, shock, depression, or other emotional upset—and physical
fatigue or pain anywhere—tend to slow stomach activity. On the
other hand, coffee and alcohol increase the churning.

Mild indigestion commonly will disappear if you do nothing
more than not eat for a few hours. You can get some relief, too,
by loosening any tight-fitting clothing and by lying down on the
right side so you put gravity to work to help the stomach move its
contents along to the small bowel.

If you experience frequent mild bouts of indigestion, it may
help to keep a record of your food intake and see if you can corre-
late eating certain foods with the upsets. If you turn up some seeming culprits, you can check them out by eliminating them for a
time. If that works, you can challenge your stomach again by trying
the suspect foods; if symptoms reappear, you can be sure of the
cause.

Use antacids? Many do without taking any other steps to end the
upsets. Antacids can provide some measure of relief. Not all, however, are useful; some may even make matters worse. (See page
206.)

When indigestion is severe or occurs frequently or chronically,
medical advice is needed. The possibility of organic disease has to
be considered.

Gastritis: the Inflamed Stomach

In gastritis, which may be acute or chronic, the stomach's mucous
membrane lining is inflamed.

The acute form, appearing suddenly, sometimes violently and
lasting briefly, is common. It can be produced by acute alcoholism,

aspirin or other drugs, hot spicy foods, foods such as milk, eggs and fish to which there may be allergy, bacteria or toxins from food poisoning or acute viral infection. Acute gastritis also may result from swallowing strong acids or alkalis, iodine, potassium permanganate, or other corrosive materials.

Symptoms may include appetite loss, general malaise, sensations of fullness, nausea, headache, dizziness, vomiting.

For corrosive gastritis, immediate hospitalization and emergency treatment are required.

Common acute gastritis is short-lived if the causative agent is removed, because the stomach replaces its mucous membrane lining about every 36 hours. Symptoms usually are gone within 48 hours. Antacids may help relieve pain, and a drug such as prochlorperazine, a prescription item, may be used to control nausea and vomiting.

Chronic gastritis produces indigestionlike symptoms, including discomfort on eating, mild nausea, burning sensations in the upper abdominal region overlying the stomach. The chronic form may be associated with chronic use of aspirin, pernicious anemia, diabetes, thyroid or other gland disorder. In addition to treatment for the cause, antacids are helpful in some cases. Bland diets have not proved useful, but any foods that appear to make symptoms worse should be avoided.

Ulcers: Healing and Keeping Them Healed

Good news for ulcer sufferers, who comprise about 10 percent of the population, is a new approach to treatment directed at not just healing an ulcer and rehealing it again and again as it recurs repeatedly, but at permanent healing.

A peptic ulcer, of course, is an open sore—either in the stomach itself (making it a gastric ulcer) or more commonly in the duodenum or first part of the small bowel (making it a duodenal ulcer). While ulcers themselves aren't fatal, complications such as internal bleeding if the ulcer erodes an artery or peritonitis if it perforates the stomach or duodenum do kill about 8,000 Americans yearly.

It used to be considered gospel that stress is commonly the reason for ulcers. More recently, however, studies have found no striking correlation between the open sores and jobs generally considered to be stressful. It's conceivable to many medical men that stress other than on the job may play a role and even that job stress could be involved to some extent (with the same job being more or less stressful to different people). But conclusive evidence, one way or the other, on stress and ulcers is lacking.

What is known with some certainty is that stomach acid is involved—too much of it as the result of some body misfunctioning. Also likely: a special vulnerability of mucous membranes of the stomach or duodenum to acid.

For years, conventional treatment has been a bland diet loaded with milk products and liberal use of antacids. Today, most gastroenterologists find no evidence that such a diet helps in healing, and it turns out that milk is actually a potent stimulator of stomach acid.

Moreover, even if a bland diet were effective, some physicians believe there are two good reasons against imposing it. For one, it is almost impossible in our society to adhere to a bland diet anywhere except at home. And, secondly, as one gastroenterologist puts it, "no patient in his right mind will be willing to adhere to a bland diet for years on end." One recent medical report even notes, somewhat cuttingly, that while some physicians using a bland diet may believe thoroughly in its usefulness, there may be others who prescribe it so that when ulcer pain recurs the patient can be blamed for violating the hard-to-follow regimen.

NEW APPROACH.   Based on some intuitive perceptions to begin with, a new approach to ulcer management was worked out 16 years ago by Dr. James L. Borland, associate professor of medicine, University of Florida, and director, Clinic for Digestive Diseases, Jacksonville. And Borland's perceptions have been validated recently by clear-cut scientific evidence produced by the work of many other investigators.

The evidence is that not only do ulcer victims secrete as much as eight times normal amounts of acid when fed a meal; also, peculiarly, the actual concentration of stomach acid stays low for the first hour after a meal, then shoots up rapidly even as the acid secretion is reduced to four times normal. So the first hour after a meal isn't the critical time, the time for antacid taking. The critical time is during the three subsequent hours.

Moreover, the commonly used six small feedings a day can be bad rather than good. They disrupt secretion rhythms. Worst of all, with the sixth feeding at ten or eleven at night, stomach acidity is high until two or three in the morning, when the patient has the fewest available defenses—which is why the nocturnal pain suffered by many ulcer victims.

As for milk, it is NOT an effective antacid. It contains calcium, and calcium produces an acid rebound. "This recently uncovered association," says Borland, "puts the lid on the potentially weight-increasing, probably atherogenic [artery-disease-inducing] milk or cream-based six-feeding bland diet."

These are highlights of Borland's treatment, which he has used for the past sixteen years successfully on many hundreds of patients to heal ulcers and prevent recurrences—a treatment he has reported recently and which is now being used increasingly by many gastro-enterologists, although it has not yet come into widespread use among physicians who are not specialists:

· Three meals a day, as much as possible at the same time every day—to take advantage of the rhythmic production of acid and to use meals and mealtimes as a timing mechanism for antacid therapy, so scheduled as to keep stomach acidity below ulcer-producing levels.

· The meals themselves, enjoyable. The only absolute proscription: pepper. Discouraged but not absolutely forbidden: caffeine (in coffee, tea, cola drinks), alcohol, smoking.

· In the beginning when the ulcer is acute, antacids may be used hourly to relieve symptoms and usually do within a day or two. After the first week, however, they're used to prevent symptoms—not taken, as many people take them, immediately after a meal when they're not needed, but one hour after eating when they have an acid-buffering effect lasting two to three hours.

· From the second through seventh week, another antacid dose is taken three hours after eating—and again at bedtime, along with a drug such as Pathilon, to help reduce acid secretion. After the seventh week, the antacid three hours after eating is dropped.

· And after the sixth month, the only medication consists of an antacid with Pathilon or similar drug at bedtime—and this for the rest of life.

The regimen actually makes minimal demands, says Borland, and most patients can count not just on healing of an ulcer but an end to the typical repeated episodes of acute flare-ups.

A NEW ANTIULCER DRUG.   A drug called cimetidine is actually the first specific antiulcer agent. It directly reduces the secretion of stomach acid by blocking the action of a body substance, histamine.

Histamine is the same material released from body cells during allergic reactions and common colds, leading to skin rashes and runny noses. In the stomach, it has a role in triggering acid secretion.

What long puzzled researchers was that the antihistamine drugs used for allergies had no effect on stomach acid.

Antihistamines act by blocking certain sites on body cells that serve as receptors for histamine. Finally, it became evident that if the usual antihistamines didn't work for acid control, it could be because there are two different kinds of receptor sites on cells, only one of which was blocked by conventional antihistamines.

Recently, investigators have developed a whole series of new antihistamines designed to block the second receptor site. Cimetidine has turned out to be the most useful. It speeds ulcer healing, greatly reduces the need for antacids to relieve pain, and reduces episodes of bleeding. Typically, in many studies, about 85 percent of patients have been free of ulceration within 28 days after being placed on the drug.

Experience to date with cimetidine indicates that over the short term it appears to be safe as well as effective. It should be useful for even the most severe cases. It may be used to promote healing, after which reliance on the Borland program may well keep the ulcer healed.

Pouches in the Gut: Diverticular Disease

A diverticulum (from the Latin *divertere,* to turn aside) is a blind pouch or pocket formed when the lining of the colon pushes into the bowel wall. Usually, there are dozens and even scores of such pockets appearing in clusters. And *diverticulosis,* the presence of such pockets, occurs in more than one third of Americans over age 40.

It's benign in the beginning: no symptoms. But the pockets may trap and hold fecal material, become inflamed and infected, resulting in diverticulitis.

Diverticulitis sometimes is called "left-sided appendicitis" because its pain on the left side of the abdomen is similar to the right-sided lower abdominal pain of appendicitis.

The attacks of pain are severe, may last minutes, hours or days, coming on at any time without relation to eating or activities. Other symptoms are distention, nausea, occasional vomiting, sometimes with chills, fever, and malaise.

Conservative treatment with bed rest, liquid diet, antibiotics usually helps. When, however, the attacks are repeated and severe, or when it is difficult to differentiate the disease from possible cancer of the colon, or when the pouches perforate or obstruction or heavy bleeding occurs, surgery may be needed and involves removing the diseased section of colon and bringing healthy segments together.

Recent studies indicate that people who live on a high-residue diet—vegetables, fruit, whole-grain breads and cereals—rarely get diverticular disease. It appears that with a low-residue diet producing small-volume stools, the colon has to clamp down harder to move the stools along, with the clamping down producing high pressures that push out the pockets. Some physicians report that a high-residue diet may even be of value in avoiding need for surgery when the diet is used once an acute attack is over.

Hemorrhoids—and, When Necessary, Removing Them Almost Painlessly

Hemorrhoids, also called piles, are stretched veins under the mucous membrane lining of the anal and rectal area. They're called internal when in the wall of the rectum above the sphincter, or circular, muscle controlling defecation, external when in the anal canal below.

One indication of hemorrhoids is bleeding from the rectum. Another is a protruding swelling that can be felt near the anus and that may protrude further with coughing or sneezing. Pain is the main symptom, especially during a bowel movement.

The main cause is straining at stool, which produces increased pressures that dilate the veins and is commonly the result of chronic constipation (page 194).

For external hemorrhoids, no special treatment may be needed. Often, they clear up within a few days. Anesthetic ointments and hot baths usually relieve any pain or itching. If large, however, the hemorrhoids may require removal.

Internal hemorrhoids, if slight, also need only conservative measures: hot baths, anesthetic ointments or suppositories. If they don't respond to such measures, they may be treated with injections of irritating solutions that scar and obliterate them (external hemorrhoids are unsuitable for injection treatment).

SURGERY. The standard hemorrhoid removal operation, hemorrhoidectomy, is simple for the surgeon, over within half an hour. But for as long as five days afterward, the patient may experience considerable pain, especially during bowel movements. For relief, local anesthetics and sitz baths (sitting in warm water) may be used. The rectal area usually becomes entirely pain-free in ten to fourteen days. Once removed, hemorrhoids cannot recur, but sometimes other veins may enlarge for the same reason the first ones did unless the constipation is overcome.

Newer surgical techniques are now in increasing use. Cryosurgery—using a special extremely cold probe to touch and freeze a hemorrhoid—can be performed in a doctor's office with only moderate pain. There is only a slight discharge for a few days and healing is good.

Another technique, rubber-band ligation, is often used for internal hemorrhoids. A special latex band is placed over the neck of a hemorrhoid with a special instrument. The band ties off the hemorrhoid, and receiving no blood supply, it dies and sloughs off, usually within three to nine days. The procedure is essentially painless and can be carried out in a doctor's office. The ligated hemorrhoid may produce a sensation of fullness for a time. When it drops off, there may be some brief blood spotting. And itching may be aggravated for a time when the dropoff occurs.

Anal Itching (Pruritus Ani)

Of all body areas, the region around the anus is one of the most susceptible to a chronic itch-scratch cycle because the skin is almost always moist and exposed to fecal matter retained in the anal folds.

Many factors can trigger itching, which leads to scratching, and in turn to more itching and more scratching. Poor anal hygiene or minor injury produced by defecation, irritating soaps and clothing can do it. So can hemorrhoids. Infectious and parasitic agents, including intestinal parasites such as pinworms, can do it. So, too, allergic conditions and some disorders such as jaundice and diabetes, which are associated with itching. The itching is usually worse at night and aggravated by heat and scratching.

If a definite cause can be established and treated, chances for cure are excellent. But more often than not, no specific cause can be pinned down. Then it's essential to stop scratching and keep the skin of the area dry and clean. Thorough drying can be accomplished with cotton or tissue, and talc or dusting powder applied frequently. In severe, persistent cases, a corticosteroid (cortisone-like) cream may be prescribed for use two or three times a day and usually brings relief. Note, however, that ordinary anesthetic or other ointments may cause more trouble by macerating the skin.

On Diarrhea—Turista and Otherwise

Dietary indiscretions such as eating unripe fruit or foods that disagree with some people (eggs, shellfish, strawberries, etc.) can cause diarrhea. Other factors include eating under stress or excitement, use of some antibiotics or other drugs (aspirin for some people).

Among diseases capable of producing diarrhea are toxic hepatitis (liver disease), hyperthyroidism (thyroid gland overactivity), blood poisoning, gastroenteritis from contaminated food, ulcerative colitis, vitamin B deficiency, amebic or bacillary dysentery, cancer of colon and rectum, flu, regional enteritis.

Turista, or traveler's diarrhea, is a strange disease of sudden onset and uncertain cause, lasting one to three days, occurring sporadically to travelers in any part of the world, usually during the first week of a trip. South of the border, it is known as turista, Montezuma's Revenge, or the Aztec Two-Step. In Asia, it appears as Delhi Belly, Teheran Trots, or Katmandu Crud.

If gastroenterologists ever doubted either its existence or severity, they no longer can do so. A few years ago, an international congress of gut specialists in Mexico was barely able to muster a quorum because so many of the participants had come down with the disorder.

Until recently, once traveler's diarrhea started, opiates such as paregoric (camphorated tincture of opium) were usually the drugs of choice (in the absence of contraindications to be discussed with a doctor before leaving home).

Now a study by Dr. Herbert L. Dupont of the University of Texas Health Center, Houston, has shown that an old patent medicine, Pepto-Bismol, is the most effective treatment yet. What ingredient in the preparation does the trick is not clear, but when turista patients received eight ounces of the medicine in doses of one ounce every half-hour for four hours, a marked reduction in diarrhea, nausea, and cramps followed within twenty-four hours. The preparation, Dupont believes, may be worth investigation as a possible means of preventing traveler's diarrhea.

Meanwhile, in terms of trying to avoid the problem, you have to be extremely careful about what you eat and drink no matter where you go outside of North America, Australia, New Zealand, and most of northern Europe.

Tainted water probably is the worst problem. Although major cities boast of pure, uncontaminated fresh-water supplies, few brag about the pipes that stretch from waterworks to hotel room. Mexico City's pipes, for instance, often crack during earth tremors. Unless you want to risk diarrhea or worse, don't drink tap water, don't gargle or brush your teeth with it, and don't use ice cubes made from it. Use bottled or canned water and sodas instead.

Eat only well-cooked food. Avoid uncooked fresh vegetables and salads. Peel your own fruit. If you like cocktails such as old-fashioneds, you're safer ordering them without fruit garnish. If the local milk isn't pasteurized, avoid it. The one universally safe dairy product, it seems, is yogurt which frees itself of disease bacteria in the natural process of curdling.

On Surprisingly Common Milk Intolerance

Abdominal bloating, unexplained cramps or diarrhea, and flatulence can result from intolerance for milk in people who are otherwise healthy and drank milk without ill effects in childhood. The intolerance has nothing to do with allergy but rather involves a deficiency of an enzyme in the intestine needed for digesting the lactose (sugar) constituent of milk.

The enzyme is present at birth and in childhood, but it now appears that much of the capacity to produce it is lost at an early age

206 · The Complete Medical, Fitness & Health Guide for Men

in many people. With that loss, intolerance develops as undigested lactose passes on through the gut to cause disturbances.

If you have milk intolerance, the diagnosis can be made by a lactose tolerance test, in which you consume a specified amount of milk and measurements are then made on a sample of blood. Otherwise, you can simply limit your milk intake or stop it entirely for a week and see if your symptoms disappear. Still another alternative is to drink two glasses of cold milk (cold seems to cause more trouble than warm) on an empty stomach, and that may be all that's needed to produce your typical symptoms and point to their relationship with milk intolerance.

Does that mean you can't have any milk at all? Not necessarily.

The foremost authority on the problem, Dr. Theodore M. Bayless of Johns Hopkins University School of Medicine, Baltimore, has found that milk-intolerant people, although unable to handle large amounts of milk, often can take smaller amounts in cereals and coffee, and also have less difficulty if they take milk with meals rather than by itself.

Ice-cold milk especially is to be avoided, Bayless has found. He has also established that the intolerant usually do well with forms of milk such as yogurt and cheese in which part of the lactose has been converted to another substance during processing.

If You Use Antacids

Antacids, of course, neutralize, at least temporarily, stomach acid and are commonly employed for heartburn, digestive upsets, and ulcer.

Cost may be one factor in selecting an antacid; except for calcium carbonate, the compounds are expensive. Palatability is a matter of individual preference; antacid products are available in varied flavors.

As for efficacy, liquid preparations definitely have the edge even if tablets win on convenience. Many tablets contain aluminum hydroxide, which tends to lose some of its acid-buffering action in the drying process used in making tablets.

Whether tablet or liquid, various antacids may differ in efficacy and side effects.

Sodium bicarbonate reacts almost instantly with acid to neutralize it. But it is not recommended for long-term use because it tends to increase blood alkalinity, which may cause shallow or irregular breathing, prickling or burning sensations in fingers, toes or lips, muscle cramps, and in severe cases convulsions. The sodium it contains also may not be advisable for anyone with high blood pressure or a heart problem.

Calcium carbonate is the cheapest antacid. Because it empties from the stomach more slowly than sodium bicarbonate, its antacid action is more prolonged. But calcium may cause increased acid secretion rebound, and some physicians oppose its use.

Aluminum hydroxide tablets are less effective than liquids. The preparations often contain significant amounts of sodium and should not be used by anyone on a sodium-restricted diet. Advantages of aluminum hydroxide include relative palatability and lack of toxic effects. The most common undesirable effect is constipation, which can be countered with use of a magnesium antacid or a preparation that combines aluminum hydroxide with a magnesium compound. Because aluminum compounds can interfere with action of tetracycline antibiotics and absorption of anticholinergics, iron, warfarin, barbiturates, quinine and quinidine, they should not be used simultaneously with these drugs.

Magnesium antacids: Magnesium hydroxide, or milk of magnesia, although used mainly as a laxative, is a relatively effective antacid. It does, however, tend to produce diarrhea as do other magnesium compounds such as magnesium carbonate, magnesium oxide, magnesium phosphate, and magnesium trisilicate. Magnesium compounds therefore are usually combined with aluminum or calcium compounds to avoid diarrhea.

On the "How" and "Why" of Restoring Fiber to Your Diet

More and more evidence supports a theory that lack of adequate fiber in the diet may contribute significantly to development of many bowel disorders—and that fiber restoration often may help control these disorders.

Until the turn of the century, man ate much fiber, the indigestible part of plant cell walls, present naturally in large amounts in grains and cereals.

With the coming of modern roller mills, it became economically feasible to remove the outer husk of cereal grain kernels and, with it, the fiber, to produce refined white flour. Currently fiber intake in the United States is one tenth of what it once was.

As fiber intake has gone down, the incidence of many bowel disorders has gone up. Appendicitis became common only in this century. Colonic cancer has become, after lung cancer, the second most common cause of cancer death. Diverticular disease is now common, constipation widespread.

Yet, as these disorders have increased in the United States and other Western countries, they have remained rare among rural Africans living on native unrefined diets containing large amounts of fiber. American blacks, whose ancestors came from African villages where even now colonic cancer, for example, remains rare, are no longer exempt. Although even fifty years ago, when black and white American menus differed markedly, bowel cancer affected two whites for every black, now, with diets virtually the same, blacks are affected as often as whites.

Fibrous foods add bulk. Once in the gut, fiber absorbs water and swells. That makes stools soft and large, preventing constipation with its small, hard, pebbly, slow-moving stools. More than a nuisance in itself, constipation leads to straining at stool. With straining, pressure in the colon is raised, leading to diverticular outpouchings. Also, with straining, pressure within the abdomen is raised and may, some investigators believe, tend to raise the stomach up through the diaphragm, causing hiatus hernia. The raised pressure also may be transmitted to leg veins, dilating them to produce varicose veins, and to veins in the anal area, dilating them to produce hemorrhoids, which are in fact varicose veins.

As for colonic cancer, there is some evidence that cancer-causing chemicals (carcinogens) are produced by bacteria in the bowel. Constipated stools may promote cancer in two ways: by giving the bacteria more time to act on the slow-moving fecal material to produce carcinogens and by giving the carcinogens more time to act on the bowel lining.

RESTORING FIBER.   Cereals with "bran" in their names contain sizable amounts of fiber. So do cereals such as old-fashioned, slow-cooking (not instant) oatmeal, shredded wheat, and whole-grain wheat cereals.

Whole-wheat breads and whole-meal flour are rich in fiber, and the flour can be substituted in many recipes calling for white flour.

Many vegetables and fruits—particularly mango, carrot, apple, Brussels sprout, eggplant, cabbage, orange, pear, green bean, lettuce, pea, onion, celery, cucumber, broad bean, tomato, cauliflower, banana, rhubarb, potato, and turnip— contain dietary fiber.

Unprocessed bran—discarded in the milling of white flour—is available in health food stores and may be in others. It can be used as a fiber supplement, sprinkled on cereals, mixed with soup, and combined with flour in baking.

To Stop Choking on Food

Choking on a piece of food, often a large chunk of meat, is a common problem, sometimes fatal, the cause of many "café coronaries" or sudden deaths in restaurants which have seemed to be the result of heart attacks.

If you should ever experience such choking, urges Dr. T. H. Ingalls of Framingham, Massachusetts, summon all the air in your lungs for one vigorous cough. Cough immediately, without leaving the table; there is no time to get to a rest room. "When you are stoppered like a bottle with a cork in it, you must hack with whatever remaining air you can squeeze from your lungs," he advises.

A "hug of life" maneuver to be used when you see a dinner partner suddenly choking on food has been developed recently and endorsed by both the American Medical Association and the American Red Cross. It is also called the Heimlich Maneuver after Dr. Henry J. Heimlich, who originated it.

To carry it out, stand in back of the victim, reach both arms around him, make a fist, and grasp the fist with the other hand. Then, placing the thumb side of the fist against the victim's abdomen, above the navel but below the rib cage, press your fist sharply upward. This raises the diaphragm, compresses the lungs, and increases the air pressure in the windpipe, forcing the food particle out. In an early test, the hug of life used on 374 potential victims, including a 9-month-old baby, led to survival for all.

Some Serious Gut Problems

Regional Enteritis

Also known as Crohn's disease, and of unknown cause, regional enteritis involves inflammation of the lower ileum, the last part of the small intestine, but sometimes may affect other areas of the gut. Symptoms include chronic diarrhea, abdominal pain, fever, weight loss, sometimes appendicitislike colic. Diagnosis is aided by x-ray studies.

Although complete recovery may follow a single attack, in most cases the disease progresses. In treatment, a high-calorie, low-residue diet may be used, with mild sedatives and anticholinergic drugs. Corticosteroids are often valuable in acute stages, lowering fever, decreasing diarrhea, improving appetite. Surgery may sometimes be required to overcome obstruction or remove the diseased area, eliminating symptoms for a period of years. Recurrences develop in more than 50 percent of cases after surgery.

Ulcerative Colitis

A chronic inflammatory disease of the colon, producing ulcerations and oozing of blood and pus, ulcerative colitis can occur at any age but most commonly affects the 20- to 40-year age group.

Usually, it manifests itself as a series of bloody diarrhea attacks, with freedom from symptoms in between. Stools may become looser, more frequent (10 to 20 a day), often consisting mostly or entirely of blood and pus. Other symptoms may include cramps, appetite loss, malaise, mild temperature rise in the evening and, later, high fever, nausea, vomiting, severe appetite loss, and anemia.

Examination of the colon, x-ray studies, and stool tests help in diagnosis. As many as 20 percent of patients recover completely after a single attack. Others suffer chronically.

Treatment may include drugs to lessen cramps and stool frequency; a high-protein, high-calorie diet; blood transfusion if anemia is severe; antibiotics or other antibacterials. Corticosteroids such as prednisone and hydrocortisone, by mouth, injection, or enema, do not cure but do produce remission of symptoms in as many as 85 percent of patients, often rapidly. When medical measures do not suffice, surgical removal of the affected portion of the colon may be required.

Gallstones

Gallstones are stonelike masses called calculi that form in the gallbladder. Why isn't known definitively, but there is evidence of a connection between stone formation and obesity.

The stones may be present without causing trouble or may lead to such symptoms as upper abdominal discomfort, bloating, belching, and nausea, especially after eating fatty foods. Such symptoms, however, can occur with indigestion and so are not necessarily attributable to stones even when stones are seen on x-ray films.

No medical treatment for stones is presently available, although currently under investigation is a promising method of dissolving stones over a period of time.

Because inflammation of the gallbladder (cholecystitis) may occur in one third or more of patients with gallstones at some point, removal of the gallbladder (cholecystectomy) may be performed even in the absence of symptoms.

Symptoms such as those mentioned may occur in chronic cholecystitis, which can develop after repeated attacks of acute cholecystitis, leaving the gallbladder scarred, shrunken, and sometimes with stones present. If stones are found, gallbladder removal may be advised; if gallstones are not present, a low-fat diet or use of antispasmodic drugs may be helpful.

Carcinoid Syndrome

This disorder stems from release of large amounts of chemicals such as serotonin, a constrictor of blood vessels, by tumors usually arising in the small intestine.

Earliest symptom usually is flushing of the skin triggered by food, alcohol, or emotions. Abdominal discomfort and repeated diarrheic episodes follow. In some cases, flushing is accompanied by asthmatic wheezing.

Treatment may include surgery and drugs such as prochlorperazine, chlorpromazine, or prednisone for flushing, cyproheptadine or other agents for diarrhea.

Cancer of the Colon

The colon, or large bowel, is a common site for malignancy. A tumor may manifest itself by blood in the stool, a change in bowel habits (from few movements to many, or from many to few), cramps, and in some cases anemia, weakness, weight loss. A large proportion of the tumors can be seen with a sigmoidoscope, an instrument insertable through the rectum for a distance of ten or more inches. A newer aid to diagnosis, the colonoscope, a flexible instrument, permits inspection of the whole length of the colon. Also helpful in diagnosis: x-ray films taken after a barium enema.

Surgery is the only definitive treatment. The growth and section of bowel containing it, plus a segment on each side, must be removed. Depending upon extent of the growth and its site in the colon, it is sometimes possible for the two remaining healthy ends of the bowel to be joined. In other cases, the end of the remaining healthy colon may be brought up to an opening in the abdomen (colostomy). Most colonic cancers are curable when discovered in early stages, some even at later stages.

Cancer of the Small Intestine

For unkown reasons, cancer is rare in the small intestine although common in the large. Symptoms may include intermittent, crampy mid-abdominal pain, stools darkened by blood pigments, anemia. Diagnosis is aided by small intestine x-ray study. Surgery is the only definitive treatment.

Cancer of the Stomach

Stomach cancer, which has been declining in incidence for some years, affects twice as many men as women and is concentrated largely at ages over 40.

Symptoms may include upper abdominal discomfort, often but not invariably worse right after eating, pain in the region over the pit of the stomach, loss of appetite, vomiting, weight loss, anemia.

X-ray examination of the stomach is a major aid in diagnosis. So is gastroscopy, in which, under local anesthesia, a lighted tube is inserted into the stomach through the mouth so the tumor may be examined and a small piece removed for microscopic study.

When a definite diagnosis of stomach cancer is established, surgery is essential. It is also advisable in cases where there is any doubt. Sometimes when a stomach ulcer is present, x-rays and tests may not be able to rule out the possibility that it is cancerous. Duodenal ulcers rarely if ever are malignant, but stomach ulcers sometimes are.

Even when a growth appears very large on x-ray films, surgical cure may be possible. The growth itself may be small but may have produced a significant inflammatory reaction around it which makes it appear larger than it actually is. In some series of patients, 15 to 20 percent of stomach cancers that seemed from x-ray studies to be inoperable proved to be curable by surgery. In surgery, much or all of the stomach may be removed, depending upon the extent of the cancer. When the entire stomach must be removed, the first part of the small intestine can be connected to the esophagus so that food goes straight from esophagus to intestine. Meals will then have to be small, perhaps half usual size, and taken half a dozen times a day.

10

The Back and Joints

On Backaches: the Misery, Myths, and Relief

A startling study in one city (Copenhagen) recently revealed that 25.7 percent of nearly 5,000 men, aged 40 to 59, employed in large public or private enterprises, experienced low back pain in the course of a single year. Eleven percent of the sample had also experienced radiation of the pain down their legs. Eight percent had to seek treatment, leaving their work. Over half had previously had low back pain.

Here, in the United States, latest available National Health Survey figures show that each year Americans make some 19 million visits to doctors' offices to complain about backache—a problem reported more frequently than headaches, fatigue, or even the common cold.

Why is this happening? What goes wrong in the well-engineered structure of the back—and what can be done about it?

Of myths about backaches there are plenty. Among the most common are three: that ever since man stood upright, he was doomed to ache behind; that almost invariably the culprit is a "slipped disk"; and that once a backache victim, always a backache victim. Yet, if you happen to be a backache victim, it's not at all likely to be for either of these "reasons," nor is it true that once a victim always a victim.

A GUYED STRUCTURE. You've undoubtedly seen guy wires supporting a utility pole. And if you keep that picture in mind briefly, you can quickly get an idea of what the human back is like and why many back pains develop.

The backbone, or spinal colmn, is a stack of 33 separate bones, or vertebrae, reaching from the sacrum at the base of the spine to the skull. Instead of being set squarely atop each other like a column of toy blocks, they're arranged in an S-shaped curve to help balance body weight, with each vertebra resting at an angle on the one below.

In between are the disks—round cushions, one quarter to three quarters of an inch thick, which act as shock absorbers. The spinal cord, a bundle of nerves encased in a protective sheath, passes behind the disks through holes in the vertebrae. Smaller nerves leave the cord between the vertebrae, much like tree branches, and the large sciatic nerves, which originate near the bottom of the spine, run like roots over the buttocks and into the legs.

Although there are ligaments to hold the vertebrae loosely together, muscles have the job of supporting the column. One hundred forty muscles attached to the spine do the work, and it's a prodigious amount. For example, if you weigh 180 pounds and just bend forward, it takes 450 pounds of muscle force to prevent you from toppling over—and almost twice as much force may be needed when you carry a heavy object.

A disk *may* weaken and tear, with part of its gelatinlike center extruding like paste out of a tube. Pain will be felt only if the extruding material happens to press on a sensitive nerve—and then, rather than focusing in the back itself, the pain will shoot into the leg.

Arthritic changes, too, may develop in the spine and produce back pain. So may fractures. And pain in the back can sometimes arise from conditions having nothing to do with the back. Heart disease on occasion may produce it; so, too, lung disease, gallbladder disease, peptic ulcer, or colitis.

In the great majority of cases—more than 80 percent—backache is unrelated to disk problems, arthritis, or other organic conditions. That has been demonstrated by at least two large-scale studies, each involving more than 5,000 patients, one carried out by a team from New York and Columbia Universities, the other at the Institute for the Crippled and Disabled, Rehabilitation and Research Center, in New York.

In the vast majority of cases, the studies show, the trouble lies with muscle weaknesses—but not weakness of muscles in the back.

Now recall the guying analogy which holds—up to a point. Stomach muscles serve as a guy wire for the back. But, in the case of a utility pole, if one guy wire breaks or loosens, the pole falls in the direction of the taut wire. It's different in the spine. With weak stomach muscles, there is some tendency to fall backward. But that is counteracted by our sense of balance, and to compensate for the weak abdominal muscles, we shift body weight, lean slightly forward, and hang on our back muscles.

Excessively loaded, the back muscles after a time may become fatigued and painful. Naturally enough, a back pain victim, feeling the pain in the back, blames the back muscles. But the ache is in back because of stomach muscle failure. Tests of backache victims show that commonly their abdominal muscles are less than a third as strong as their back muscles.

SELF-TESTING. While many tests can be used to check for weakness of various muscles that may lead to back pain, often a simple quick test can pinpoint the cause.

Lie flat on your back on the floor, hands clasped behind your neck, knees bent so heels are close to buttocks. With somebody holding your ankles down, try to roll or curl up into sitting position.

If you don't make it—and you fail no matter how strong and heavily muscled you are elsewhere—you'll be in the large company of those with weak abdominal muscles and far more prone to back troubles than others.

Add this: The test is actually only a check for minimal abdominal muscle strength. If you pass, doing the sit-up once, and your work is light and you never go in for vigorous sports or any strenuous activity, your abdominals may be strong enough. But if you do exert on occasion, you may need much more strength, evidenced by ability to repeat the sit-up several times without difficulty.

DOING SOMETHING ABOUT IT. To strengthen flagging stomach muscles requires a specific exercise program. Although many sports and other activities can be counted on to provide a workout for many muscles, they may not do much for the abdominals.

Specific exercise programs, many of them, have been developed —but often have called for long periods of workout, as much as an hour and even more daily. Few people keep them up.

Some years ago, Dr. Lawrence W. Friedmann, then medical director at the ICD Rehabilitation and Research Center, began developing and testing abbreviated programs which had proved successful. They have been reported in a book, *Freedom from Backaches*, by Dr. Friedmann, written with the author of this present volume (Simon and Schuster, 1973).

Even for men with three, four, or more muscle deficiencies, 15-minute sessions twice a day suffice. For abdominal muscle deficiency alone, 5 minutes in the morning and another 5 in the evening may be adequate.

A PERSONAL PROGRAM.   To strengthen your abdominal muscles, you can make use, according to your need, of exercises that have proved effective in thousands of men, and these are noted below.

You don't do all at one time but rather move progressively through them, from one level of difficulty (and increased muscular strengthening) to the next, staying within the daily allotted time period.

To begin, you experiment to find your starting level. You do the first exercise indicated. If you can do it five times without difficulty, move to the next. Move from one to the next until you arrive at an exercise that you can't do readily. That's your *key* exercise.

After that, you proceed daily in this way: Start your exercise period with 5 repetitions of each of the two exercises preceding the key exercise; next do as many repetitions of the key exercise up to 5 as you can; finish with 3 repetitions of the two preceding exercises in reverse order.

At any point where 5 repetitions of the key exercise become easy for you, try the next exercise, which becomes your new key exercise. Begin your sessions with 5 repetitions of the exercise preceding the former key exercise, followed by 5 of the latter, then as many as you can without strain of the new key exercise. Finish with 3 repetitions of each of the first two exercises of the session in reverse order.

In the same way, you can move on through the whole program, dropping the easier exercises as you go, always staying within the time period you set, and progressively building greater abdominal muscle strength.

And, having arrived at the strength you need, you can maintain it in sessions in which you do just 5 repetitions each of the last three, most demanding exercises.

THE EXERCISES. 1. *The pelvic tilt.* Lie on your back on the floor, squeeze buttocks together and tighten stomach muscles, sucking abdomen in toward spine and also up toward chest while flattening the back against floor. Hold a few seconds, then relax a few seconds, then repeat. Flexed knees make it easier.

Because the pelvic tilt is actually a step in many of the other exercises, getting the "feel" of it is important. A simple way is to lie on your back on the floor and let a family member slip a hand in the hollow of your back, in the space between back and floor. squeeze buttocks together, tighten stomach muscles, and try to press your low back against the hand. As you tighten your stomach muscles, they may quiver a bit, but this is normal with weak abdominal muscles and should be ignored.

In doing the pelvic tilt, try to equalize the time of muscle contraction and relaxation. Relaxation is important, since it allows blood to flow more freely to the muscles, bringing in nutrients and removing wastes.

2. *Tilt and head raise.* On your back on the floor, with knees bent, exhale, squeeze buttocks and tighten stomach muscles to achieve the pelvic tilt—and, at the same time, slowly raise head toward knees as far as you can without strain. Make the head-raising slow and deliberate.

3. *Knee kiss.* Proceed as in 2 and, while raising your head, also raise one knee, trying to bring head and knee as close together as possible. Repeat with other knee.

4. *Double knee kiss.* Start as in 3, doing the pelvic tilt, but now, without raising the head, bring both bent knees toward the chest.

5. *Knee kiss, neck flex.* Repeat the movements in 4—but now, while bringing bent knees toward chest, bend neck and raise head and shoulders to bring head and knees as close together as possible.

6. *Straight leg raise.* Important in strengthening the hip-flexing muscle needed for more advanced abdominal muscle development,

this exercise begins with the pelvic tilt. Now, with one leg bent at both hip and knee, raise the other leg to about 30 degrees while keeping that knee straight. Keep leg elevated 3 to 5 seconds, slowly return it to floor, repeat with other leg. During this exercise, stomach muscles, contracted for the pelvic tilt, should remain contracted.

7. *Progressive sit-ups.* Sit-ups can be done in various ways so that the exercise can be made easy to begin with and progressively more difficult and valuable. In all sit-ups, the pelvic tilt is the first step. Note, too: When you begin—doing sit-ups with knees and feet kept straight—the abdominal muscles are aided by the hip-flexing muscles and this is desirable. Then, in advanced sit-ups, as you bend knees and hips more and more, hip-flexing muscle aid is progressively reduced and finally the abdominals do all the work.

For the beginning sit-up, lie on back on floor, feet and knees straight, with feet tucked under bed, sofa or bureau, arms stretched out parallel to floor. Don't jerk up; that's useless. Rather, curl up, raising head first, then shoulders, then chest. Hold position briefly, then slowly lower to starting position.

For progressive abdominal strength buildup, modify arm position. Do the sit-ups next with arms in front of face, bent at elbows, with each elbow held by the opposite hand. Then modify progressively by letting forearms touch waist; next by clasping arms behind head, forearms alongside ears and elbows facing forward; finally, by clasping arms behind head and bringing elbows as far back on each side as possible.

8. *Increasingly advanced sit-ups.* Place feet as before under a heavy furniture piece but now with soles on floor so knees can be bent to 45-degree angle between thighs and calves. Do the sit-ups with arms behind head, elbows back. Then, in a first modification, do them with knees bent to a 90-degree angle; in a second modification, with knees bent enough so calves are directly against thighs and heels against buttocks.

The next step is to position feet straight out with knees straight, clasp hands behind head with elbows far back, and twist the upper body so arms and shoulders are turned to the right. Curl up while maintaining the twisted position of the upper body, then repeat with upper body twisted to the left. This exercise strengthens the oblique abdominal muscles which run at an angle.

In another advanced sit-up series, you use weights held in the hands, starting with 1 pound and working up to 5 pounds (food cans are useful). Go from 1 to 5 pounds first with hands behind neck, elbows back, feet supported, knees straight. Next, do the same with knees bent to 45-degree angle, then bent to 90, and again bent so calves are against thighs and heels against buttocks.

In the final advanced series, you start at the beginning of the preceding sit-up exercises and work gradually through them all— but now without any support for the feet.

RESULTS. When, as it so commonly is, abdominal muscle weakness contributes to or is the major cause of backache, muscle-strengthening can be curative, not just relieving symptoms but also eliminating the cause. It has worked for many seemingly hopeless cases, including some not aided by surgery.

It is not, of course, a panacea. If it does not help, if pain persists or increases, something more than, or other than, muscle weakness may be responsible, and expert medical diagnosis and treatment should be sought.

OTHER AIDS. To prevent back problems or recurrences, experts offer these recommendations:

Posture: Stand and walk with back straight, shoulders not rounded, chin and pelvis tucked in. Avoid exaggerating the natural curvature of the spine or misplacing the center of gravity. If you shove your pelvis forward or let the abdomen sag or even use a ramrod military posture, you create a swayback, which is bad.

Sitting: Avoid very soft chairs. Best is firm, shaped to natural back contour, with support at small of back, and permitting you to sit with feet flat on floor. If you must sit for much of the day, it's a good idea to get up and move around periodically. If you drive for long periods, keep the car seat forward and a cushion behind your lower back.

Sleeping: Avoid soft, sagging or lumpy mattresses. Use a firm one, even with a bed board. Avoid sleeping on your stomach. Sleep on back or side with knees and hips slightly bent.

Lifting: Bend at the knees and hips, keeping your back straight, when lifting something heavy. As much as possible, lift heavy objects close to the body. Also avoid using your back to push or pull; instead, use the whole body with knees and hips bent slightly.

The Proper Way to Relieve an Acute Backache Attack

You've just been struck with an agonizing backache. Maybe you know why; maybe, not. At the moment, the ultimate cause is not important. With severe pain, even a skilled physician wouldn't be able to determine the cause and probably wouldn't even try. The immediate, urgent problem is to relieve the pain.

Often you can do that with simple home remedies—provided you use them properly and don't stop short, as victims commonly do, with one or two which don't do the job when a combination of several would.

The immediate problem actually is spasm—involuntary contraction of back muscles. When any muscle anywhere is severely strained, that muscle and often others nearby go into spasm. Meant to be protective, spasm contracts the strained muscle fibers to prevent additional damage. Unfortunately, however, when tightened in spasm, the fibers can't get adequate blood flow and nourishment and can't dispose of waste materials. The result before long is pain. A vicious cycle then ensues. The spasm has produced pain. The pain leads to more spasm. The added spasm leads to still more pain. And on the cycle goes.

If relief is to be quick, both spasm and pain must be attacked. Aspirin, heat or cold, rest, massage, and even gentle movements and exercises help to control both.

The first step when a backache strikes: Take two aspirins and lie down; get into bed as soon as you can.

But that's not enough. Go on to apply heat at once. You can use a heating pad wrapped in a towel. Apply for half an hour, then change position to avoid stiffness. For some people, cold provides quicker relief than heat; if you happen to be one, you can spray on ethyl chloride or, in the absence of that, gently rub the painful area with ice cubes or crushed ice in a pillowcase.

After that, ask your mate to gently rub down the painful area with a counterirritant (any commercially available one will do).

Continue the aspirin (if you're sensitive to it, you can use a non-aspirin type of analgesic such as acetaminophen). Most people can take two tablets of one or the other every three to four hours without trouble.

Repeat the heat or cold applications. If you can make it to the bathtub, soak in a hot bath for 30 minutes at a time, four or even more times a day. And ask your mate to repeat the gentle, easy-rubbing massage several times a day.

Chances are good you'll find the pain beginning to dampen down within 24 hours or even by next morning. Continue the aspirins, hot or cold applications, and massage—and now begin to move the arms and legs gently and arch and curve the back to avoid stiffness.

With further easing of the pain, start gentle exercises—pulling in your stomach muscles, holding them that way briefly, then relaxing, and flattening the curve of your back against the mattress. Use the exercises about every half hour.

If your attack is relatively mild, you may not require bed rest. But do ease off on all physical activities and use aspirin, hot or cold applications, counterirritants, and massage until pain is gone.

Bursitis

A bursa is a sac or pouch located around a joint and containing a small amount of lubricating fluid. It aids in making joint motion smooth and gliding. The delicate structure can become inflamed, and the inflammation is known as bursitis.

Inflammation of a bursa may be traceable sometimes to a general body disorder such as gout. By far the most common cause, however, is excessive or improper use of the adjacent joint. The bursas in the shoulder are most commonly affected, but almost any bursa in any joint in the body may become inflamed, and some of these inflammatory conditions have earned special names such as "tennis elbow."

In an acute attack of bursitis, great pain develops with any effort to move the joint. The joint area is tender, warm, often boggy, and the muscles in the area are tense and spastic. Often a calcium deposit appears in the affected bursa.

A sling with cold packs and a sedative often may provide relief. Aspirin may be used, or aspirin with codeine. Antiinflammatory steroid (cortisonelike) drugs or phenylbutazone given by mouth are helpful in easing the pain. In most cases, the calcium is absorbed, usually in seven to ten days.

Another treatment sometimes used: needling the inflamed bursa under local anesthesia to drain the fluid and instill a small amount of a steroid solution. This may produce immediate relief. On occasion, however, it may exacerbate the pain.

Sometimes, when bursitis becomes chronic, surgery may be used, if the pain and disability justify it, to remove calcium deposits or eliminate any adhesions that may be present.

TENNIS ELBOW. Also known as epicondylitis and radiohumeral bursitis, tennis elbow may occur after not only tennis playing but also an activity such as screwdriving. Pain may radiate from the elbow to the outer side of the arm and forearm. It can interfere with normal activities and in some cases be severe enough at times to keep the victim awake.

In relatively mild cases, avoidance of movements causing discomfort may produce gradual improvement. In other cases, one or more injections of hydrocortisone or prednisolone may bring relief. Uncommonly, if medical measures fail, surgery may be used and may consist of manipulation under local anesthesia or, rarely, removal of an inflamed bursa.

Tennis elbow tends to be a common problem, particularly among less experienced tennis players. According to a study by one expert in the field, Dr. Robert P. Nirschl of Northern Virginia Doctors Hospital, Arlington, an experienced player uses the power source of shoulder muscles as well as body weight force in swinging a racket, reducing strain on the elbow. The inexperienced player, on the other hand, usually tends to rely on the force of the forearm, which transmits much strain to the elbow, especially in backhand strokes.

The type of racket used also appears to be a factor. Metal rackets, particularly stainless steel alloys, Nirschl finds, tend to apply least force against the elbow when swung. He also recommends a stringing tension not greater than 50 pounds.

Another study by Dr. James D. Priest of Stanford University Hospital, Stanford, California, suggests similarly that use of a steel or aluminum racket and, in addition, of a two-handed rather than one-handed backhand stroke increases the likelihood of avoiding tennis elbow.

If a player experiences immediate pain in the elbow after a game, he should apply ice over a 24-hour period, advises Dr. Nirschl. If the pain persists, he should get medical help.

After another study involving 871 tennis elbow patients, Drs. H. B. Boyd, Emeritus Professor of Orthopedic Surgery at the University of Tennessee, Memphis, and A. C. McLeod of Hattiesburg,

Mississippi, have reported that only 40 did not respond to medical treatment and needed surgery. In almost all cases, when surgery is required, it can relieve pain and restore full motion, with the patient usually able to resume work and hobbies in six weeks, but three to six months are required for regaining full forearm strength.

TENNIS ELBOW: ADDED PREVENTIVE MEASURES. These recommendations come from Drs. Nirschl, Priest, and other orthopedists, all of them tennis players themselves and researchers in the field:

Before going on the court, do some brief exercises—including reaching with arms high and wide, bending, stretching legs, and jogging in place for a few minutes.

Wear a warm-up suit or sweater until your body is hot. Keep your elbow warm by wearing a Neoprene bandage (which also helps hold the joint firm), elastic band, or even an old sock.

Use light balls—not any of the pressureless type.

Avoid carrying suitcases or other heavy objects with palms facing body. Instead carry them in your arms whenever possible, with palms up.

Daily exercises to strengthen muscles extending from elbow to hand can help. They include lifting a 3- to 5-pound weight from the wrist with your forearm on a flat surface, palm facing down, and trying to twist in opposing directions with both hands on a broom handle.

Frozen Shoulder

Well named, a frozen shoulder involves a motion-limiting adhesion of joints. It can be caused by bursitis or injury but commonly is of unknown cause.

The pain, deep in the shoulder, may sometimes involve arm, chest, or back and tends to be worse at night.

Treatment may consist of rest, suitable exercises, injection of an anesthetic into the shoulder, and heat applications. Improvement is slow at first, but after about 50 percent of normal range of movement has returned, it speeds up. In some severe cases, expert manipulation, under suitable anesthesia, may be needed to loosen the adhesions.

Although frozen shoulder understandably can make a victim impatient and sometimes even desperate, almost all cases clear up after six to twelve months.

Shoulder Dislocation

A shoulder dislocation makes any motion painful. The shoulder's normal roundness is gone, the shoulder looks disjointed, and the affected arm may seem longer or shorter than the other. It may occur as the result of swimming or other sports or strenuous activities. In some men, however, it may follow nonstrenuous activity, even just getting into a coat. According to some experts, if a first dislocation occurs before the age of 20, chances of recurrence may be as high as 90 percent.

Treatment requires replacement of the shoulder under anesthesia by a skilled physician, with three to four weeks thereafter needed for healing, during which a sling and swathe may be required.

When a shoulder is easily and repeatedly dislocated, surgery is usually effective.

Heel Pain

This can be the result of bursitis due to ill-fitting shoes or ligament bruising or inflammation from strain. Often, flatfoot is a contributing factor and requires treatment. Proper shoes, sometimes with adjustment of heel height, may be prescribed. For pain under the heel, a ring of felt or sponge rubber may minimize pressure on the painful area, which, if necessary, can also be injected with hydrocortisone.

Trick Knee

An injury on either side of the knee that tears one or both cartilages lying between the two major bones of the joint leads to trick knee when a bit of the torn cartilage gets caught between the joint surfaces. The knee then may suddenly give way or become locked.

Treatment may involve expert manipulation, splinting, or removing some of the bloody fluid from the joint through a needle. In some cases, surgical removal of the bits of torn cartilage may be required.

Sprained Ankle

A sprain can be mild, with stretching but not tearing of a ligament; moderate, with an incomplete tear; or severe, with a full tear.

Strangely, there may be more swelling and pain with a mild sprain. No cast is needed. When a tear has occurred, a walking cast is needed for about six weeks, followed by taping of the ankle for about two weeks more. Even after that, all activities that might strain the ankle must be avoided. It takes about three months before the ankle is back to normal. When a complete tear has occurred, as demonstrated by x-ray studies, surgery may be used.

Sprained or Strained Wrist

A strain is a wrenching of a tendon or muscle, whereas a sprain involves stretching or tearing of a ligament. Symptoms may include pain, swelling, and reddish-blue bruise marks caused by bleeding into the wrist joint.

Many seeming sprains are really fractures, and a good rule is that every sprain should be x-rayed for a possible hidden break, especially if the pain or swelling does not diminish within a few days.

Treatment for a sprain or strain may include immobilizing the wrist, application of ice packs to reduce swelling over the first 24 hours, followed by hot moist packs or hot water soaks for 30 minutes at a time several times a day. Gentle exercises as soon as tolerable help to prevent adhesions.

Trigger Points and Neck, Shoulder, Back, and Chest Wall Pain

The *myofascial syndrome* is a painful condition of skeletal muscles rather than joints but it is included here because it can produce what may seem to be joint pains—and even, on occasion, what may seem to be pain from a herniated spinal disk or, confusingly, a chest pain similar to that of angina associated with heart disease.

The hallmark of the syndrome is the presence of one or more small, highly sensitive areas called trigger points. When stimulated by pressure, these points shoot out pain, sometimes to considerable distances. The pain can be knifelike, stiff, boring, or aching.

In the typical patient, onset of pain is associated with some kind of injury, which may be specific, such as a sudden twist, strain or sprain, or sleeping with the neck crooked. But chronic muscle injury due to poor posture and prolonged strain can produce the pain. Such factors as fatigue, chilling, and anxiety may contribute to onset of symptoms.

The myofascial syndrome often may go unsuspected. It should, experts say, be considered especially when there is sudden onset of neck and shoulder pain, chest wall pain, or back pain following mild trauma.

Finding a trigger point helps confirm the diagnosis. Trigger points can be detected by the physician as he presses with his fingertips. Usually, when he touches the trigger point involved, there will be a sudden intensification of the patient's pain.

Treatment involves injecting a local anesthetic such as procaine or lidocaine into the trigger point. Although there will be pain during the injection, within several minutes afterward the pain and tenderness disappear dramatically. After successful injection, gentle exercise is prescribed along with application of heat.

The pain relief after a single injection may be permanent or there may be recurrence. In the latter case, repeat injections usually produce more lasting results.

Gout

Almost exclusively a disorder of men (only 5 percent of cases are women), gout affects half a million or more Americans and in many cases is hereditary.

The immediate cause of gout with its excruciating joint pain is an excessive accumulation of uric acid in the body. Because of an abnormal metabolism or body handling of certain compounds called purines in foods, an increased level of a purine breakdown product, uric acid, builds up in blood and body tissues. When the excess is deposited in joints, it can inflame the joint tissues, producing severe pain, swelling, and stiffness. The joints usually affected are those of the lower extremities, particularly the great toe, but any other joint in the body can be involved. The arthritis of gout can be severe and disabling if untreated and may lead to permanent deformity. Also, changes leading to impairment of vital organs such as the kidney may occur.

Not everyone with gout develops arthritis; in many cases there are no symptoms. People in sedentary work are more likely than manual laborers to have clinical gout.

A first attack is usually sudden in an otherwise healthy man. The affected joint is red to purplish red, shiny, swollen, excuciatingly painful to the touch, so even the lightest clothes cannot be tolerated. There may be fever and chills. An attack can last up to four days, or even longer if untreated.

Gout is an ancient affliction and until relatively recently its victims, in efforts to head off attacks, were placed on diets that banned many "rich" foods (those with high purine content). That's no longer necessary except for such items as sweetbreads, anchovies, liver, and kidney in some cases.

Effective measures are available both for relieving an acute attack and for minimizing likelihood of recurrences.

Colchicine, made from the autumn crocus, brings relief in 24 hours or less. How it works is not entirely clear, but it is so effective for gouty arthritis and for so few if any other diseases that the very fact of its providing relief confirms the diagnosis of gout. For those unable to tolerate colchicine because of side effects such as nausea and vomiting, another agent, the antiinflammatory drug phenylbutazone is effective.

Drugs such as probenecid are available to promote excretion of uric acid via the kidneys, thus reducing the amount in the tissues, and when taken regularly help to prevent recurrent attacks.

A more recent addition to preventive treatment is allopurinol, a drug that blocks the enzyme that converts materials into uric acid, thus minimizing uric acid formation. At the same time, allopurinol stimulates the breakdown and excretion of uric acid deposits that may already have accumulated.

Allopurinol has had to be taken regularly three times a day. In more recent research at the University of Pittsburgh, a triple-strength tablet of the drug has been found effective when taken just once a day.

An interesting sidelight about gout: Uric acid and genius have long been thought to be linked. Among the famous reported to have been tortured by gout are Kublai Khan, Alexander the Great, Goethe, Francis Bacon, Isaac Newton, Charles Darwin, and Benjamin Franklin.

And among studies tending to support the idea of a link is a very recent one by Yale and University of Michigan researchers who took blood samples from 155 high school and college boys and correlated the blood levels of uric acid with grades, test scores, and other data. Their finding: uric acid is positively associated with overachievement, high grades, college entry, participation in activities, and speed in completing certain aptitude tests.

Airplane Ankles

Many men who have to make long airplane flights complain of ankle swelling. The cause, a British investigator reports, seems to be sitting for prolonged periods with knees bent, allowing blood to pool in the legs and, because of the reduced circulation, permitting fluid to accumulate in tissues, leading to ankle swelling.

Normally, it's the movement of leg muscles which produces a pumping action that aids in moving blood upward from legs to heart. Even the relatively little leg muscle movement carried out while riding in a train or car seems enough to maintain circulation, reports Dr. H. D. Johnson of the Royal Postgraduate Medical School, London. His recommendation for airplane ankle sufferers: exercise at least the toes and ankles briefly every half hour while on a plane.

Stiff Spine (Ankylosing Spondylitis)

Ten times as common in men as in women, often occurring in relatively young men, ankylosing spondylitis is an arthritislike disorder affecting the small joints of the spine. Spinal joints and ligaments stiffen, making movement increasingly painful and difficult. The stiffening may extend to the ribs, limiting flexibility of the rib cage and impairing breathing.

The disease is chronic. But if pain can be relieved to permit posture-maintaining exercises, it is often possible to avoid crippling and achieve a productive life.

Cortisonelike drugs have not been particularly helpful for ankylosing spondylitis. Gold therapy has been ineffective.

Two drugs found effective are phenylbutazone and indomethacin. About 90 percent of patients are satisfactorily helped by either drug. The drugs may sometimes cause side effects, which can be eliminated when they are withdrawn.

Aspirin, too, may be effective in some men, a study by a nationwide team of Veterans Administration and university hospitals investigators indicates. In the carefully designed study, the patients received all three drugs, one at a time, at different times—six weeks for each—and with the medications placed in look-alike capsules so that neither physicians nor patients knew which drug was being used when until the trial was over.

Although phenylbutazone and indomethacin proved superior for most of the men, in 12 percent both pain relief and improvement in spinal mobility were greater with aspirin. Aspirin, the study suggests, deserves a trial for anyone with ankylosing spondylitis before resort to other, more potent and more expensive agents.

Arthritic Joints

Arthritis, or joint inflammation, our most widespread chronic disorder, afflicts 20 million Americans, about one in every eleven. One third of the victims are men. The causes remain obscure—and there is no cure.

There are many degrees of osteoarthritis—which tends to develop with advancing age and is also called "wear-and-tear" and "degenerative" arthritis—and of rheumatoid arthritis, an often more crippling problem.

In some cases, drugs—ranging from commonplace but valuable aspirin to more potent agents—are helpful. In others, relief may be found in broader treatment programs that vary with individual needs and may include combinations of medication, rest, exercise, physical therapy, heat, and mechanical aids.

But there remain those with severe osteoarthritis or rheumatoid arthritis who fail to benefit adequately from medical care and suffer severe pain and crippling. For many of these, now, the rapid advance of joint replacement surgery offers already significant and growing promise.

CHOOSING A DOCTOR. For any arthritis sufferer, proper choice can be crucial. Not all physicians can or will provide the time-consuming, ongoing care an arthritic can need. Dr. John Calabro of Tufts University, a leading rheumatologist, in his book, *The Truth About Arthritis Care* (McKay), has suggested that internists are more likely to provide this care than general practitioners or surgeons, and offers seven criteria for choosing the best possible doctor: (1) He is not vague. Usually he will give an exact diagnosis, and say what his treatment will be and what to expect. (2) He will invest time, especially at the start, when he must explain the disease. (3) He will not promise a cure. (4) He does not rely on drugs alone. (5) He inspires confidence that he will be there, ready and able to help, when his care is needed. (6) He will not resist a patient's quest for additional help through consultation with, or referral to, another doctor. (7) You will like and trust him.

THE MAINSTAY DRUG. This is aspirin, although it is often not properly used. Aspirin, in fact, is a remarkable compound. Along with pain- and fever-relieving activity, it is also antiinflammatory. And inflammation as well as pain is a critical problem in arthritis.

If properly used, aspirin can do much for a large proportion of rheumatoid arthritics. When it is not properly used, it may be because of failure of a physician to provide understanding for the patient.

As a recent report emphasizes, in order for aspirin to have antiinflammatory activity, a certain blood level—18 to 25 milligrams percent—is needed. For this to be attained, 3 to 6 grams of aspirin per day—that is, 12 to 20 five-grain tablets—are needed. Below that amount, aspirin has pain-relieving but little antiinflammatory effect.

Adult patients, the report indicates, usually can be started on 12 aspirin tablets a day—3 taken halfway through each meal and, again, at bedtime with food. If necessary, the dose can be increased gradually every three to five days until side effects occur. Ringing in the ear (tinnitus) is a side effect that indicates high therapeutic blood levels of aspirin. If this occurs, the dosage can be reduced by one tablet every two to three days until the ear ringing stops. If gastric upset occurs, antacids can be used. Once the proper dosage is established, it can be continued for years.

In some patients, however, therapeutic-dose levels of aspirin, even with antacids, produce intolerable side effects. For them, other agents of approximately the same potency—one such is Motrin, a newer drug—may be used and may not produce undesirable effects.

OTHER DRUG TREATMENTS. Sometimes useful as an additional aid along with aspirin is the injection into an actively inflamed joint of a long-acting form of a steroid, or cortisonelike drug, such as prednisone, prednisolone, triamcinolone, or dexamethasone. The effect usually lasts one to two weeks but sometimes may persist for several months. Injection may be repeated every two to three weeks several times, then every six to eight weeks.

When rheumatoid arthritis fails to respond to aspirin, more potent agents may be used. Gold therapy is often helpful, producing improvement in about 70 percent of patients, often with complete elimination of symptoms. Gold, some rheumatologists indicate, appears to be the only drug capable of stopping the progression of rheumatoid arthritis. It must be employed carefully.

Gold is given weekly by intramuscular injection. Small test doses are used first to check for any possible allergy or sensitivity to gold. Thereafter, 50-milligram injections are used weekly for up to about 20 weeks.

Beneficial effects of gold usually do not appear until 500 to 800 milligrams, occasionally more, have been used. Once improvement appears, a regular maintenance program of one injection every three to four weeks is established.

The most common undesirable effects of gold are mouth ulcers and itching skin rash, which disappear with discontinuation of treatment and may not return when treatment is resumed. Routine blood checks are needed to make certain that blood disturbances do not occur.

Systemic steroids, once considered potential arthritis wonder drugs, now elicit less enthusiasm. They may relieve pain but there is no evidence they have any major effect in retarding or stopping the disease. They may be used sparingly in some cases under close supervision.

Potent antimalarial drugs sometimes may be employed. One such agent, hydroxychloroquine sulfate, has been reported useful in about 60 percent of rheumatoid arthritics. Rarely does improvement appear before six weeks; in some cases, six months are needed. Improvement takes the form of progressive reductions of pain, stiffness, and swelling. Possible side effects include rash, nausea, vomiting, cramps, diarrhea, vision blurring, muscle weakness, and hair loss, which may be reversible with lowered dosage.

Recent research has suggested other agents that may be useful. Dr. Donald Garber of Downstate Medical Center, Brooklyn, New York, has found that rheumatoid arthritis patients have abnormally low levels in their bodies of L-histidine, a natural amino acid constituent of protein. He has reported that several dozen patients given L-histidine supplements have experienced pain relief and general improvement in joint strength and function.

For some time, too, evidence has been building that rheumtoid arthritis patients have much lower levels in their blood of a metal, zinc. In a trial to determine whether zinc supplements might be helpful, Dr. Peter A. Simkin, a University of Washington, Seattle, rheumatologist, added zinc sulfate three times a day to existing treatment of one group of patients while, for comparison, another group on the same existing treatment received dummy capsules.

The zinc-treated felt better and experienced more relief from joint swelling and morning stiffness; they could also walk farther and longer. When, later, the comparison group also received zinc, they too showed the same improvement. Says Dr. Simkin: "These encouraging results indicate that oral zinc sulfate deserves further study in patients with active rheumatoid arthritis."

WATER EXERCISE THERAPY. What one arthritis specialist believes may well be the first truly helpful innovation in physical therapy of arthritis in the past hundred years has been made by a woman arthritis victim, Dvera Berson. At age 60, she had been a rheumatoid and osteoarthritis victim for six years, had been getting progressively worse despite medical treatment, and was in danger of permanent crippling.

Exercise for arthritis is not new. But for arthritics, exercise has been painful, and pain has limited its use and value. Yet if exercise is carried out in water, Mrs. Berson found in her own case, it could be pain-free and, when carried out intensively, could reverse many of the consequences of arthritis.

In a recently published book, *Pain-free Arthritis* (Simon and Schuster, 1978), Mrs. Berson has detailed the water exercises she has used to free herself of neck brace, back support, need for traction in a hospital bed several times a day, finger deformity, and constant pain.

The exercise program is no cure but rather a means of achieving, at no small expenditure of effort, a strengthening of muscles, ligaments and bones, and freedom from pain after weeks or months, which can be continued, Mrs. Berson writes, as long as the program is continued on a maintenance basis.

Arthritis Surgery and Joint Replacement

No area of arthritis research has moved as rapidly in recent years as arthritis surgery, including replacement of severely diseased joints with man-made prostheses.

SYNOVECTOMY. The synovium, a membrane lining body joints, produces a fluid that lubricates joint surfaces. In severe rheumatoid arthritis, swelling and inflammation of the synovium may distend a joint, stretch and damage ligaments and tendons, and lead to deformity.

In the operative procedure synovectomy, swollen membrane is removed, stretched ligaments are repaired, and displaced tendons are restored to normal location. The operation can be employed for hands, fingers, knees, shoulders, elbows, and other joints. It is palliative, not curative. It appears that not all synovial membrane can be removed from a joint, and there may be recurrence of disease. But in carefully selected patients, the procedure may be of value.

ARTHRODESIS. Arthrodesis is the surgical fusion of a joint. It may be used when disease twists and gnarls a joint, producing disabling pain and deformity. It is often effective in relieving pain and improving function.

Fusion to fix the wrist, for example, in a neutral undeformed position has been reported to produce gratifying results in as many as 96 percent of patients, leading to increased grasping power and making the wrist pain-free and more useful. With a bone graft, the wrist is fused so that it no longer bends, but patients report that the increased function stemming from pain relief and increased strength more than compensates for the loss of bending.

HIP REPLACEMENT. The first dramatic development in joint replacement was a workable artificial hip in the 1960's. Its success encouraged other prosthetic advances.

The hip, the largest joint, bears body weight. The difficulty in replacing it was to find a material strong enough to withstand many millions of body weight-loading pounds over the years. The material also had to be elastic enough to mimic the energy-absorbing qualities of living bone and cartilage, durable, self-lubricating, and slip-proof.

The hip prosthesis developed by Dr. John Charnley of England fulfilled all the requirements. It uses stainless steel or Vitallium for one component, polyethylene plastic for the other, with both cemented into place. Pain disappears almost as if by magic, and most patients are walking virtually normally within weeks.

At first, hip replacement was limited to patients over 60 because of uncertainty about how long the prosthesis might last. With a decade of satisfactory experience, surgeons are implanting artificial hips now in younger patients, even in some children. Currently, 40,000 people a year in the United States alone are receiving the hips.

KNEES, ANKLES AND TOES.   The knee was long considered to be a "nightmare" joint to try to replace because of its complexity. It bends, rotates, locks when extended, has a mechanism for shifting body weight during bending and straightening, without which we would never manage to get up from a squatting position.

Yet several knee joints have now become available. At New York City's Hospital for Special Surgery, Dr. John N. Insall has used the Freman-Swanson knee (named for its English developers) to replace more than two dozen rheumatoid- and osteoarthritis-crippled knees with excellent results in terms of pain relief, motion and stability.

In other medical centers, other knee prostheses—a "polycentric" knee, a "geometric" knee, and a "UCI" (University of California at Irvine) knee—now have been used successfully in hundreds of patients. Pain is relieved. After a rehabilitation period during which crutches or a walker may be used temporarily, most patients no longer need help in walking.

Until very recently, artificial ankles were of limited usefulness. The natural ankle is an intricate hinge that not only supports body weight but allows the foot to rotate and tilt through many angles. The best artificial ankle of the past consisted of a hinge allowing only up-and-down motion.

A new ankle joint developed by Dr. Theodore Waugh at the University of California, Irvine, permits side-to-side as well as up-and-down movement of the foot. A T-shaped metal piece that screws up into the shin and rocks on a rounded runner that covers the talus ankle bone, it can be implanted in half an hour. Most patients receiving it have been walking on crutches five days after surgery, with many walking unaided less than a month later. Some of the patients, Waugh has reported, unable to walk without crutches for years, are now playing golf and tennis.

Toe implants, too, have been developed to overcome foot deformities. They include half-joints, spacers, and hinged devices suited to individual problems. At UCLA Medical Center, Los Angeles, Dr. Andrea Cracchiolo III has reported on 19 patients receiving 25 implants to relieve foot pain and improve toe alignment. Ten now walk without limitations; five others, up to six blocks at a time.

FINGERS AND KNUCKLES.   Arthritis can twist and gnarl hands into grotesque shapes that even bear descriptive names such as "swanneck" and "buttonhole" deformities.

Finger joint implants now often help. A typical one, made of silicone rubber, resembles a piece of taffy pulled out at both ends. After a deformed joint is removed, the ends of the implant are positioned in channels in bones, with the thickest part of the device lying between and keeping the bones properly aligned.

Dr. Alfred Swanson, a hand surgeon of Blodgett Memorial Hospital, Grand Rapids, Michigan, who developed the joints, has reported that they provide 75 percent of the efficiency of natural, healthy joints. They are now being implanted in many medical centers.

Very recently, successes with new prosthetic knuckles have been reported by Dr. Robert J. Schultz of the Hospital of the Albert Einstein College of Medicine, Bronx, New York. They are for patients with hands deformed so gripping, pinching, and opening the hands widely to grasp large objects are no longer possible.

The replacement knuckles, of stainless steel and polyethylene, are implanted in two hours, and patients begin to use their hands on the fourth day after surgery. In the first 150 implanted and followed for as long as two and a half years, there have been no undesirable effects—and the joints, reports Dr. Schultz, "are not perfect, but close."

SHOULDERS AND ELBOWS.   A new shoulder joint has been developed at the Michael Reese Medical Center, Chicago, by a team headed by Dr. Melvin Post. Somewhat like the Charnley hip prosthesis, it replaces damaged shoulder surfaces with a metal-to-plastic ball-and-socket joint. And because the shoulder is subject to extreme twisting forces, the device has a special plastic collar that locks around and helps prevent dislocation.

After implantation, the arm is immobilized for four weeks, then gentle motion exercises are begun. The prosthesis is showing promise in allowing patients to carry out ordinary shoulder movements and perform tasks that were painful or impossible before.

Very recently, too, Dr. Frederick C. Ewald of Harvard Medical School reported success with a new elbow joint. Previous models could provide only limited motion and tended to loosen. The new one consists of a cuplike plastic element and a ladlelike metal component. The cup goes on top of the ulna bone on the inner side of the forearm; the handle of the ladle fits into the long humerus bone of the upper arm. Cemented into place, the two elements work together like a natural elbow.

In the first 28 patients to receive the prosthesis, all with complete elbow joint destruction and intractable pain for 3 to 10 years, pain has been relieved, better than 90 percent normal arm function has been restored, and all patients have been able to resume usual daily activities.

REPLACING MANY JOINTS.   Arthritis, of course, can affect more than a single joint severely. When necessary, because of extreme and intractable pain and inability to function, more than one can be replaced.

Often, the most troublesome may be replaced first, with other replacements following. Sometimes, however, order of priority may depend upon the particular joints. When, for example, hip and knee joints require replacement, rehabilitation is easier if the hip is replaced first. Once use of the hip is regained, the knee joint can be replaced.

The great needs in arthritis remain—better understanding of causes and improved means of medical control and even prevention. Until those needs can be met, however, the new prosthetic developments make possible rehabilitation for many people once considered virtually hopeless.

11
Hair and Skin

"Hair Today—Gone Tomorrow"

For three days not long ago, a special international symposium on human hair was held in Atlanta. It was sponsored by the Hair Research Task Force of the National Program for Dermatology and hosted by Emory University School of Medicine, Atlanta. Dozens of university dermatologists plus researchers from the cosmetics industry and academic laboratories presented papers on every aspect of hair.

When it was over, a medical publication was moved to report sadly: "Bald is a four-letter word for millions of men who discover to their mortification that their hair is leaving them. Alopecia is a five-syllable euphemism used by dermatologists as a kind of verbal hairpiece to cover the bald fact that they are helpless to reverse, arrest, or cure falling hair.

"Less is known about the root causes of alopecia (let alone its therapy) than about cancer.... Pending a billion-dollar government grant program for a moon-shot attack on hair dysfunction, the most concrete proposal was that projected by one of the few female participants, Dr. Marjorie Muir. She presented a number of scanning electron micrographs but concluded it all by projecting this message: 'Hair today—gone tomorrow. Betta getta wig.' "

It's not really all *that* bad; there is, at least, an alternative to a wig.

Plumage Plus: Some Facts, Some Myths

If human hair is ornamental, it's also protective even if not indispensable. Atop the head, it's a kind of pillow for blows and sunscreen as well. On the face, it's protective, too—but not always. The practice of shaving is thought to have begun with Alexander the Great to keep the enemy from using the beard of his warriors in hand-to-hand combat.

Man has about the same quantity of hair as the ape—so man, the so-called naked ape, is actually a hairy ape, but with finer hair. Atop the head, there are from 90,000 to 150,000 hairs, more than 1,000 per square inch of scalp.

Hair is constantly changing. Quite normally, about 80 hairs are shed daily. A follicle that has shed its hair may rest awhile, then produce another. Pluck out a hair, and as long as the follicle is normal, a replacement appears in due course. At any time, about 90 percent of hair follicles are actively at work while the remaining 10 percent are resting in preparation for getting back to work. You can figure that, in your lifetime, your scalp hair will be replaced about a dozen times.

Does hair ever become gray overnight? Not really. Sudden graying may occur when, because of illness or emotional shock, a lot of hair may be lost temporarily, and much of what remains happened to have already turned gray. Once gray, hair doesn't return to original color—without some help from the bottle. Pigment determines hair color. And hair grays because, for some reason still not understood completely, air spaces form in the hair shaft replacing pigment—usually in middle age, though it may happen prematurely.

The Scalp Massage Myth

Despite the common notion that scalp massage is valuable for the hair, it has no value—and, in fact, may help accelerate hair loss, according to a late report by Dr. J. B. Jerome of the American Medical Association.

Vigorous massage (with or without shampoo, and regardless of whether the hair is dry, wet, or being toweled dry) and vigorous manipulation (by brushing, combing, or during shampooing) tend to break hair mechanically.

Hair grows relatively slowly (less than half an inch a month) and mechanical loss may exacerbate, at least in appearance, the normal daily hair loss. Suggests Dr. Jerome: Shampoo and dry gently and avoid scalp massage; neither scalp nor hair roots need it.

Dandruff

A certain amount of dead cells, oil, bacteria, and dirt accumulating in the hair is natural and readily controllable with regular shampooing and rinsing. In dandruff, however, there are excesses and complications. The outer layer of scalp peels off in little white scales. The flakes become large, greasy, yellowish. They may block sebaceous gland openings so the hair becomes dry, but more often dandruff is associated with increased gland activity, and the hair becomes oily. This latter condition is called oily seborrhea. And the scalp condition may be accompanied by greasy patches of skin on face, neck, and body.

Many factors may operate in dandruff: impaired physical health, nervous tension, infecting organisms, lack of absolute cleanliness. You may be able to clear dandruff by increased attention to good nutrition and general health care. Keeping hair and scalp scrupulously clean by shampooing and rinsing every few days may help. It's important to keep comb and brush clean. A moderate amount of sunlight may be valuable.

Almost every type of dandruff, including the most severe, will improve when treated with a selenium sulfide preparation. Full-strength selenium requires a prescription, but half strength is available in a number of commercial preparations. If the dandruff is severe, full strength is needed. The hair should be shampooed with the selenium preparation, which should be allowed to remain for five minutes or so, with care taken that none gets into the eyes or mouth, since it is toxic. Afterward, another shampoo with a conventional shampooing preparation will remove the toxic material. Hands and fingers should be scrubbed clean.

Baldness

Since it sometimes may begin in the early 20's, baldness is not just a sign of aging. There is, of course, a hereditary factor. Usually, a bald man will pass on his bald pattern characteristics to about half his sons.

Some eight different types of bald pattern characteristics have been distinguished, ranging from type 1, with no hair loss at all, through type 8, with virtually all hair lost in due course. The intermediate common type 4 is characterized by a bald spot in the center of the crown and hair receding at the temples. Only an estimated 4 percent of white men are lucky enough to be type 1, with no hair loss at all.

Is production of testosterone, the male sex hormone, an important factor in baldness? There's no clear-cut answer yet. Aristotle, who was bald, observed that eunuchs did not get bald. But not all eunuchs, it appears, have full heads of hair, and a small percentage of women are bald. There have been some reports of experiments in which testosterone applied in cream form produced a bit of fuzz on bald heads—nothing at all to make it useful, but enough to suggest that elimination of testosterone wouldn't be a universal panacea for eliminating baldness.

A lot of light, passing, and sometimes facetious observations have been made about bald men, including that of one prominent non-scientist American: that men bald in front tend to be thoughtful, those bald in back sexy, while those bald from front to back just think they are sexy.

A cure for baldness? Not for ordinary baldness. Of false claims there are many, but no shampoos or other preparations have been demonstrated to protect against or cure baldness. Any miraculous cures you may hear about have nothing to do with ordinary baldness, only with special types. For example, in a condition called alopecia areata, the hair suddenly falls out, often in clumps. The disease, not fully understood, appears to be connected with emotional disturbances. In many cases, the hair will grow back after the illness has subsided; and if the sufferer has been using a "hair restorer," he may sign a testimonial in good faith crediting it with his new hair growth.

Hair Transplantation

The theory behind hair transplantation—that if hair follicles are moved from their original location to another area, they will behave as they did in their original site—has proved valid. More than one million transplants have been carried out since the technique was first devised in the 1950's by Dr. Norman Orentreich of New York City.

The success rate for survival and continuing growth of transplanted hair, when the procedure is done by a well-trained surgeon, now approaches 100 percent. There have been poor results, however, in the past—with a national average for graft survival of only about 40 percent as recently as the early 1970's—largely traceable to doctors who undertook to do the seemingly simple procedure without knowing very much about it.

What's involved is the punching out of a plug of hair from an area where there is plenty and transferral to a bald site. One plug commonly contains 8 or 9 hairs but may contain as many as 15 if the hair is fine. Surgeons may differ somewhat in technique. Some punch out the plugs by hand and may graft from 10 to 50 in a session. Some use a special power-driven cutter operated at slow speeds which may permit more plugs—as many as 50 to 70— to be grafted in a session.

Surgeons may differ in other respects. Some prefer not to transplant in young men still losing hair and favor waiting until hair loss is complete. Others favor early hairline restoration. The transplants may be started as soon as thinning becomes noticeable if the hair loss is in the crown area only. If there is hairline recession or if both hairline and crown are affected, reconstruction of the frontal hairline first is favored by some surgeons. They may begin grafting when the hairline has receded to the point where the man feels he would be satisfied if further recession can be prevented. The hairline then can be strengthened at this point, and grafts can be implanted to replace hair loss as it continues, both in back of the reconstructed hairline and in the crown.

TRANSPLANTS FOR COMPLETE BALDNESS. Some men, completely or almost completely bald, have no scalp hair to be grafted. Recently, Dr. Orentreich, the pioneer of the original transplant procedure, has been experimenting with homografts, or hair plugs taken from others for implantation in the completely bald.

The problem here is the same as with grafts of donated kidneys and other organs: rejection by the body of something foreign. Orentreich, after trying many approaches to counter rejection, has recently resorted to injecting corticosteroids, or cortisonelike drugs, into the site of a transplant. The injections have to be continued once a month to keep the grafts going. Some patients who have volunteered for trials of the experimental technique have retained their donated hair, thus far, for as long as three years.

A NEWER TRANSPLANT PROCEDURE.   A so-called instant hair operation, now being used by a few surgeons in the United States, was devised by Dr. Jose Juri, a Buenos Aires plastic surgeon who has employed it for some 600 patients over a 10-year period. It uses techniques developed for grafting skin in severe burn patients.

In the procedure, as many as three flaps of scalp, each as wide as an inch or an inch and one-half and as long as 8 or 9 inches, are raised from the sides and back of the head and stretched across the top of the head, with original blood supply still maintained. Eventually, the bald scalp is cut out, and the flaps are sutured in its place.

The procedure is complex, done in three stages, over a period of some weeks, with the final stage requiring major surgery with the patient under general anesthesia. Discomfort afterward is reported to be minimal; convalescence takes a week or two; the scalp itself remains numb for about a year. Most of the sutures can be removed within two weeks, at which point the hair can be combed and styled.

Speed and density of hair obtained are the main benefits of the procedure, according to those who favor it—benefits not achievable with punch grafts of hair. One flap is the equivalent of more than 300 punch grafts. And while hair can be styled within 2 weeks after the flap operation, at least six months must elapse before hair grows long enough to be combed and styled after a punch graft transplant session.

OTHER USES FOR HAIR TRANSPLANTS.   In addition to their use for common male baldness, hair transplants recently have been proving useful for other types of hair loss—from scars, burns, accidents, operations, radiation, infections, and systemic diseases. In addition to scalp hair loss, they have been used to remedy eyebrow loss, reports Dr. Robert Auerbach of New York University School of Medicine, with continuing good results and indications that the grafts will continue to function effectively for a lifetime.

The Skin

One of the most versatile body organs, the skin is also the largest, weighing about 6 pounds and having an area of 17 to 20 square feet in an average 150-pound man. It extends into the nose and other body cavities in the form of thin mucous membrane which secretes lubricating fluids.

The skin keeps body fluids in and foreign agents out, shields against harmful rays, helps regulate body temperature, forms the body's shape, contains the sense of touch, is a main organ of sexual attraction. It even reflects much about the body's state of health, as you may have noticed in the sick, and about the state of mind, as evidenced when anyone blushes with embarrassment or pales with fear.

A single square inch contains some 70 feet of nerves, 650 sweat glands, 15 to 20 feet of blood vessels, 65 to 75 hairs and associated muscles, 100 oil glands, and hundreds of nerve endings for detecting pressure, pain, heat, cold.

The outermost of the three layers of skin, the *epidermis,* is actually made up of dead rather than living cells, because living cells cannot survive exposure to air. Microscopic layers of cells from the epidermis are constantly being lost through bathing and rubbing against clothing. They are replaced from underneath by new cells formed in a deeper layer of the epidermis.

In this deeper layer, the skin may be colored by a pigment, melanin, which helps to prevent tissue damage from the more dangerous rays of the sun. Skin color is also influenced by another pigment, which is yellow, and by the presence of blood vessels in the dermal layer.

Beneath the epidermis is the *dermis,* sometimes called the "true skin." At the top of the dermis, a layer of tiny, rounded ridges called papillae project outward, some 150 million of them throughout the body. On the fingertips, they form the lines and whorls of fingerprints.

The dermis carries the skin's blood supply, in the form of tiny capillary vessels with thin walls. When the body becomes too warm, the capillaries dilate, giving them more surface area, and increasing the rate of evaporation and cooling. When the body becomes cold, the capillaries constrict, reducing heat loss through the skin.

Along with blood vessels, bundles of nerve fibers enter the

skin and branch out in profusion. In addition to involuntary muscles in the skin, which dilate and contract the capillaries, an erector muscle connected to the side of each follicle, or hair pocket, can contract to make the hair stand upright. It is this which makes furred animals appear larger when in danger and also provides an insulating air layer between the hairs as protection against cold. Some investigators believe that the action of the erector muscles in man, which produces "goose pimples," stems from the days when our ancestors had hairy bodies.

The *subcutaneous* layer under the skin is attached loosely to inner body structures such as bones and muscles. Along with blood vessels and nerves, the subcutaneous layer contains fat globules, which both insulate against heat and cold and cushion inner organs against bumps and jolts. If fatty tissues become too thick, graceful movement of muscles may be hindered. With aging, the fatty tissue may be absorbed, causing outer skin layers to form uneven folds, or wrinkles.

Skin Care

Regular cleaning of normal skin with soap and water removes oily secretions, sweat, dead skin, and bacteria, as well as any dirt present. There is no particular mystique. A clean washcloth serves the purpose; soap need not be massaged in, and it should always be rinsed off thoroughly.

Normal skin often tends to become dry with middle age; a plain cold cream or oily lotion can be useful. If the skin is excessively oily, a moderately drying soap helps. If oiliness persists, an astringent two or three times a day on the oily areas of nose, chin, and forehead may solve the problem.

Germicidal soaps and antiseptics are not essential, since healthy skin is unaffected by germs landing on it.

Athlete's Foot

Also known as ringworm of the foot and tinea pedis, athlete's foot can be a stubborn problem. At its height, with malodorous, soggy, whitish, itching between-the-toes outbreaks, it can be distracting.

A long-held concept has been that the trouble lies with a fungus, or microscopic plant growth, that thrives in locker rooms, public showers, and swimming pool walkways, and also on the dead cells of skin between the toes.

But recent research indicates that's only a half-truth. Athlete's foot does start as a fungal infection, at which point it produces no symptoms, only some dry scaling. When it becomes troublesome— with odor, itching, other symptoms—the fungi are not responsible and may not even be present. Bacteria are the culprits.

After discovering that fungi were absent in the vast majority of all typical, advanced, symptomatic cases, investigators, particularly a group at the University of Pennsylvania Hospital, have arrived at this picture of what goes on:

First comes fungal infection, with the fungi multiplying between the toes, producing some skin scaling. At some point, excessive moisture is introduced—because of exercise, hot weather, tight shoes, even emotionally induced excessive sweating. The moisture is ideal for bacterial growth. And bacteria, including some previously harmless types present in small numbers between the toes, multiply, drive out the fungi, and produce the symptoms.

Given this setup, the investigators concluded that what was needed for effective treatment was some preparation that could assure drying. If it also had broad antibacterial activity, that would be to the good.

Trials of many preparations on prisoner volunteers in Philadelphia, all suffering from athlete's foot, finally led to an effective one: a solution of 30 percent aluminum chloride ($AlCl_3.6H_2O$, which any druggist can prepare at a cost in the area of $2 to $3 for four ounces).

In the Philadelphia studies, the solution, dabbed on twice daily with a cotton-tipped applicator, relieved itching and ended malodor within 48 to 72 hours, markedly abating all symptoms within a week. Usually the solution can be applied until complete clearance; thereafter, it may be needed only once a day in especially hot, humid weather.

Rarely does it produce irritation. In cases where this has occurred, a fissure, or narrow deep slit, has been present, allowing the solution to penetrate deeply, below the scaling and horny skin, to living skin. In uncommon cases where fissures are present, the solution should not be used.

Dry Foot Skin

Fungal infections can cause dryness of the skin of the feet. So may ichthyosis (with roughness and scaliness as well) resulting from failure of normal shedding of keratin produced by skin cells. For dry foot skin conditions from these and other causes, urea is reported to be a valuable agent. The compound increases water uptake by the skin and promotes useful, mild peeling of the horny skin layer.

In one study, every one of 75 patients using a urea preparation (Carmol Cream) experienced relief of itching, heel fissuring, cracking, and other symptoms. The preparation also promoted healing.

Excessive Underarm Perspiration

A new medical treatment promises to benefit many men with excessive underarm sweating that resists all the usual measures. At the Hospital of the University of Pennsylvania, Drs. Walter B. Shelley and Harry J. Hurley, Jr., have been able to achieve sustained underarm dryness with a preparation of 20 percent aluminum chloride hexahydrate in anhydrous ethyl alcohol (200 proof).

It has proved regularly effective, they report, in patients following their instructions to apply it at bedtime to the dried, unwashed underarm area, which is then covered with a plastic sheeting such as Saran Wrap kept snug against the skin. In the morning, the plastic is removed and the area washed. Once-a-week application keeps the area dry indefinitely.

Sweaty Palms

For this problem, an effective treatment has been reported recently by Dr. H. H. Gordon of the Southern California Permanente Medical Group, Fontana.

Gordon began studies with a 10 percent aqueous glutaraldehyde solution, not alkalinized, and found it to be a rapidly effective antiperspirant for the palms but with a disadvantage of staining. In further trials, a 5 percent solution, used three times a week, proved effective, with staining minimized. Thereafter, used when necessary, a 2.5 percent or even lesser solution is effective. Some possibility of an allergic reaction to glutaraldehyde exists, but thus far, Gordon reports, no patient has developed one.

Itching

Among the many possible causes of itching are insect bites, fungal and yeast infections, ringworm, hives, eczema, anemia, and more serious disorders such as jaundice, diabetes, kidney disease, and cancer. Not infrequently, itching may stem from tight or irritating clothing, reactions to paint, varnish, insecticides, dusts, dyes, even overhot baths.

Scratching doesn't really help. It may seem briefly to relieve the discomfort, but it actually lowers the itch threshold and often brings on a cycle of itch-scratch-itch–more scratch–more itch. As an alternative, some itchers pinch nearby skin; others apply extreme cold, which helps temporarily but is followed by greater itching.

Medical help—particularly from a dermatologist—may be needed when itching is complicated. But when it isn't, this recommendation from a recent medical journal editorial: "If the skin is dry, moisten it; if moist, dry it; if the skin has no oil, oil it; if the skin shows evidence of attack by any of the itch-producing agents or organisms, protect the skin against them."

Fever Blisters

Caused by the herpes simplex virus, these lip sores that start out with burning and itching and then become yellowish and crusted are occasional nuisances for many people, repeatedly recurring ones for some. No drug has been of value.

Recently, however, two medical reports indicate that ether, the volatile liquid that has been used for anesthesia, may be of significant benefit.

A team of Indian dermatologists used ether-laden pads pressed onto fever blisters for five minutes on two consecutive days in a trial with 11 patients. All pain disappeared within two minutes, the blisters dried up within 24 hours, healed completely in 48 hours. Four of the 11 had no recurrences; of the others, 3 had greater intervals between recurrences.

In the United States, Drs. G. R. Nugent and S. M. Chou of West

Virginia University Medical Center, Morgantown, report having patients use an applicator stick soaked in ether, dabbing it onto a developing blister ten times and repeating the application three times a day, with blister development stopped in its tracks and healing beginning almost immediately.

Canker Sores

Painful ulcers on the mucous membranes of the mouth, appearing singly or in groups, bother some people often, as frequently as monthly.

Although evidence has not been conclusive, the same herpes simplex virus involved in fever blisters has been believed responsible. More recently, some evidence has appeared that some forms of a bacterial organism, alpha streptococcus, may be responsible. The latter finding has led to trials of antibiotic syrups with some reported success.

A common procedure is to hold a teaspoon of tetracycline hydrochloride syrup (250 milligrams per cubic centimeter) on the sore or sores for five minutes, then swallow, and repeat four times a day.

Skin Cancer

The most curable cancer, that of the skin is also the most common, particularly in the fair-skinned, with men much more prone than women, probably because of greater exposure to the elements.

The most common type, basal cell cancer, which generally starts as a pearly, pale, translucent nodule that slowly enlarges and ulcerates, is least dangerous because it rarely spreads to other parts of the body. Squamous cell carcinoma, next most common, starts as a small raised area or patch that may darken or redden and become hard. After a period of months or years, it may grow and form a crusted ulcer. It can arise on normal skin. A common site is the lower lip. It seldom involves other organs.

Most dangerous is the black melanoma, which is relatively rare, usually develops from a mole, spreads rapidly, and may involve other organs. Unlike the other two major types, which are almost 100 percent curable, melanoma is often deadly.

Sunlight, especially certain wavelengths of ultraviolet light, seems directly related to skin cancer: the more intense the sunlight, the higher the skin cancer rates—very much higher, for example, in Dallas than in Minneapolis. Skin cancer also appears more frequently in people exposed to too much x-ray, coal tar, beryllium, and nickel.

The best detection center for skin cancer is yourself. Any skin change that does not heal promptly or properly needs medical examination. When a pigmented patch of skin present for years suddenly changes appearance, color or size, it is particularly suspicious.

Most of the vast number of skin conditions are not malignant. A biopsy (study under the microscope of a small sample of tissue) can establish the true nature of the lesion. When skin cancer is detected early, surgery done in the physician's office often is enough to provide complete excision and cure. Radiation and chemotherapy are also effective. With early detection of melanoma and use of newer treatment techniques—including combinations of anticancer drugs and sometimes drugs to stimulate the immune or defense system—the outlook is beginning to improve, with benefits moving upward from 25 to 30 percent of patients to higher percentages.

Avoidance of overexposure to sun, needless x-rays, or other cancer-producing agents may help to prevent skin cancer.

Sunburn

Mild amounts of sunbathing may have some value. But sun-worshippers can do themselves considerable harm. Tanning causes premature skin aging, induces wrinkles, impairs tone and elasticity of the skin, and can produce hard, horny, dark gray precancerous changes called keratosis.

The fair-skinned burn more quickly and more severely than others, and commonly blonds and redheads cannot tan but break out in freckles.

However hazy or even cloudy a day, it can still lead to a severe burn. Thin clothing is no shield from burn-producing sun rays; plate glass is. Sunshine effects are greatly increased by reflection from water or snow. Snow blindness—a burn on the cornea of the eye—can be extremely painful.

Overexposure to the sun may produce redness, itching and tolerable pain in mild cases. In severe cases, in addition to angry reddening of the skin, blisters develop, and there may be chills, fever, headache, nausea, vomiting, weakness, even shock lasting as long as a week and followed by considerable peeling.

Often helpful: a cold compress of whole milk or of saline solution (one teaspoon of salt in a pint of cool water). Severe cases should be treated by a physician, who may provide a soothing steroid ointment and treatment to prevent infection.

Severe sunburn can usually be prevented by limiting first-day exposure to a maximum of 30 minutes, with a maximum of 7 or 8 additional minutes added on each succeeding day until tanning has developed.

An Effective Sun Screening Agent

Although suntan lotions applied before exposure can help in keeping the skin moist and loose, avoiding tightness, they do not totally protect against sunburn.

An effective sun screening agent—capable of filtering out burning rays, preventing sunburn while permitting tanning, and helping to minimize other harmful effects of the sun—has long been sought. The most effective currently available, according to recent studies, is PABA (para-aminobenzoic acid). It is being used as an ingredient in some commercial preparations, as indicated on the labeling.

For the Extremely Sun-Sensitive

A sensitivity to sunlight so extreme that its victims have had to spend much of their lives sheltered from exposure results from a disorder, erythropoietic protoporphyria, in which the body is unable to properly handle a natural chemical, porphyrin. After even a few minutes of sunlight, the buildup of excess porphyrin in the skin becomes poisonous and causes intense itching, burning, and swelling.

A promising treatment for such people has been reported by a team of investigators headed by Dr. Micheline M. Matthews-Roth of Harvard Medical School, Boston: 30-milligram doses of beta-carotene, a yellow pigment found in yellow and green leafy vegetables and yellow fruit.

Carotene appears to be a specific, acting to prevent light-exposed porphyrin from causing trouble. In first studies with 53 patients, 46 had a fourfold or greater increase in time they could tolerate sunlight without discomfort, and 3 others experienced a doubling. Most of the patients now can engage in outdoor activities that were impossible before.

All told, in the first 135 patients treated, only 5 have not benefited. And in the six years since tests first began, no side effects have been noted.

Tinea Cruris

A fungal infection of the genital area and thighs, tinea cruris produces burning, itching, and pain. A newer topical drug—miconazole nitrate (MicaTin Cream)—with activity against many fungi, yeasts, and bacteria, is reported to be effective. In a study at the USAF Medical Center, Keesler Air Force Base, Biloxi, Mississippi, 93 percent of patients were freed of signs and symptoms of infection, with relief often occurring within 24 hours.

Rosacea ("Rum Nose")

Acne rosacea, a skin disorder that produces facial flushing, particularly of nose, chin, and forehead, with the nose becoming bulbous, sometimes occurs in a young adult but is more common in middle age. Such appellations as "rum nose" and "whiskey nose" are unfair, since the problem occurs in teetotalers as well as drinkers. Other symptoms include dilation of capillaries, pimples, dandruff.

The role of diet is controversial, although in some men certain foods—coffee, tea, nuts, chocolate, hot peppers, alcohol, and spices —appear to exacerbate the condition by their ability to dilate blood vessels.

Suspected foods can be checked for by two- to three-week elimination trials.

Other factors that may contribute to rosacea and may need avoidance or treatment include extreme heat or cold, exposure to sun and wind, and chronic gastrointestinal disorders. Antibiotics may sometimes be used. In severe cases, excessive nose tissue may be treated surgically.

Recently, some investigators have reported that metronidazole, a drug sometimes used for genitourinary infections, controls the acnelike lesions, though not the flushing, in about 70 percent of patients taking 200 milligrams daily (and abstaining from alcohol, because the combination of alcohol and drug may produce head-ache).

Psoriasis

A chronic disease that affects skin, scalp, and nails, psoriasis is marked by reddened patches which become covered by thick silvery scales. The patches favor elbows, knees, scalp, groin, chest, lower back, and body folds, rarely affecting the face. There is itching in many instances, and the name comes from the Greek *psora,* meaning "to itch."

The cause of the disease, which is not contagious, is not clear. The fact that it seems to occur in families with previous histories of the problem suggests a hereditary factor. It comes and goes over many years, and occasionally may clear up entirely. Many patients benefit, some to the point of almost complete clearance, by tanning in sunshine.

Many treatments have been employed with varying degrees of success. In recent years, topical corticosteroids, or cortisonelike drugs—particularly fluocinolone acetonide, flurandrenolide, and triamcinolone acetonide—have come into use. They are often more effective when applications are made at bedtime and the area covered with a plastic film. In some cases, injection of triamcinolone acetonide directly into small, localized psoriatic lesions is used.

Other treatments have included a tar-sulfur-salicylic acid com-bination for the scalp, anthralin ointment applied once a day to body outbreaks, and various forms of tar, including colorless tar distillate preparations.

A method of treament called the Goeckerman regimen, which usually requires hospitalization, often is effective for severe out-breaks. Crude coal tar ointment is rubbed thoroughly into all affected areas except the scalp nightly and removed with mineral oil in the morning. The areas are exposed daily to sunlight or ultraviolet radiation, which is gradually increased to the point of mild skin reddening. In many cases, improvement is marked within 10 to 14 days.

For very severe, extensive psoriasis, a drug called methotrexate has come into use. Sometimes employed for cancer, methotrexate acts on an essential enzyme and in doing so may interfere with cell division. It is given by mouth and must be used with great care under close supervision because of the possibility of toxic effects.

Several years ago, Drs. E. M. Farber and D. E. Harris of Stanford University School of Medicine, Stanford, California, began to use a modification of the stiff anthralin paste that had been employed for psoriasis in the past. Almost like peanut butter in consistency, the new paste produces less irritation and staining and allows even seriously affected patients to treat themselves at home after treatment is begun in the hospital.

Reporting on the first 50 patients treated, the physicians indicated clearance in 47 during hospital treatment. They then continued treatment at home, using the paste overnight three times a week, then at less frequent intervals. A follow-up of 36 of the patients after two to seven months of home treatment found 28 without recurrences or with good control of the disease.

More recently, at the Letterman Army Institute of Research, Dr. Isaac Willis, now at Johns Hopkins University, and Dr. David R. Harris, now at the VA Hospital, Palo Alto, California, tried applying a low-strength anthralin paste, then a solution of methoxsalen (see below), followed by black light to activate the methoxsalen. Their patients, all men with chronic psoriasis that had failed to respond to other treatment, exhibited complete clearing within one to three weeks, with the clearing maintained with occasional repeat treatments.

The newest treatment, one with apparently major promise for the future, though still considered experimental, is currently being tested by researchers across the country.

Actually, the early Egyptians followed a practice of treating some skin diseases with some success by swallowing a powder from a local plant and exposing themselves to sunlight.

Methoxsalen, or methoxypsoralen, is a drug extracted from the Egyptian plant. In the new treatment, which is referred to as PUVA (for psoralen plus ultraviolet-A light), a specially developed light device is employed to activate the methoxsalen.

About two hours after taking the drug in pill form, the patient either lies on a bed or is slid under a horizontal arch lined with ultraviolet light tubes, or stands in a cylindrical chamber somewhat like a shower stall, for 8 to 30 minutes, depending upon the individual case. The cells in psoriasis patches multiply as much as ten times faster than do normal cells, and the combination of drug and light apparently slows the multiplication process to the point where scales do not form.

First reported by Harvard Medical School investigators, PUVA has been used with marked success on hundreds of patients both in Boston and in Austria in related research carried out by Dr. Klaus Wolff of the University of Vienna. In the first 300 patients, complete clearance has been obtained in over 93 percent.

Side effects have included itching in one sixth of patients, mild nausea in one sixth, severe nausea in 2 percent, localized reddening in 9 percent, generalized reddening in 1 percent, and localized blistering in 2 percent.

More testing is needed before the treatment can be considered safe for the long term. More research may also permit reduction of presently known side effects. Further research is also needed to determine whether patients may be able to discontinue treatment. Several who, for one reason or another, could not continue treatment have remained clear of psoriasis for as long as six months. Others who stopped have had only mild recurrences.

A cooperative 16-center trial has been launched with plans to treat 1,600 patients in an effort to establish both safety and efficacy in a larger series, possible long-term deleterious effects, and possibly more effective and less troublesome dosages of both drug and radiation.

Boils and Carbuncles

When friction, irritation, a scratch or break in the skin allows bacteria on the surface to penetrate the outer skin layer, a local infection based in a hair root may develop. The result: a boil or furuncle, as large numbers of white blood cells travel to the site and attack the invading bacteria, some white cells as well as the bacteria are killed, and they and their liquefied products form pus.

The boil shows on the surface as a dark red, swollen, hot area, tender and quite painful. A carbuncle is a group of interconnected boils. Boils most often develop in the neck but also occur on the face, back, buttocks, and in the armpits. Carbuncles, most frequent in men, commonly develop on the nape of the neck.

A single boil may be treated with moist heat to bring it to a head so it can be incised and the core removed. Sometimes single boils and commonly multiple boils and carbuncles, require antibiotic treatment.

Boils may afflict healthy people but often their appearance is an indication of low resistance, commonly as a result of poor nutrition or illness. People suffering from skin disorders or untreated diabetes tend to be particularly susceptible.

Chilblain

A common complaint, chilblain is a painful burning, itching sensation of fingers, toes, ear, nose, or feet, followed shortly by redness and swelling on exposure to cold. The basic cause is not so much cold temperature as sensitivity to cold, which may result from poor health, poor nutrition, or circulation. The problem may be overcome by good diet and exercise, and by use of warm, loose clothing rather than tight, restricting garments.

Frostbite

Frostbite, or injury by cold, sometimes is generalized but commonly affects toes, fingers, nose, and ears—areas with lesser degrees of blood circulation. Early warning of developing frostbite is a tingling, numbing sensation. The skin reddens and becomes painful, and burning, itching, and swelling may follow. When all feeling is lost and the skin becomes white, complete frostbite has occurred.

There should be no rubbing with snow or anything else. In generalized cold injury, blankets may be used to prevent further body heat loss and permit natural slow rewarming. In local frostbite, an often-recommended treatment is application of warm water to encourage rapid rewarming, with the water kept between 100 and 104 degrees Fahrenheit, never warmer or colder, and a thermometer used to check its temperature. Other parts of the body are kept warm and whiskey or a drug such as papaverine, which dilates blood vessels, may be used.

Sunstroke (Heatstroke, Hyperpyrexia)

Prolonged exposure to heat or sun, often combined with exercise, may cause body temperature to rise to 106 degrees or higher. Symptoms may include headache, dizziness, nausea, with flushing, hot and dry skin, sometimes muscular twitching or cramps, confusion, and sometimes convulsions.

Heat hyperpyrexia (excessively high fever) can threaten life and constitutes an emergency, requiring immediate medical attention. Meanwhile, often-recommended first aid treatment is to place the victim, if possible, in an ice-water tub bath or cover him with a water-soaked blanket and apply vigorous skin massage to bring rectal temperature down to 101 but not lower, with cold applications discontinued when that temperature is reached but massage continued. If temperature keeps dropping, the patient must be kept warm.

Preventive measures for heat hyperpyrexia include undertaking no vigorous work in high temperature until the body has adjusted to the heat, use of unstarched clothing and a hat or other head covering, free intake of fluids.

Heat Exhaustion

Similar to sunstroke in producing such symptoms as headache and dizziness, heat exhaustion is relatively minor and unlike it in other respects. The skin, instead of being hot and flushed, is cold and clammy, sweating is usually profuse, and there is no steep rise in temperature.

Advance warnings of heat exhaustion include a sudden feeling of faintness, dimming or blurring of vision, weakness.

Heat exhaustion can be overcome by lying down in a cool place with head lower than body and by compensating for lost fluids by slowly sipping water for half an hour and taking salt tablets.

Shingles

Caused by the same virus that produces chickenpox, shingles is an acute nerve inflammation with a skin outbreak. It often begins, before any outbreak appears, with chills, fever, malaise, and even gastrointestinal discomfort. In a few days, blisters erupt along the course of the affected nerve, on one side of the body, usually going from the back around to the abdomen. In about five days, the blisters begin to dry and scab.

In mild cases, no treatment may be needed except for aspirin or use of a Neocalamine lotion. In painful cases, codeine or another strong analgesic may be used, and a corticosteroid drug such as prednisone may be helpful. Large doses of vitamin B_{12} have been reported to be helpful in some cases.

Most patients recover without any aftereffects except for some scarring, but in some, neuralgic pain may persist.

Efforts to find new and more effective treatments for acute shingles itself and for its aftermath of neuralgic pain continue. One recently reported: injection of procaine or another local anesthetic into an affected nerve pathway. In all patients in whom the measure was tried, immediate relief occurred. The same treatment provided relief in slightly more than one third of patients with persisting neuralgic pain.

Corns and Calluses

Corns, which are commonly caused by friction or pressure from poorly fitting shoes or hose, are of two kinds: the hard corn, usually located on the outside of the little toe or on the upper surfaces of the other toes, conical in shape; and the soft corn, a white sodden mass usually found between the fourth and fifth toes and kept soft by moisture.

Corns can be treated by soaking in warm water for 15 minutes or more, applying a 10 percent solution of salicyclic acid in collodion, and covering with corn pads for about four days. At that point, with further soaking, they usually come out readily.

Calluses, commonly due to excessive use of an area, are localized thickenings of the skin. One often-recommended treatment: application of 10 percent salicylic acid and paring, with iodine applied if live flesh is cut.

Unusually troublesome corns and calluses are best treated by a podiatrist. Anyone with diabetes or a circulatory disorder should never attempt self-treatment of the feet.

Warts

Small skin growths, warts are virus-caused and contagious. A few are flat but generally they are firm and irregular in shape and painless, except for the plantar wart on the sole of the foot.

If not troublesome, warts can be left alone. If uncomfortable or unsightly, they can be removed by various means, including topical agents, electric needle, and freezing with liquid nitrogen.

Vitamin A acid has been reported useful for people with flat warts too numerous for freezing or other treatment. A 0.05 percent solution of the acid, also known as tretinoin, is applied twice daily.

For difficult-to-treat plantar warts, glutaraldehyde in a 25 percent solution has been reported effective. Applied daily, it hardens the warts, making them easy for the patient or a family member to pare.

Hypnosis for warts? Despite many suggestions that it may work, evidence has been lacking. But a recent study at Massachusetts General Hospital, Boston, indicates that, in fact, hypnosis often may be useful.

Seventeen patients with an average of 30 warts each were treated hypnotically once a week for five weeks and were told under hypnosis that warts on one side of the body (chosen by each patient) would soon disappear. Another 7 patients, serving for comparison, received no hypnosis. Three months later, both groups were checked.

Of the hypnotized, 9, or 53 percent, showed marked improvement. Sudden loss of all warts occurred in 4 of the 9, gradual fading in 4, and 1 experienced sudden successive loss of individual warts. None of the nonhypnotized patients showed improvement; of these, 4 subsequently received hypnotherapy and 3 improved.

12
The Senses

Hearing

On Your Risk of Hearing Trouble

Survival once, in primitive times, depended on good hearing to detect the presence of predators. Survival today, in the business world, often depends on ability to hear face-to-face and by phone.

Not every man becomes hard of hearing. But some degree of hearing loss commonly affects men after 40, and some men are affected earlier.

Although all forms of loss are not amenable to treatment, many are and some are avoidable.

The Three Ears

Involved not only with hearing but also with a sense of equilibrium, balance, and orientation, the human ear is made up of three parts. The *outer ear* consists of the lobe and the ear canal, into which sound funnels. The canal, about an inch long or a little less, dead-ends against the eardrum, or tympanic membrane.

Just across the drum, the *middle ear* contains three tiny bones of hearing (or ossicles)—the incus, malleus, and stapes. The bones relay the vibrations of the drum—set up by sound waves entering the outer canal—to the fluid-filled cavity of the inner ear. The middle ear is connected by a tube, the eustachian, to the rear part of the throat. The tube serves to adjust pressure of air in the middle ear to outside pressure.

The vibrations transmitted by the bones are further transmitted through an oval window, another membrane, to the *inner ear*. There, a snail-like coil, the cochlea, contains the organ of Corti, consisting of specialized nerve cells with hairlike projections. The organ of Corti transforms the incoming vibrations into nerve impulses which the brain interprets as sound.

A good ear has remarkable sensitivity. It can respond to sound waves that deflect the eardrum by one 0.00000001 millimeter. It can assess some 1,600 frequencies from high to low, some 350 intensities from quietest to loudest. It can measure the intensity and frequency of sound waves oscillating between 20 and 20,000 cycles per second.

Also within the inner ear is the organ of equilibrium, or balance. It consists of three semicircular canals and two small sacs next to the cochlea. The canals are set in different planes and contain a gelatinous material along with nerve receptors. The movement of the gelatin in the canals as the head is moved causes the nerve receptors to flash to the brain the information that the head is changing position. A somewhat similar system in the sacs next to the cochlea transmits the messages, which, in effect, always let you know which way is up.

The Three Types of Hearing Impairment

One is conductive; another is perceptive, involving nerve loss; the third is a mixture of the two.

A physician can determine, with a tuning fork, whether hearing loss is conductive or perceptive. A vibrating fork is placed close to the ear and then against the bone behind the ear. If the sound is heard better on the bone, the loss is conductive in type. In addition to the fork, an audiometer can be used to establish the degree of any nerve damage loss.

A SELF-TEST FOR HEARING LOSS. If you suspect you may not be hearing as well as you once did, answering several questions can be helpful.

Do you frequently have some difficulty in understanding talk on television? Hear better on the phone than in other conversation? Sometimes misunderstand what people are saying? Cock your ear to hear better? If you place a watch at the ear opening and then on the bone behind the ear, is your hearing more acute on the bone? If you answer yes to any question, you are experiencing some hearing loss.

Conductive Loss

Commonly, anyone with this type of hearing impairment will tend to speak in a low voice because he hears his own voice at amplified levels through bone conduction.

Interference with sound conduction may occur anywhere along the route through the ear canal and middle ear. It can stem from wax and water in the ear, blockage of the eustachian tube during a cold, puncturing of the eardrum, infection, or otosclerosis ("hardening of the ear").

IMPACTED WAX. Blockage of the external ear canal by impacted wax is perhaps the most frequent cause of conductive hearing loss. In addition to interfering with sound wave passage, the wax also may serve as a culture medium for bacteria which can produce infection. Impacted wax sometimes can act, too, through reflex to produce an annoying dry cough.

Normally wax works its way out unnoticed bit by bit. But in some people the wax simply does not come out in this way.

Although wax solvents for instillation in the ear are available, the best bet is to have a physician remove impacted wax. If infection is present, rather than syringe the wax out, he can remove it with a special instrument, a cerumen curette, avoiding possible spread of infection. If you happen to be one of those people who accumulate a lot of wax, yearly or even more frequent removal by a physician may be in order.

BLOCKAGE OF THE EUSTACHIAN TUBE. When the eustachian tube function is impaired by a bad cold or allergic episode, by an enlarging tumor mass or adenoid enlargement, or by a fast descent in an inadequately pressurized airplane, the middle ear cannot get the air it needs. Negative pressure then may develop within the ear, drawing the eardrum inward. If this goes on for some time, fluid may be withdrawn from the bloodstream, filling the middle ear around the ossicles, impairing hearing. Other symptoms may include fullness in the ear, crackling sounds during swallowing, noises in the ear, and a sensation of fluid present in the ear. If nose drops or a nasal spray fail to overcome the blockage, medical help is needed. A short course of steroid treatment may clear the ear. If not, the fluid can be withdrawn through a needle placed through the anesthetized eardrum.

EARDRUM PUNCTURING. The eardrum can be punctured accidentally when toothpicks, Q-tips, or other objects are used to clean the ear canal. It's also said that insertion of the tip of the tongue during a passionate kiss can, on sudden withdrawal, sometimes create enough suction to rupture the drum.

Along with loss of hearing, there may be severe pain, dizziness, nausea, and vomiting. Blood may appear in the ear canal.

Help from an ear specialist is needed. A drug may be used to ease pain. A small perforation may heal on its own. Sometimes, if the perforation is large, medical treatment may help bring about healing. If necessary, a graft may be used to seal the drum and improve hearing.

EAR INFECTION. Boils can occur in the ear canal, producing pain along with diminished hearing. They are commonly caused by staphylococcal bacteria gaining entry through a small crack or fissure in the skin that may be caused by scratching an itchy ear or by use of implements to clean the ear.

Swimming in polluted waters may cause a fungal infection in and around the ear canal, causing temporary hearing loss and itching. Other types of infection may also affect the ear canal. Effective drugs are available for medical use in overcoming boils and the other infections.

Middle ear infection (otitis media) may occur as a complication of a nose or throat infection. Symptoms can vary, depending upon the type of infection. There may be hearing loss, sense of fullness in the ear, earache, ringing noises, sometimes fever. Chronic infection may cause adhesions that impede sound transmission and may affect eardrum, ossicles, and other structures. Antibiotics and other medications may be used, and often surgical drainage of the middle ear is essential. Barring complications, hearing will return to normal with effective treatment.

264 · The Complete Medical, Fitness & Health Guide for Men

OTOSCLEROSIS. Usually diagnosed in the 40's and 50's and affecting millions, otosclerosis is one of the most common causes of defective conduction.

The stapes, the innermost of the three small bones of the middle ear, is stirrup-shaped and fits into and closes the oval window in a membrane that separates the middle from the inner ear. When the stapes moves, it agitates fluid in the inner ear into vibratory waves.

In otosclerosis, the stapes hardens and becomes rigid and fixed, unable to transmit the sound waves. Hearing is impaired and there is ringing of the ear in about 70 percent of cases.

Otosclerosis today is surgically correctable. The operation, stapedectomy, is performed under local anesthetic supplemented by other measures to induce drowsiness. The eardrum is lifted to expose the middle ear, and the stapes bone is removed. The opening into the inner ear is then covered with a small piece of vein or other material. A tiny section of plastic or wire is connected to the incus bone to form a strut between the incus and the graft covering the inner ear window. The eardrum is then replaced. Often the patient can be discharged from hospital on the second postoperative day.

Stapedectomy is highly successful but not foolproof. There is some possibility that the operation may not improve hearing. About 92 percent of patients benefit. Usually hearing loss from otosclerosis occurs in both ears, and patients who have had successful surgery on one ear want similar surgery on the other. Many surgeons believe that a second stapedectomy should be done only after a six-month to year interval.

Through tests prior to surgery which indicate the level of function of the auditory nerve, it is possible for surgeons to predict how much hearing can be restored through stapes surgery.

For patients with normal nerve function, operation is likely to result in complete hearing restoration, and if a hearing aid was required before, it can be discarded. If there is some degeneration of the auditory nerve with a loss of upper-frequency sounds, successful stapedectomy will allow normal hearing in most situations but will not eliminate some limitations in other situations. On the whole, hearing will be satisfactory without a hearing aid. With marked nerve degeneration, hearing will improve enough to justify surgery: it will be possible to hear close conversation and to hear comfortably on the phone, but for most social and business purposes a hearing aid may be needed. When nerve degeneration is advanced, so much so that a hearing aid was of no value, the aim of surgery is to permit use of an aid effectively. Age is not a factor in suitability for stapes surgery. The basic requirement is sufficient auditory nerve function.

SUDDEN DEAFNESS. A recently discovered reason for sudden deafness appears to be rupturing of the membranes separating the middle and inner ear. The membranes may break in response to a sudden buildup of pressure in spinal fluid, which circulates in the spinal canal and the brain and may be in communication with fluids in the inner ear. If spinal fluid pressure increases suddenly—as might happen with sudden physical exertion—membrane rupturing may occur. One possible result: mixing of various fluids in the inner ear which normally do not mix, with destruction of delicate nerve endings.

The hope lies in immediate treatment when such sudden deafness occurs. In some cases, persistent deafness may be prevented by prompt and complete bed rest. In others, membrane patching with a graft may be required.

FLUCTUANT HEARING LOSS. Feelings of fullness with ringing of the ears, fluctuation in hearing acuity, and vertigo or dizziness occur, usually in that order, in an inner ear disorder called fluctuant hearing loss. Most often, the problem appears in middle age and not infrequently affects both ears.

Abnormal fluid retention in the inner ear is known to be involved. The disorder appears to stem from many possible causes, including diabetes, syphilis, excessive blood levels of fat, excessive smoking, high salt intake, and even anxiety.

At the Memphis Otologic Clinic, Drs. J. J. Shea and A. E. Kitabachi have found abnormal glucose tolerance, suggesting latent diabetes in 57 percent of cases, and in 50 percent the intolerance had not been noted previously. Excessive smoking was the next factor in order of frequency (10 percent), followed by others such as high blood-fat levels (7 percent) and allergy and anxiety (each 7 percent).

Correction of any of these factors can be useful. And often, the two investigators have reported, the problem can be managed by treatment that includes a low-salt diet, use of a diuretic such as

Dyazide (promoting elimination of excess fluids), and inhalation of a mixture of oxygen and carbon dioxide to dilate blood vessels in the inner ear and promote circulation.

Additionally, when warranted in individual cases, a low-carbohydrate, low-calorie diet is used to control glucose intolerance; a low-fat diet to reduce elevated blood-fat levels; allergy-producing agents are eliminated in those with allergy if possible or an antihistamine, cyproheptadine, is prescribed. Such treatment has produced good results in preserving hearing and controlling dizziness.

On hearing aids. If you experience a conductive hearing loss not amenable to medical or surgical correction, you may benefit from use of the right hearing aid.

Emphasis is on "right."

There are two types of aids. The air-conduction type is worn in the ear; the bone-conduction type is worn against the bone behind the ear. A hearing aid can only improve hearing, not restore it to normal.

And if it is to provide maximum improvement with minimum discomfort, it should be prescribed by an expert, an otologist or an audiologist at a speech and hearing center, and dispensed by a reputable dealer. Anyone with hearing loss has unique needs that require a carefully chosen and well-fitted aid, a matter for an expert. Just getting a hearing aid off the shelf is likely to prove a waste of effort and money.

In a striking study, investigators in Houston not long ago, working with 298 hearing-impaired patients, selected several aids for each patient that, theoretically, on the basis of the characteristics of the aids themselves and the needs of the patients, should have provided peak performance. Yet, in actual use, effectiveness varied greatly. In 47 percent of the patients, there were differences of 20 percent or more in speech discrimination between what proved to be for them the poorest and best performing aids. In 86 percent, there were differences of 10 percent or more.

Such marked differences, the study suggests, justify the effort and expense involved in having an expert otologist or audiologist not merely choose an aid that should be, theoretically, suitable but go on to evaluate various aids for an individual patient.

If you can't get such help, you may have to rely on your own tests of performance, checking for tolerability, freedom from internal noise, intelligibility of ordinary and faint speech, difficult words, and adequacy under difficult conditions.

Ideally, though not all dealers will oblige, you should have a trial loan period with each of several instruments for testing at home or in the office. If necessary, rental for trial periods may be worthwhile.

Get the help of a friend or family member with a good normal voice who will be willing to spend a little time first practicing and then speaking test words and reading passages from a book or magazine repeatedly in the same tone and with the same loudness.

Internal noise will be obvious. For intelligibility, have your helper read to you repeatedly in normal and then very quiet voice. Have him also read such difficult words as bat, bite, boot, beat, boat, and bout for distinguishing vowels, and vie, by, high, thy, shy, why for consonants.

Tolerability is important but difficult to test unless you've used an aid before. Sounds uncomfortably loud at first often become tolerable with wearing. Except for very severe loss, you may do better at first with an instrument of only medium or low power.

Perceptive Loss

With perceptive, or nerve-involved, hearing loss, there is a tendency to speak loudly, since one's own voice is heard only faintly.

High-frequency sounds and sounds like *p, k, t,* and hard *g* are difficult to hear although other sounds may be heard well. As a result of hearing a word such as "play" sound as if it were "lay," there may be difficulty in making sense out of what is heard in some situations.

With perceptive loss, you may depend for understanding speech on quite small differences among sounds you actually hear, much as a normal listener depends on small differences when speech can just about be heard above a background noise.

You are also likely to find annoying a phenomenon known as recruitment of loudness, which means that while faint or moderate sounds are difficult or impossible to hear, there is little or no loss in the sense of loudness for loud sounds. This is why commonly people with perceptive loss may first complain that they cannot hear a speaker and then, when he raises his voice a little, complain that he is shouting at them. Recruitment is one reason why it is often more difficult to tolerate a hearing aid with perceptive loss compared with conductive loss.

CAUSES. The possible causes of perceptive loss are many. Nerve injury may sometimes occur with a blow to the ear. Exposure to a single, sudden, overwhelmingly loud blast or chronic exposure to loud sounds may produce loss.

In presbycusis, which is associated with aging, there is loss of ability to perceive or distinguish sounds.

Perceptive loss may result from complications in such diseases as streptococcal infections, meningitis, syphilis, mumps, measles. It can stem from brain and acoustic nerve tumor. Hearing loss may be a symptom of Meniere's disease.

In those who are sensitive to them, some drugs such as quinine, streptomycin, and some other antibiotics may cause loss, with recovery sometimes possible if their use is discontinued promptly enough. In the sensitive, too, excessive use of aspirin and related compounds can cause hearing loss.

ACUPUNCTURE AND TRANSDERMAL STIMULATION. There have been some reports of the value of acupuncture in improvement of hearing in cases of perceptive loss. But data have been sparse and there have been other conflicting reports of no value.

In one recent study, investigators from Vanderbilt University and Central Michigan University checked 111 patients who had undergone acupuncture treatment. They found that only 4 percent showed some improvement while an equal proportion showed a decrease in hearing.

Another experimental method of treatment, "transdermal electrostimulation," which involves electrical stimulation through electrodes across the head, has been under study since 1969, but thus far, the investigators found, does not appear to be effective.

Their conclusion: Neither acupuncture nor transdermal stimulation can be dismissed; either or both, with further research, may prove to have some usefulness, but no evidence presently exists warranting the use of either for the hearing-impaired.

EXPERIMENTAL HEARING IMPLANTS. Implantable electronic devices that may allow partial restoration of hearing in perceptive loss are under study. One device consists of a wire which a surgeon threads partway into the cochlea, where it stimulates the hearing nerve, bypassing damaged sensory cells. The wire's other end leads under the skin to a button behind the ear connected to a microphone.

Other devices are being tested in a considerable amount of research encouraged by the National Institutes of Health and presently under way at many university research centers, medical centers, and private organizations.

Vertigo

Vertigo—a sensation of being whirled about in space or of objects whirling about the sufferer—often is accompanied by nausea, pallor, and sweating.

The possible causes are many, since vertigo involves a disturbance of the equilibratory or balancing apparatus, which consists of structures in the inner ear, brain areas, and sensory nerves of muscles, joints, and tendons.

Vertigo thus may stem from ear infections or inflammations or Meniere's disease (see next). General infections may produce it, as may medications such as quinine, aspirin and related compounds, streptomycin and some other antibiotics, tumors, eye problems such as glaucoma or ocular imbalance, and even, on occasion, alcohol, caffeine, nicotine, and various sedatives.

Cure, of course, depends on determining and eliminating the cause. Symptomatic treatment may include use of a tranquilizer such as perphenazine or an antihistamine such as dimenhydrinate, which has a depressant effect on an overstimulated labyrinth.

Recently, in studies at Mount Sinai School of Medicine, New York City, another antihistamine, meclizine hydrochloride, has been found to be valuable in reducing both the severity and frequency of vertigo attacks.

Meniere's Disease

A disturbance of the labyrinth of the inner ear, Meniere's disease commonly begins with a mild perceptive hearing impairment coupled with vertigo and tinnitus (or ringing in the ear). The attacks often come on abruptly, last for minutes to hours, and are often associated with nausea and vomiting. The course of the disease can vary. Sometimes the vertigo stops but the hearing impairment and tinnitus continue. Or the vertigo may stop only when hearing loss is complete.

There is no one universally accepted treatment. Many approaches have been used, some helpful for some patients, others for others.

Among the drugs that may be used are antihistamines, diuretic agents to reduce fluid accumulations, and niacin and nicotinyl alcohol to help expand blood vessels and improve circulation. Relief for a severe attack sometimes can be provided by an injection of atropine or scopolamine.

In severe, incapacitating cases, surgery has been employed. If the labyrinth disturbance affects one ear and useful hearing in that ear is lacking, electrical coagulation of the labyrinth has been helpful. Good results also have been reported with use of high-frequency sound waves (ultrasound) to selectively destroy the labyrinth while preserving the hearing apparatus.

A NEW DIURETIC TREATMENT. Promising results with chlorthalidone, a diuretic, have been reported recently by physicians at the Akademiska Sjokhuset, Uppsala, Sweden. In a first study, 34 patients were treated with the drug and followed for seven years. Improvement was experienced by 24, with the most pronounced benefit being reduced prevalence and intensity of vertigo.

In a second study, 220 severely incapacitated patients who had been hospitalized for possible surgery received the drug. In 133, the improvement on chlorthalidone was sufficient to avoid need for operation.

The Swedish investigators report that they have no evidence that the drug arrests the course of the disease, but it does in some cases appear to reduce need for surgery and help allow active lives.

LITHIUM TREATMENT. Lithium carbonate is a drug often used for manic-depressive illness. Its use in Meniere's has been studied at the University of Copenhagen, Denmark, by Dr. Ole Rafaelson.

Very quickly, 10 of 40 patients in whom lithium was tried discontinued its use because of weight gain. Of the remaining 30, 21 found the drug valuable. Sixteen of the 21 remain on lithium; 5 could stop all treatment after 10 to 18 months with complete elimination of symptoms.

Weight gain, a common though not invariable side effect, usually runs 11 to 22 pounds.

Food allergy and Meniere's. That in at least some cases Meniere's may be due to food allergies—with elimination of symptoms when offending foods are identified and avoided—has been reported by Dr. Jack D. Clemis of Northwestern University Medical School, Chicago. The food groups most commonly responsible: wheat, corn, eggs, and milk.

Clemis has made use of a test developed by Dr. William T. K. Bryan of Washington University, St. Louis, to simplify detection of specific food allergens. With the white blood cells present in just a small sample of blood, 70 common food allergens can be checked. If there is sensitivity to a specific food, the white cells distintegrate when that food is added to the sample.

One patient reported by Dr. Clemis was a 55-year-old surgeon faced with early retirement because of severe vertigo and hearing loss. Surgery on the labyrinth in the right ear had provided relief for three months. But then hearing fluctuations increased in severity, tinnitus persisted on the right side and occurred intermittently on the left, ear fullness and pressure developed, and there were episodes of imbalance.

The blood testing revealed a large series of allergies—to oats, rice, barley, safflower, cottonseed, milk, eggs, tuna, shrimp, crab, herring, mustard, tomatoes, cane sugar, coffee, bananas, cantaloupe, yeast, soy, almonds, and peanuts.

During six weeks on a diet eliminating these allergen foods, the surgeon lost 15 pounds but had a marked gain in hearing, although some fluctuations in hearing persisted. After three months, hearing was back to virtually normal levels in his left ear, and other symptoms were relieved.

In Dr. Clemis' experience, once foods are removed from the diet, they can usually be reintroduced in small amounts beginning about a month after all symptoms have cleared, although it is not likely that they can ever again be consumed in as great a proportion as before Meniere's developed.

Blood fat levels and Meniere's. Recent work has suggested the possibility that some sufferers from Meniere's disease and similar inner ear disturbances producing hearing loss and vertigo may be helped by reduction of high blood levels of cholesterol and triglycerides (fats) through diet.

High cholesterol and triglyceride levels have, of course, been linked to atherosclerosis, the artery-clogging disease that leads to heart attacks and strokes. A clue to their possible role in some hearing problems came several years ago when Dr. Samuel Rosen, a New York ear specialist, surveyed hearing loss in many areas of the world and found that hearing levels tended to be reduced wherever the incidence of elevated cholesterol, atherosclerosis, and heart disease was high.

It occurred to Dr. Rosen that, in fact, atherosclerosis might sometimes first affect the delicate inner ear structures and that hearing loss might even be a first indication of athersclerosis in some cases.

If that were so, might a change in diet to lower blood fat levels overcome hearing loss? Dr. James T. Spencer, a Charleston, West Virginia, ear specialist, himself a victim of hearing loss and vertigo, decided to try to find out.

For five years, Spencer had experienced progressive loss of hearing with periods of vertigo. In addition, he had discomfiting allergy problems. Aware of sensitivity to wheat, he decided half a dozen years ago to eliminate wheat from his diet.

Over the next several weeks, he lost a few pounds, felt a little better, but was far from well. At that point, he had laboratory tests done and discovered that his levels of cholesterol and triglyceride were quite high. He then went on a diet that eliminated refined sugar, kept total carbohydrate (sugars and starches) low, and increased intake of protein with minimal saturated fat.

Not only did he lose more weight (14 pounds) and achieve a satisfactory reduction in blood fat levels, but within three months, to his astonishment, he had regained 87 percent of his lost hearing.

At that point, while wondering how a diet to lower blood fat levels as a means, hopefully, of cutting atherosclerosis risk could influence hearing, he recalled the work of Rosen.

Not long afterward, he was confronted by a patient who had been medically discharged from the Marines because of hearing loss, vertigo, and ear ringing that had persisted for four years despite repeated hospitalization and study.

The man had a severe roaring in his right ear, a 60-decibel hearing loss in that ear, and a 30-decibel loss in the left ear, was experiencing frequent vertigo attacks with nausea and vomiting, was overweight, and had very high blood-fat levels.

Five weeks after being placed on the diet Spencer had used for himself, the man had a 12-decibel gain in the right ear. Two weeks later, he had lost 25 pounds and was reporting some improvement of hearing in both ears. After another month, he had lost 10 pounds more and his hearing acuity had increased further.

Over the next three years, during which he saw 444 patients with inner ear problems, Spencer found that 207 (46.6 percent) had high blood-fat levels, and another 46 (10.3 percent) were borderline. Their symptoms varied. Many had hearing loss mainly in one ear, with some deterioration in the other ear. Many also experienced ear noises, fullness, or pain. Some had acute vertigo attacks. In some cases, headaches were a problem. Many were overweight; some were obese.

Spencer at this point had begun to fit diets to individual patients. In some cases, only blood cholesterol was elevated; in others, triglycerides; in still others, both were elevated.

The essential diet features included reduction of cholesterol intake, reduction or elimination of saturated fats and increases in polyunsaturated, controlled carbohydrate intake, elimination of sugars and concentrated sweets, with greater or lesser emphasis on one or more features depending upon the individual patient.

Spencer has reported benefits in most patients. Hearing loss progression has been halted, and in some cases gains of as much as 30 decibels in an affected ear have followed. Vertigo attacks have either stopped or become less frequent and severe. Headaches, pressure in the head, and ear fullness have been among the first symptoms to be relieved.

Vision

On Vision Risks You Run

Current estimates indicate that about half a million people in this country are legally blind, and 1.5 million have such serious difficulties that they are unable to read ordinary newsprint, even with the help of glasses. Another 10 million have a serious impairment of vision, and somewhat more than 100 million either wear glasses or should do so.

So vision risks are real. They increase with age. In addition, of course, to the refractive errors that may appear at any age, with aging commonly presbyopia arrives, signaled by the need to hold reading matter farther and farther from your eyes, to the point where you may complain, "My arms are getting too short."

As you grow older, too, the risk—as distinguished from inevitability—increases for cataracts, glaucoma, and detachment of the retina.

The Eye

The human eye, which presents us with a world of space and depth and a continual variety of sights, packs into a single cubic inch of space more than 150 million light receptors.

The outermost layer of the eyeball forms the white of the eye and at the front becomes the transparent cornea.

The next layer is the iris, which has an adjustable aperture, the pupil, which becomes larger or smaller depending upon the amount of light entering.

Just behind the iris and its pupillary opening is the oval-shaped and elastic lens, which bulges out when its muscles contract, and flattens when they relax, thus adjusting to properly bend and focus light rays on the retina.

The retina, which lines the eye and serves as the "film," contains the light receptors that react to incoming images. The responses of the receptors are transmitted along a million nerve fibers which form one outgoing cable, the optic nerve, at the back of each eye. The exit of the optic nerve leaves a "blind spot"—without receptors.

According to some estimates, 85 percent of everything we learn comes to us through the eyes.

Actually, the eyes are light-transmitting machines and the brain does the seeing. This is the process: Light rays strike an object and are reflected to the eyes. The rays pass through the cornea, the clear front window, the aqueous humor (a watery liquid behind the cornea), the pupil, and the lens. The lens bends and focuses the rays on the retina. As the rays impinge on the light-sensitive pigments in the retina, chemical reactions take place that send impulses through the optic nerve to the brain. There, images are received upside down because the lens inverts them, but the brain has learned to respond to and interpret them in accord with reality.

Central vision—what you use when you look straight at an object—is sharpest. But you also have side, or peripheral, vision. And while peripheral vision is not very acute, it is important: without it, you would bump into things and be unaware of objects approaching from the side. You can demonstrate side vision simply enough: With both eyes open, hold your right thumbnail 16 inches in front of your face and focus on it. Have someone hold a wrist-watch at arm's length to your left and gradually move it toward your thumb. Without moving your eyes, you will be able to identify the watch probably when it is about 15 inches away from your thumb. Chances are, though, that you will not be able to tell time until the watch is about 2 inches away.

Interestingly, each of us has his own individual view of the world. For one thing, the eyes can transmit millions of impulses per second, but the brain chooses details on the basis of individual past experience, mood, and interests at the moment.

How we see things also can be affected by their meaning for us. In one experiment, for example, when subjects were asked to estimate the size of coins and cardboard disks that were exactly the same size, they guessed, on the average, that the coins were one-fourth larger than the disks—and the poorer off financially a subject was, the more he overestimated coin size.

The eyes even serve a purpose beyond seeing. They have an effect on taste, as shown by studies with volunteers fed in a completely darkened room. Unable to see food, they could detect no difference between white and whole-wheat bread, or between other foods.

Eye Signals

The eyes, like the rest of the body, will produce warning signals when something is not quite right. In fact, they can mirror and warn of some diseases originating elsewhere. Sometimes an ophthalmologist can detect diabetes before its presence is revealed in blood or urine tests because of distinctive characteristics left on tissue at the back of the eye. He may also detect arteriosclerosis or hypertension by observing the shape and color of the blood vessels on the retina.

Early signals from the eyes about possible problems of their own include some of the following:

FLOATERS. These small black dots which float across the center of the eye are a common complaint. They may mean nothing at all, particularly as you get older. But if a sudden increase of the dots occurs, it could be an indication of hemorrhage in the eye and calls for examination by an ophthalmologist.

As you pass your 40's, the vitreous humor, a jellylike material which makes up the bulk of the eye and among other things gives it shape, begins to change to a more watery substance. Normally, floaters are no indication of disease but simply pieces of the dissolving vitreous casting a shadow on the retina.

The appearance of floaters, however, can be a particularly opportune time for an ophthalmic checkup, since the vitreous sometimes may stick to the back of the eye, leading to a retinal break, which in turn may cause a retinal detachment. Retinal breaks can be detected early and repaired with little or no complication.

LIGHT FLASHES. Flashes of light in the peripheral vision area, especially if they occur some years after floaters have been noticed, may indicate a retinal tear or detachment. There is no pain. A quick checkup by an ophthalmologist is called for.

VISION BLURRING. In the young, of course, this usually indicates a refractive error: the eye is either too long or too short. If too long, the image is focused in front of the retina, producing myopia, or nearsightedness. If too short, the image is focused behind the retina, producing hyperopia, or farsightedness. Either can be corrected by glasses.

Vision blurring after about age 40, causing difficulty with close reading or near detail, results from changes in the lens of the eye and is the most common complaint after 40.

The lens is actually a bit of pinched-off modified skin incorporated inside the eye in the embryo. Like the skin, it grows continuously. Unlike the skin, however, its products of growth cannot be sloughed off outside the body. In appearance, the lens somewhat resembles an onion, with each layer of skin winding around the previous layer, forming a layer over layer structure. With the passage of years, the lens gets bigger, producing problems in reading, requiring things to be held farther away if they are to be seen clearly.

By the time you are holding a dinner menu out at arm's length so you can see the fare clearly, your first prescription for corrective glasses is overdue.

As the lens gets bigger, there is a tendency for the middle part to get harder and farther away from the source of nutrition, and this may be a contributing factor in cataracts.

REDNESS OF THE WHITE OF THE EYE. Continual redness, persisting over a period of several days, can be caused by some conditions that are relatively minor, some that are major.

The possible sources are eyelid roughness irritating the eye; infection or inflammation of the eye; blockage of a tear duct, cutting off lubrication; or, conceivably, glaucoma.

PAIN IN OR AROUND THE EYE. This is a warning signal of a potentially serious problem. It may be an eye infection or inflammation, or it could be a form of glaucoma—acute angle closure glaucoma—which must be corrected by surgery, which is generally highly successful.

EXCESSIVE TEARING. Two small holes on the nasal side of the eye lead into the nasal passage and provide outflow channels for tears. When these become blocked, tears overflow out of the eyelids. Annoying but of little danger, the condition can be corrected by an ophthalmologist who unplugs the drain holes.

BOTHERED BY LIGHTS. Pain in and around the eyes can reflect a sensitivity to light which causes eye muscles to constrict when the light is excessive. But if lights take on a halo appearance at night and no one else sees the halo or it is not foggy or rainy, it may be an indication of swelling of the cornea caused by one of the glaucomas. An ophthalmologist should be consulted.

Glaucoma

Glaucoma is often referred to as the "sneak thief of sight" because the common chronic type develops gradually and painlessly.

The less common acute form strikes suddenly, producing cloudy vision, severe eye pain, redness of the eye, headache, and nausea and vomiting that may be so severe that the problem may be mistaken for a gastrointestinal disorder. Because of acute glaucoma's imminent threat to sight, it should be regarded as an emergency situation calling for immediate consultation with an ophthalmologist to bring down the pressure within the eye.

Actually, there are numerous different glaucomas, but all have in common increased pressure within the eyeball because fluid cannot get out.

As noted before, the hollow area inside the front of the eye is partly filled with a circulating fluid, aqueous humor, which continuously forms and drains off so it remains at the same pressure level. In glaucoma, drainage is impeded and pressure builds up, inhibiting the blood supply and leading to damage of nerve cells.

The damage begins at the edges, slowly moving toward the center. The victim loses side, or peripheral, sight and has "tunnel vision," which makes him seem to be viewing things through a telescope. He may also have blurring of vision and may see halos or rainbow-colored rings around lights.

Glaucoma rarely appears before age 35; about two million Americans over 40 have it; by age 65, about 10 percent of the population are affected. Glaucoma causes 13.5 percent of all blindness.

The disease can be arrested and controlled when detected early enough. The only way to detect it, however, since it can be silent in early stages, is by a test, using the tonometer, which measures the tension and pressure within the eyeball. Simple, painless, requiring about a minute, the test involves placing the tip of a small instrument against the front of each eye. It is advocated for all people over 35.

MEDICAL TREATMENT. When glaucoma is detected, eye drops of pilocarpine or other drugs are prescribed to drain fluid from the interior of the eye and thus lower the tension. Commonly, they are effective in controlling the disease.

SURGICAL TREATMENT. When it is impossible to achieve control with drops, surgery is indicated.

Iridectomy, the simplest operation, which may be used in early stages of glaucoma, involves cutting off a segment of the iris through an incision in the white of the eye at the edge of the iris. A small, almost invisible opening remains and allows increased drainage. The operation may be performed under either local or general anesthesia, and the patient is out of bed within a day or two and home from the hospital a few days later.

Iridectomy is effective in about 95 percent of acute glaucoma cases. Usually, acute glaucoma will affect both eyes, one at a time. Surgery will usually be done for the affected eye and at a little later date a preventive operation may be advisable for the still unaffected eye. When acute glaucoma has not led to extensive eye damage, iridectomy will be followed by return of normal vision.

Other surgery. For chronic glaucoma, iridectomy may be used, or a filtering procedure may be carried out under local anesthesia. In one such procedure, *sclerectomy,* a tiny hole is made through the outer coat of the eye into the space under the sclera, the outer white eyeball sheath, opening a new fluid drainage channel. In some cases, a section of iris may be drawn into the new channel to act as a wick for the fluid. The procedure is called *iridencleisis.* No scar is visible. Sutures of a type that can be absorbed may be used so no suture removal is needed. A change of glasses may be needed following operation, and in some cases drops may be continued.

Delicate as it is, surgery for glaucoma is not life-threatening; the success rate for avoiding blindness is high, and in many cases restoration of good vision is achieved.

Cataracts

Opaque spots that form on the lens and spread throughout the lens over a period of time, cataracts keep light rays from getting through to the retina.

Among possible causes are intraocular diseases such as glaucoma and detached retina. Cataracts also can be congenital, and some may be associated with infection inside the eye, diabetes, injury such as a contusion of the eye or penetration of the eye by a metallic or other object, and rarely exposure to chemical or physical poisons. But in most cases they are called *senile* cataracts and appear to be part of the aging process.

Blurring and dimming of vision are often the first indication. Paradoxically, although distant vision is blurred in the early stages of cataracts, near vision may be somewhat improved, so that if you have had to use glasses for reading you may find you do better without them. Such "second sight," as it has been termed, often foretells the need for cataract removal in the not distant future.

With continued clouding of the lens, you may find you need brighter reading lights or must hold objects closer to the eyes. There may be double vision. A need for frequent changes of glasses may be caused by cataracts.

Cataracts commonly occur in both eyes, although the rate of progression in each eye is seldom equal.

An ophthalmologist's examination with an ordinary light shined into the eyes can detect cataract formation, and further examination with an ophthalmoscope reveals the extent of the opacity.

SURGICAL TREATMENT. The only known effective treatment for cataracts is surgery. No drops, ointments, or other medical measures can dissolve a cataract.

More than one quarter of a million cataract operations are performed yearly in the United States. Once it was considered necessary to wait, sometimes for years, for a cataract to ripen, or spread throughout the lens and in the process loosen the lens from its capsule, before surgery could be undertaken. With the ripening, it was easier to get out all of the lens, leaving nothing behind to cause possible vision interference later. Now, new techniques permit ready removal of the lens at any time without need for an extended period of partial blindness. Cataract removal is indicated when vision is impaired to the extent of interfering with work or other normal activities.

Cataracts can be removed under local anesthesia. Through an incision at the point where clear cornea and white of the eye meet, the lens can be reached and then can be loosened by injecting an enzyme, chymotrypsin, that dissolves the lens ligaments without affecting other eye structures.

The lens can then be lifted out with forceps, or a freezing rod that grips it securely, or an instrument with a suction cup. After lens extraction, fine sutures are used to close the incision; in some cases, the sutures are absorbable and do not require later removal. The eye is bandaged for several days. Many surgeons now encourage the patient to be out of bed the first postoperative day.

Cataract surgery, although delicate, is more than 95 percent successful in allowing vision restoration.

Since a lens is needed for focusing, glasses are required after surgery. They have thick, conspicuous lenses and tend to make objects appear somewhat larger, but most people adapt to them quickly. Contact lenses, for those who can wear them, often make for better vision.

When both eyes are affected by cataracts, it has been customary to remove one cataract at a time, with an interval of one to six months between. In some cases now, as the result of improved techniques, both cataracts may be removed during the same hospitalization.

Currently under study, several new techniques may further simplify cataract removal.

One new instrument is built around a hollow needle in which a tiny whirling blade, working somewhat like a food blender, pulverizes the lens, which then is drawn off through a tube. In another new instrument, a needle vibrates at ultrasonic speed, 40,000 beats a second, to detach the cataract, and a system emits fluid to flush away the lens debris. With both devices, only a one-tenth-inch slit is needed to get at the lens, in contrast to an incision about three quarters of an inch long used in conventional surgery. The smaller incision, which can be closed by a single suture, heals faster.

Also under study is the possibility that patients may not really need a week to ten days of hospitalization but may be released safely in much less time, possibly even the day of surgery.

Detached Retina

One in every 10,000 Americans each year suffers a detached retina. Although more common in older people, detachment can occur at any age, with or without physical injury.

The retina is held in place in the back of the eye by the vitreous humor, the transparent gel-like material filling much of the eyeball. When a tear or hole occurs in the retina, the fluid may seep behind and lift the retina, causing its detachment, which is partial at first but if untreated becomes complete.

With detachment, flashes of light, or stars, are seen, followed by a sensation of a curtain moving across the eye. The extent of vision loss depends upon the location of the detachment.

Diagnosis of detachment is made with an instrument, the ophthalmoscope, which discloses folds, tears, or other irregularities in the retina.

SURGICAL TREATMENT. Surgery is required for retinal detachment, and the earlier the better.

With a local anesthetic dropped into the eye, an incision is made in the white of the eye. Through a needle, fluid behind the separated portion of the retina is withdrawn. The remaining fluid filling the eyeball then has a chance to press the detached area back into place. When this is achieved, the retina is sealed in place by any of several methods—an electric needle, freezing rod, or laser light beam.

In another type of operation, a small plastic implant is sutured to the eyeball over the area of detachment and acts to push and hold the choroid against the detached portion of the retina.

Surgery for detachment is not painful. Both eyes may be bandaged for another week or so. Complete bed rest may be advisable for ten days to two weeks to prevent bleeding within the eye and minimize risk of jarring the retina loose. Thereafter, it may be necessary to stay home from work for as long as three or four months as a precaution against jarring.

The smaller the detachment and the earlier surgery is done, the more likely a successful result. Overall, four of every five patients can expect to benefit.

Tobacco/Alcohol-Induced Eye Disorder

Excessive use of tobacco and alcohol, especially in combination, can sometimes produce toxic amblyopia, a reduction in the acuteness of vision believed due to a toxic reaction in part of the optic nerve. Affecting both eyes, it begins as a small central or peripheral area of depressed vision which may slowly enlarge, increasingly interfering with sight. The outlook is generally good if smoking and drinking are stopped or greatly moderated. It should be noted that toxic amblyopia also may be caused by prolonged exposure to carbon monoxide, carbon tetrachloride, arsenic, lead, benzene, or quinine; and improvement may follow avoidance of exposure to these agents.

Drug-Induced Eye Disturbances

Many valuable drugs produce side reactions (undesirable effects) in a minority of users. Like other organs of the body, the eyes may sometimes be affected. If you experience vision disturbances during treatment with any drug, they should be checked with your physician. A change of dosage or a switch to another drug may solve the problem.

Vision blurring: Among the more or less commonly prescribed agents which may produce this are Aldoril, Ambenyl Expectorant, Antivert, Artane, Bellergal, Benadryl, Bendectin, Bentyl, Bentyl/Phenobarbital, Butazolidin, Butazolidin Alka, Combid, Compazine, Dalmane, Dimetane, Donnagal-PG, Donnatal, Diupres, Diuril, Doriden, Elavil, Etrafon, Hydrodiuril, Indocin, Lanoxin, Lasix, Librax, Librium, Mellaril, Norgesic, Periactin, Phenergan preparations, Placidyl, Pro-Banthine, Regroton, reserpine, Salutensin, Serax, Sinequan, Stelazine, Sterazolidin, Talwin, Tandearil, Tigan, Tofranil, Tranxene, Triaminic, Triavil.

Color vision disturbance may accompany the use of Aldoril, Esidrix, Hydrodiuril, Hygroton, Rauzide, Regroton, Salutensin.

Double vision may occur with Ambenyl Expectorant, Benadryl, Dimetane, Periactin, Polaramine, Serax.

Blepharitis

This inflammation of the eyelid margins, often caused by bacterial infection, produces itching, burning and redness of the lid margins, swelling of the lids, loss of eyelashes, irritation of the conjunctiva, excess tearing of the eyes, and sensitivity to light. Treatment is with antibiotic ointments or solutions or combinations of antibiotics and corticosteroids.

Conjunctivitis (Pink Eye)

ALLERGIC CONJUNCTIVITIS. Producing itching, tearing and redness of the eye, this disorder may be part of an allergic disturbance such as hay fever or may occur alone from contact with pollens, dusts, animal danders and other airborne substances or from contact with drugs or other materials carried by the fingers to the eyes. Avoidance of a known or suspected cause is advisable. Antihistamines may be helpful. In severe cases, an ophthalmic ointment containing a corticosteroid drug may be used.

ACUTE CATARRHAL CONJUNCTIVITIS. Caused by various bacteria and highly contagious, this form of conjunctivitis occurs most often in fall and spring. Symptoms include tearing of the eyes, watery discharge that later becomes mucus- or pus-laden and often seals the lid margins overnight, redness, itching, smarting, burning of the lids, and sensitivity to light. An antibiotic or sulfa ophthalmic preparation may be used several times a day.

CHRONIC CATARRHAL CONJUNCTIVITIS. Caused by the same organisms that are involved in the acute form, the chronic produces itching, smarting, redness, sensations of a foreign body in the eye. It tends to be worse at night and can come and go over a period of months or years. Elimination of any irritating factors such as wind, smoke, and dust may help. Treatment may include use of a combination of antibiotic and corticosteroid, with special lid massage.

"SWIMMING POOL CONJUNCTIVITIS." Known formally as *inclusion conjunctivitis,* this disorder is caused by organisms with some of the characteristics of both viruses and bacteria. Symptoms may include lid swelling, pinkness, discharge of mucus and pus. One or both eyes may be affected. In treatment, an antibiotic may be applied to the eyes and taken by mouth as well.

SPRING (VERNAL) CONJUNCTIVITIS. Considered allergic in nature, this chronic conjunctivitis produces intense itching, tearing, light sensitivity, and a sticky mucoid discharge. Symptoms usually recur in spring, persist through summer, disappear in winter, although in some cases they may last year-round. Corticosteroid eye preparations, sometimes supplemented with small doses of corticosteroids by mouth, may be prescribed. In some cases, desensitization injections to increase tolerance for pollens are helpful.

Corneal Ulcer

Ulceration of the clear transparent front covering of the eye is caused by bacteria that invade after injury of the cornea or by spread of infection from nearby infected areas. Symptoms include pain, light sensitivity, tearing, and eye muscle spasm. Treatment may include antibiotics applied to the eye and administered orally, cauterization of the base of the ulcer, hot compresses, local anesthetics, patching, and sometimes use of corticosteroid drugs.

Choroiditis

This inflammation of the middle vascular coat of the eye, and often of the retina as well, produces varying visual disturbances —in some cases, distortion of size of objects; in others, blurring; in still others, reduced central vision. Its cause commonly is obscure. Corticosteroid drugs are used to suppress the inflammation until the cause can be determined and eliminated or disappears on its own.

Dacrocystitis

An inflammation of the tear sac of the eye, dacrocystitis produces pain, redness and swelling about the sac, overflow of tears, fever, conjunctivitis, and inflamed edges of the eyelid margin. It is caused by narrowing of the nasolacrimal duct, a downward continuation of the tear sac that opens within the nose, or by injury to the nose, deviated septum, polyps, or other nasal problems. In treatment, hot compresses, penicillin by mouth or injection, and antibiotic ophthalmic preparations are used. If an abscess has formed, it is incised and drained.

Fat on the Lids

Occurring mostly in older people, flat or slightly elevated nodules of fat on the eyelids (xanthelasma) are painless and may result from excessive levels of blood cholesterol. Diet and medication may be helpful. The nodules, if unsightly, can be removed surgically by an ophthalmologist.

Iritis

This inflammation of the iris, the colored portion of the eye with the pupil in its center, can produce severe eye pain, often radiating to the forehead and becoming worse at night, with the eye red and pupil contracted and sometimes irregular in shape, extreme sensitivity to light, vision blurring, and tenderness of the eyeball. The inflammation may be acute, with sudden pronounced symptoms, or chronic, with less severe but longer-lasting symptoms. It may be associated with rheumatoid arthritis, diabetes, syphilis, tonsillitis, other infection, or injury. In treatment, the pupil is dilated with atropine drops, and local corticosteroids may be applied to reduce inflammation. Systemic cortiscosteroids also may be used while the cause is sought and if possible eliminated.

Keratitis

This inflammation of the cornea produces pain in the eyeball, a sensation of a foreign object in the eye, heavy tearing, redness, sensitivity to light, and blurring of vision. The usually clear cornea in front of the iris and pupil becomes cloudy, and a colored spot may appear on the eyeball. The most common causes are viral or bacterial infections. Immediate treatment is essential to prevent permanent clouding and scarring of the cornea. Treatment may include use of an antibiotic or antiviral agent, sometimes with a corticosteroid.

Nystagmus (Abnormal Eyeball Movement)

Involuntary rhythmic, horizontal, vertical or rotatory oscillation of the eyeball may result from poor vision caused by congenital abnormalities or, when it appears in later life, from inner ear disease, multiple sclerosis, prolonged use of eyes with bad light and in strained position, fatigue of eye muscles from myopia or astigmatism. It may be relieved in some cases by correction of refraction errors and other causes of eyestrain, or by treatment of underlying disease. In other cases, eye muscle surgery may be needed.

Optic Neuritis

An inflammation of the optic nerve almost always affecting one eye, optic neuritis may produce vision disturbances ranging from slight contraction of the visual field to blindness. Possible causes include meningitis, encephalitis, syphilis, acute fever-producing diseases, multiple sclerosis, and poisoning with various substances such as methyl alcohol and carbon tetrachloride. Immediate use of corticosteroids, either systemically or injected behind the eyeball, often helps.

Retinitis

An inflammation of the retina of the eye, retinitis may be caused by injury, drugs, smoking, or excessive use of alcohol. Symptoms include loss of visual acuity, distortion of size and shape of objects, and eye discomfort. Corticosteroid drugs often help. The vitamin thiamine may be prescribed along with elimination of tobacco and alcohol.

Retinitis Pigmentosa

An inherited disease in which there is progressive degeneration of the retina, retinitis pigmentosa may appear in childhood or later in life, producing narrowing of side vision with a "looking-through-a-tunnel" effect. No cure is available. Central vision often remains clear for a long period, sometimes a lifetime.

Retinopathies

These noninflammatory diseases of the retina may be caused by severe high blood pressure, arteriosclerosis, diabetes, or excessive smoking. Symptoms include blurring of vision, blood spots in the eyes, sometimes a bloodshot appearance. If high blood pressure is involved, it can be reduced. Elimination of smoking may be advisable. Corticosteroids are useful. Treatment with a laser beam to coagulate hemorrhaging retinal blood vessels is showing promise.

Sty

An infection of one of the sebaceous glands of the eyelid, a sty may begin with a foreign body sensation in the eye, tearing, and then pain and redness of the lid margin and appearance of a pimple-like lesion. Often, a sty can be localized by hot compresses applied for 10 to 15 minutes every few hours. An antibiotic may be prescribed to increase the likelihood of clearance without pus formation and discharge. A sty forming deep inside the eyelid is usually more severe and painful and may have to be removed surgically under local anesthesia in the physician's office.

Taste and Smell

What's Normal

Man has about 3,000 taste buds, mainly on the tongue, although a few are on the palate, tonsils, and pharynx. There are four primary or basic taste sensations—sweet, bitter, sour or acid, and salt. You can't taste all flavors on all parts of the tongue. Sweet flavors register near the tip, sour on the sides, bitter on the back, and salty all over.

The sense of smell is located in odor receptors in the upper passage of the nasal cavity. The size of the membrane containing the odor receptors is only about one-fourth square inch in man as against an area 40 times as great in the dog. The organ of smell, which can detect things at a distance, is obviously more important as a danger warning system in animals than in man.

It's because of the location of the receptors that you may not smell delicate odors at first. It takes several whiffs to get the odor into the upper nasal passage.

Before you can taste anything, the substance must be moistened, and the salivary glands supply the moisture. And to be smelled, an odor must be dissolved in the mucus secreted by the nasal membranes. Smell receptors in man, although they don't have the same capacity as in lower animals, still are sensitive enough to allow you to detect a substance diluted to as much as 1 part in 30 billion.

Taste and Smell Disturbances

Although there are no definitive statistics, disturbances of taste and smell are now known to affect surprising numbers of people. The disturbances range from loss of all taste or smell to distortions in which there are revolting taste and smell sensations.

The disturbances in the past were often looked upon as psychological in origin. More recently, however, at least two readily correctable physical causes have been found for them.

A few years ago, at the National Institutes of Health, Bethesda, Maryland, Dr. R. I. Henkin and a medical team began to look into taste and smell aberrations. The team was to work with more than 3,000 patients, many of whom had been dismissed as neurotic. Some had little or no ability to smell or taste anything. Others suffered from revolting taste and smell sensations. Some were affected to the extent of having to limit themselves to a few foods such as lettuce, rice, bland cheeses, apples; almost everything else smelled and tasted, as some put it, "like manure or decayed garbage."

The NIH physicians found that many of the patients had one thing in common: low blood levels of zinc, a mineral that, although present in only minute amounts in the body, is known to be an essential factor in many critical enzyme systems.

When these patients were given zinc sulfate in doses of 25, 50, or 100 milligrams four times a day, all showed increases in zinc blood levels, about two thirds regained normal taste and smell sensations, and the remainder experienced marked improvement.

Meanwhile, at Barnes Hospital in St. Louis, Dr. Robert J. McConnell has developed evidence that in some patients with the disturbances, the fault may lie with hypothyroidism, or underfunctioning of the thyroid gland. In a study of hypothyroid patients, Connell found that half were aware of either diminished or distorted sense of taste, and one third had both. Many also complained of defects in the sense of smell. After correction of the hypothyroid condition by thyroid replacement treatment, four of every five of the patients were cured of the taste and smell disorders, the earliest in sixteen days.

13

A Concise Manual
of Diverse Problems

Neurological

The Brain and Nervous System

One measure of the intricacies of the human brain is that it weighs only about 12 ounces at birth and 3 pounds in a full-grown adult, yet can store more information than is contained in the 9-million-plus volumes of the Library of Congress.

Another is that if necessary we can do with only half the brain, and after removal of much of one side of the brain because of tumors, physicians, lawyers, and others have been able to carry on their regular work.

The brain has some 15 billion nerve units which allow storage of memory images and learning. It also has vast numbers of connections to control the 600-plus muscles of the body and other connections from eyes, ears, and nerves in the skin to allow recording and remembering what we see, hear, feel, smell, and taste.

The brain is made up of several parts. The *cerebrum* takes the form of two hemispheres divided by a groove. The cortex, or surface, of the cerebrum is gray matter formed by the cell bodies of nerve cells. Fibers from these bodies lead inward to form the cerebrum's white matter, crossing over so that those entering the brain from the left side of the body cross to the right side of the brain, which is why the right side of the cerebrum controls most of the left side of the body, while the left side controls the right.

At the base of the cerebrum are three structures: pons, medulla, and cerebellum. The *pons* connects the medulla with higher brain centers. The *medulla,* just below the pons and at the upper end of the spinal cord, is a switching center for nerve impulses to and from higher brain centers. It also has centers that act through the autonomic nervous system to control heart activity, breathing, and other involuntary functions. The *cerebellum,* or little brain, has areas that control muscle tone and equilibrium and coordinate voluntary movements.

The skull, a tough bony cage surrounding the brain and protecting it, is itself protected by the scalp, which is made up of five layers: skin and hair, cutaneous tissue, a tough layer of fibrous tissue, loose tissue, and periosteum, which covers the bone of the skull.

And additional protection is provided for within the brain by four ventricles, which are reservoirs containing cerebrospinal fluid which circulates around the brain so that in effect the brain floats on and in fluid, a good shock-absorber system. Also, within the bone of the skull the brain is wrapped in layers of tissue, one of which, the dura mater, is especially tough and protective.

With the brain serving as a control center, the nervous system is like a two-way communications network for informational messages flowing to the control center and command messages transmitted from the center. The informational or sensory messages come from eyes, ears, other sense organs, and from billions of receptors throughout the body concerned with various body functions.

In fact, we have two nervous systems—central and autonomic. The *central* includes brain and spinal cord, the latter suspended within a cylinder formed by the spinal bones (vertebrae). From the brain and cord emerge forty-three pairs of nerves that connect to every part of the body. Twelve cranial nerves from the brain go to the eyes and other sense organs, the heart and other internal organs. The thirty-one other nerve pairs go to skeletal muscles, coming off the cord between spinal bones, one of a pair going to the right side of the body and the other to the left.

The central nervous system works in more than one way. If, for instance, you touch a hot object, pain stimulates a sensory nerve which shoots informational impulses to the spinal cord; there the impulses are transferred quickly to a motor nerve to muscles which jerk your hand away—a reflex action, taking place in a fraction of a second, no thought needed.

Even as this is transpiring, impulses from the sensory nerve are also transferred to another sensory nerve traveling up the spinal cord to the cerebrum, and as you feel pain, you examine your finger, look at the hot object, and associate the two—and because of knowledge stored in memory centers in the cerebrum, you quickly put your fingers under cold water.

The other nervous system, the *autonomic,* provides for automatic control of internal organ functioning. It has two opposing or balancing parts: sympathetic and parasympathetic.

The *sympathetic* begins at the base of the brain, runs along both side of the spinal column, and nerves from it go to glands, muscles, heart, stomach, intestines, and bladder. The *parasympathetic* has two major nerves: the *vagus* coming from the medulla and sending branches through chest and abdomen; and the *pelvic* coming off the spinal cord in the hip area and sending branches to organs in the lower part of the body.

The sympathetic system dilates the pupil of the eye, speeds the heartbeat, raises blood pressure; the parasympathetic constricts the pupil, slows the heartbeat, and lowers blood pressure.

Emotions strongly influence the autonomic system.

Neuralgia

Neuralgia means paroxysms of severe throbbing or stabbing pain along the course of a nerve for which no cause usually can be found. A neuralgia may subside after a time in some cases, persist in others. Hot or cold applications and aspirin or other pain-relieving agents may help. In very severe, otherwise unyielding neuralgia, a drug such as diphenylhydantoin sometimes is helpful; another agent, carbamazepine, reduces attack frequency in more than two thirds of patients. When necessary, alcohol injection of an affected nerve or cutting of the nerve may be used.

One form of neuralgia sometimes may seem like heart trouble. This is neuralgia of the intercostal nerve, which is distributed to the muscles and skin of the chest, back, and upper abdomen. *Intercostal neuralgia* can produce pain in the chest wall.

In *glossopharyngeal neuralgia,* pain usually begins in the throat and base of the tongue, radiates to the ears and sometimes down the side of the neck.

In the best-known neuralgia, *trigeminal,* also called *tic douloureux,* pain shoots from the top of the head down the face, lasting only a minute or so, with periods between attacks stretching out to weeks or months, but with the intervals later shortening. The pain may also be in the forehead, lip, nose, tongue, and gums.

Neuritis

Neuritis is an inflammation which may affect one or many nerves (polyneuritis). If a sensory nerve (of feeling, sensation) is affected, it becomes painful along its course. Other symptoms may include tingling, numbness, burning, and loss of sense of touch or insensitivity to heat or cold. If a motor nerve is affected, the muscle supplied by that nerve may become weak and often paralyzed.

Neuritis may result from mechanical causes such as injury, pressure on a nerve during sleep, a prolonged cramped position (for example, using an electric drill for a long time), or violent overexertion; from an infection such as botulism or diphtheria which may attack nerves; from poisoning with lead, arsenic, mercury, tin, zinc, other metals and alcohol, carbon monoxide, carbon tetrachloride, and other toxic materials; and from blood vessel disease, gout, diabetes, and other conditions that may cause nutritional deficiencies, notably vitamin B_1 deficiency.

Treatment may include rest of the affected area, use of aspirin or a stronger analgesic, heat, and passive exercises. The underlying cause should be discovered if possible and corrected.

Parkinson's Disease (Shaking Palsy)

A chronic nervous system disorder most common in middle age and later, parkinsonism produces palsy, muscle rigidity, and slowness. The face loses mobility, and there may be an unblinking, wide-eyed, staring appearance, with mouth partially open and drooling. Posture is stooped, gait shuffling, hands trembling, with tremor sometimes involving the whole body.

In some cases, the disorder may result from viral infection or carbon monoxide or other poisoning, but usually the cause is unknown.

A drug, L-dopa, relieves symptoms for many patients. Other drugs, such as diphenhydramine and biperiden, may also be helpful. A surgical technique which involves cooling a small portion of the brain has shown promise in relieving tremor and rigidity.

Brain Injury (Concussion)

A fall or blow on the head may produce concussion, with dizziness, impaired vision, and severe headache. If the concussion is very serious, consciousness may be lost and breathing may become irregular.

Anyone who has suffered an accident in which there is any likelihood of brain (or spinal) injury should be kept lying down, covered with coat or blanket (even in warm weather), with no attempt made to give stimulants or bandage any bloody bruises. If breathing begins to fail, artificial respiration should be used. If the concussion is uncomplicated, the victim will regain consciousness and revive in a short time. In any case, a doctor should be summoned.

Brain Cancer

Although possible at any age, brain tumors most commonly occur in early adult and middle life. They are, however, a relatively rare disease.

Symptoms are produced by pressure of a growth and depend upon where in the brain the pressure is exerted. Despite a common belief, headache is not invariably the first symptom. Often slow progressive disturbances in sight, smell and balance or muscle weaknesses precede headaches, which, when they appear, may be shortlived at first, later becoming severe and constant.

Any or many of a variety of other symptoms may accompany a brain tumor: nausea and vomiting, drowsiness, lethargy, personality changes, convulsive seizures, impaired mental processes, psychotic episodes, paralysis, ringing in an ear, hearing impairment in one ear.

Diagnosis requires thorough neurological study, with vision and hearing tests, skull x-rays, electroencephalograms, and other tests. Treatment is by surgery, which is becoming increasingly effective (in terms of being able to remove most or all of a tumor without harm to other areas of the brain). Radiation also may be used, sometimes with drug therapy.

Meningitis

An inflammation of the meninges, the membranes covering the brain and spinal cord, meningitis may produce stiff neck, persistent headache, fever, vomiting, intolerance to light and sound. Confusion, weakness, and coma may develop.

The disease results from infection by bacteria, viruses, or fungi. An epidemic type, meningococcemia, is caused by meningococcal bacteria and is very contagious because the bacteria also are present in the throat. Tuberculous meningitis is produced by the same organisms responsible for lung TB. Most viral meningitis in the United States results from mumps and polio viruses, less frequently from others such as herpes simplex, which is also responsible for cold sores.

Diagnosis of the disease is established definitively by identification of organisms in a sample of cerebrospinal fluid. Treatment is with a suitable antibiotic administered by vein. Corticosteroids also may be used. In fungal meningitis, a special antifungal antibiotic, amphotericin B, is often effective.

Still a dangerous disease, meningitis is no longer 90 percent fatal. With prompt, effective treatment, 95 percent of victims recover.

Multiple Sclerosis (MS)

Of unknown cause, MS mostly affects young adults (20 to 40), leading to the formation of hardened patches in the brain and spinal cord which interfere with normal nerve activity. Almost the entire body may be affected.

Early symptoms often are mild disturbances of vision, fatigability of an arm or leg, some difficulty with bladder control or urination, mild and puzzling emotional upsets.

Later, many of a wide variety of symptoms may appear: double vision or loss of part of the visual field, pronounced weakness and fatigue, tremor or shaking of limbs, slowing and monotony of speech, impaired balance, unsteady walking, unbending knees, stiff gait, loss of bladder and bowel control, paralysis in any part of the body.

Although not a killer, the disease can be extremely disabling. It is peculiarly subject to spontaneous periods of improvement, with virtual freedom from all symptoms, and periods of exacerbation.

There is no specific treatment. Many drugs have been tried without notably effective results. Helpful measures include avoidance of fatigue and excessive pressures, massage for affected limbs, exercise, muscle retraining, and physical therapy.

Tics

Sometimes called habit or mimic spasms, tics are sudden, quick, repetitive, purposeless movements such as eye blinking, grimacing, head nodding or shaking, throat clearing, shoulder shrugging. Almost always without physical cause, they most commonly affect children 5 to 12 years of age, but can occur at any time of life. They often are fleeting and disappear spontaneously. When they don't, psychotherapy, tranquilizers, or mild sedatives such as phenobarbital have been used with some success.

Headaches

Headaches are virtually universal. It's estimated that 7 of every 10 American adults use pain-killers for headaches at least once a month, and for at least 1 of every 12, headaches are a chronic problem.

Except for headaches from brain tumors (rare) and from advanced (and untreated) high blood pressure, headaches are painful, even disabling, but not sinister threats to life.

CLUSTER HEADACHES. Usually untouched by common analgesics, cluster headaches are excruciatingly severe. One-sided, they involve eye, temple, neck and face, with tearing of the eye and a thin, watery discharge from the nose. They get the name cluster because, characteristically, they may appear out of the blue, recur every day for many days or weeks, disappear for a time, then return in another clustered batch.

Some recent success has been reported by Dr. A. V. Giampaoli at Stanford University, Stanford, California, in treating cluster headaches with adrenaline in aerosol form. Three to six inhalations, 15 to 20 minutes apart, may break the cyclic pattern; and the headaches, when they return, are less intense. In some cases, ergotamine, a drug often used in migraine, helps when added to the spray.

Recently, too, Dr. Lee Kudrow of Encino, California, has reported on 32 chronic cluster headache patients treated for up to

32 weeks with lithium, a drug often used for depression. Six couldn't tolerate lithium and gave up using it. But of the 26 others, 25 obtained improvement.

MIGRAINE. Although men are less likely to be affected than women, there are still scores of thousands of male migraine sufferers.

Although the cause is not completely understood, migraine is believed to be associated with constriction and then dilation of brain arteries. It is also thought to have a psychological aspect, since it often follows emotional disturbances. It also tends to run in families.

Symptoms can vary. Typically, an episode may begin with changes in vision, such as flickering before the eyes, flashes of light, or blacking out of part of sight. The headache is severe, often on one side, sometimes accompanied by nausea and vomiting.

Aspirin is usually of little help. Ergotamine tartrate is a long-used drug that works in many cases.

Some success in helping migraine patients with biofeedback has been reported. In the biofeedback procedure, a patient, with temperature sensors taped to finger and forehead, sits in front of a machine and learns to make a needle on a meter move in a direction that indicates he is relaxing blood vessels in the hands and thus increasing hand temperature; the relaxation and warming of the hands causes a redistribution of blood that reduces pressure in blood vessels in the head, ending the migraine. With adequate training, the patient can do without the machine, accomplishing the same blood redistribution to cut short a migraine attack. As many as 74 percent of migraine sufferers have been reported to benefit.

Recently, too, the drug propranolol, often used for heart patients and for hypertensives, has been showing promise in reducing the frequency and severity of attacks and, in some cases, eliminating them.

Another new development, sleep treatment, has been reported by Dr. David Coddon, director of the Headache Clinic at Mount Sinai Hospital in New York City. Deep sleep is induced by an intravenous injection of three drugs: Valium, Compazine, and amobarbital. Waking from six hours of such sleep, a migraine victim is likely to feel a little groggy but be free of headache. He may remain free of attacks for many months after a single sleep treatment, and possibly much longer after a repeat treatment. Dr. Coddon has reported efficacy in better than 90 percent of more than 4,000 patients.

Various diets have been resorted to by migraine victims. Despite many misconceptions about diet and migraine, Dr. Donald J. Dalessio of the Scripps Clinic Medical Institutions, La Jolla, California, has found some dietary measures useful. In the migraine-prone, he reports, certain foods, because of their effect on blood vessels, can lead to attacks. They include red wine and champagne, aged or strong cheese (especially cheddar), pickled herring, chicken liver, pods of broad beans, and canned figs. Their avoidance is worth a trial. So, too, avoidance of cured meats, such as frankfurters, bacon, ham, and salami—which, in some cases, have adverse effects. For some, excessive amounts of monosodium glutamate can be a migraine trigger. It's also helpful for migraine sufferers to avoid low-blood-sugar states (hypoglycemia), and for this reason, Dalessio advises, they should eat three well-balanced meals a day and avoid excessive amounts of sugar and starches at any one meal.

Recently, too, Dr. John B. Brainard of St. Paul, Minnesota, has found that salted snack foods such as pretzels, potato chips, and nuts may trigger a migraine attack within 6 to 12 hours, especially if taken on an empty stomach. Brainard studied a dozen long-time migraine victims, who recorded attack incidence for six months before and six months after avoiding salted snack foods before meals. In 10 of the 12 subjects, avoidance markedly reduced the incidence.

TENSION HEADACHES.   These account for as many as half of all headaches. They involve muscle contraction.

When a job requires a fixed head position—for example, driving against bright headlights—the muscles of neck, jaw, and scalp may be set in pain-causing postures. Commonly, the same thing happens as a reaction to psychological pressures. Tension headache victims, one physician has remarked, "symbolically carry a great weight on their shoulders." Upon feeling anxious, they set scalp and neck muscles and develop headache. Some researchers have established that the degree of muscle tension they can measure with instruments is directly related to the degree of anxiety.

Can such headaches be prevented? There have been some reports that as many as two thirds of victims can help themselves if they seriously try to reduce the number of things ordinarily done in one day, plan regular periods of rest and relaxation, and end over-concern about things being "just so." Some headache specialists urge patients to keep a daily activity record and analyze it to see under what conditions the headaches recur, then try to modify those conditions.

Biofeedback also appears to be promising for helping avoid tension headaches. Hospitals now are beginning to use it in outpatient clinics. Typically, sensor electrodes are applied to the forehead to record tension. If the level of tension is high, the biofeedback machine emits a series of rapid beeps; as tension is reduced, the beeps slow. The patient learns over a period of time to slow the beeps, using the machine, and thereafter may be able to use the same technique, without need of the machine, to reduce muscle tension whenever it begins to develop.

To relieve the pain of a tension headache, aspirin may work in a mild case. But no analgesic alone or sedative alone does much good for more severe, persistent pain. A double-pronged approach is needed: the pain threshold must be raised, achievable with an analgesic; and tension must be reduced at least somewhat, achievable with a sedative. Gentle massage of neck muscles and applications of moist, warm compresses to the back of the neck are also helpful.

DEPRESSIVE HEADACHES. Mental depression is often peculiar in the sense that the fact of depression, of "blue" feelings, is buried under one or more overriding physical complaints that command attention. It now appears that many people who used to be considered victims of tension headaches suffer in reality from depressive headaches.

According to Dr. Seymour Diamond of Chicago, a prominent headache specialist, these are people who experience a constant steady headache, present all day, usually worse in the morning, with generalized distribution over the entire head. Often the headache is associated with sleep disturbance in the form of frequent awakening during the night and early awakening in the morning. There may be other physical symptoms such as chest pain, gastrointestinal complaints, and loss of weight. There may also be psychic problems such as loss of interest in work and in sex.

Reports Diamond: "They are actually suffering from depression and can be helped by their physician through the use of tricyclic antidepressant drugs. Recently, in resistant cases of this type, we have used a combination of both the tricyclics and the mono- amine oxidase inhibitors with little risk and good results."

Blood

Anemias

Red cells in blood contain hemoglobin, a pigment that carries oxygen from lungs to body tissues. Anemia occurs when either the number of red cells or the amount of hemoglobin in them is re- duced below normal.

Although there are many types of anemia, some symptoms are common to all. Lack of energy and easy fatigability often charac- terize mild anemia. With more severe anemia, shortness of breath on exertion, pounding of the heart, and rapid pulse may develop. In severe cases, there may be weakness, dizziness, headache, ringing of the ears, spots before the eyes, drowsiness, irritability, euphoria, psychotic behavior, loss of libido, low-grade fever, varied gastroin- testinal complaints. Diagnosis of anemia, and of the particular type, is made by blood studies.

IRON DEFICIENCY ANEMIA.   Far more common in women, this type of anemia nevertheless can affect men. Iron is needed for hemo- globin. A deficiency of iron may result from chronic loss of blood —through excessive menstrual flow in women and, in both sexes, through slow bleeding from a peptic ulcer, hemorrhoids, stomach lining injuries caused by aspirin or other drugs in those sensitive to them, stomach or intestinal tumors. Failure to get adequate iron in a limited diet may sometimes be involved. Treatment includes use of an iron preparation, dietary changes if needed, and, especially in a man, search for and treatment of underlying cause.

PERNICIOUS ANEMIA.   For red blood cell production, which takes place in the bone marrow, vitamin B_{12} is essential. The vitamin is present in adequate amounts in any well-balanced diet. But its ab- sorption requires the presence in the stomach of a substance called intrinsic factor. In pernicious anemia, intrinsic factor is lacking or inadequate.

In addition to the common symptoms of anemia (previously listed), pernicious anemia can produce a red, sore tongue, difficulty in swallowing, pale lemon skin color, and in some cases numbness and tingling of the legs and fingers, unsteady gait and impaired memory.

Treatment with injections of vitamin B_{12} to get around the intrinsic factor lack, which prevents adequate absorption in the gut, can completely eliminate the anemia and symptoms.

APLASTIC ANEMIA. Any damage to the bone marrow, where red blood cells are produced, may cause aplastic anemia. Not only are red cells reduced in numbers; so, too, are white cells, which help to combat infections.

In addition to the general symptoms of anemia (previously given), which are usually severe in aplastic anemia, there may be brown skin pigmentation, blood seepage into the skin and mucous membranes, severe sore throat, lowered resistance to infections.

Some cases of aplastic anemia are of unknown cause. In others, it is traceable to exposure to drugs or chemicals such as benzene, methotrexate, nitrogen mustard, quinacrine, phenylbutazone, chloramphenicol, gold compounds, some sulfa drugs, and insecticides.

Treatment requires blood transfusion until the marrow can resume functioning, control of infection with antibiotics, avoidance of any materials that may be involved in depressing marrow function, and sometimes use of cortisonelike agents and compounds related to the male sex hormone, testosterone, which may help to stimulate marrow functioning.

HEMOLYTIC ANEMIA. In this type of anemia, the problem is excessive destruction of red blood cells.

In addition to symptoms common to other anemias, hemolytic anemia usually produces some degree of jaundice, because the destroyed red cells release their hemoglobin which is converted into jaundice pigments.

An acute form of hemolytic anemia may appear suddenly with chills, fever, nausea, vomiting, abdominal pain. The cause may be a drug to which the patient is sensitive, a severe infection, cancer, or Hodgkin's disease. If the cause can be removed (an offending medicine) or cured (an infection), the outlook is good. Prompt hospitalization is usually needed so fluids can be injected and transfusions of packed red cells and cortisonelike medications can be given.

A chronic form of hemolytic anemia may last for years and, if neglected, lead to gallstones, leg ulcers, or spleen enlargement. In some cases, surgical removal of the spleen may be required and produces great benefit.

OTHER ANEMIAS.   Other hemolytic anemias may sometimes result from mismatched blood transfusions, industrial poisons such as benzol and aniline, and other substances such as sulfa drugs, quinine, lead, fava beans. The outcome depends upon how quickly the cause can be found and eliminated as well as upon prompt treatment with fluids, transfusions, and other measures.

Still other anemias are associated with various diseases. For example, the anemia associated with low thyroid function yields to thyroid treatment; anemia associated with intestinal parasites yields when the parasites are eliminated with suitable drugs; anemia associated with lead poisoning yields when the poisoning is treated effectively; and anemia accompanying chronic infection clears when the infection is cured.

Polycythemia Vera

This disorder of unknown cause produces gradually developing symptoms that may include headache, dizziness, breathing difficulty, disturbances of vision, itching, numbness and tingling sensations, and lassitude.

In polycythemia vera, the blood-forming tissues in the bone marrow overgrow, leading to production of abnormally large amounts of red cells, with thickening of the blood and increased tendency to formation of blood clots.

Treatment is aimed at reducing the red cell numbers and blood viscosity. Venesection, or bloodletting, is often used and may be done at first once or twice a week, later every three or four months. In some cases, in addition to or instead of venesection, injections of radiophosphorus may be used to irradiate and slow down the rapidly dividing red cells. Sometimes, drugs such as busulfan and melphalan are of value.

Allergic Purpura

Caused by an allergic reaction that leads to effusion of blood into surfaces under the skin and mucous membranes, this form of purpura produces red spots which gradually darken and become purple, with itching, often accompanied by fever and malaise, and sometimes by joint and abdominal pain. Except for eliminating any suspected allergy-producing agents, treatment is symptomatic to relieve fever and pain. The condition usually lasts one to six weeks and may or may not recur.

Idiopathic Thrombocytopenic Purpura

Of unknown cause, this type of purpura produces bleeding into the skin and formation of small, round, purplish-red spots, sometimes accompanied by nosebleeds and bleeding into the gastrointestinal or genitourinary tract. It involves overactivity of the spleen, which removes too rapidly from the blood the platelets that help prevent bleeding.

Spontaneous disappearance of the disorder is common. A corticosteroid such as prednisone may reduce bleeding and increase the platelet count if bleeding is severe. If the disorder persists and is severe, spleen removal often produces complete, permanent remission. In some cases, a similar type of purpura, with the same symptoms, may result from exposure to a drug or from infection; treatment is then directed at eliminating the cause.

Endocrine

The Glands

Until a century ago, the nervous system was believed to be the one controlling force for complex body processes. But then, as too many phenomena appeared to have no relationship to the nervous

304 · The Complete Medical, Fitness & Health Guide for Men

system, it became evident that some other influence must be at work.

It proved to be the endocrine system of glands which are not at all like the salivary, sweat, and other exocrine glands of external secretion that pour their products through ducts or tubes to provide purely local activity. Endocrine glands have no ducts; instead their secretions, hormones, go into the bloodstream, and their effects are felt in areas far removed from the gland sites.

The endocrine glands are widely separated in the body. The *pituitary* is a round mass about the size of a large green pea, attached by a stalk to the brainstem. It produces many secretions that regulate the activities of the other glands in the endocrine system and influence growth, water balance in the body, and smooth muscle activity in the digestive system and elsewhere.

The *thyroid,* deep in the throat, in front of the Adam's apple and just above the breastbone, regulates the rate at which the body utilizes oxygen and food and at which various organs function. The *parathyroids,* tiny glands embedded near the thyroid base, regulate the body's use of calcium and phosphorus.

The *adrenals,* rising like mushrooms, one atop each kidney, secrete about thirty hormones involved in controlling salt and water content of the body, sugar and protein metabolism, and many other processes. One of its hormones, adrenaline, acts, when you become fearful, angry, or excited, to speed heartbeat and produce chemical changes that prepare the body for action.

The *pancreas,* lying against the back wall of the abdomen, contains the islets of Langerhans which secrete insulin, the hormone that enables the body to use, or burn, sugar and starch after they have been converted by digestive juices into glucose, or blood sugar.

The endocrine system also includes the *gonads,* or sex glands, the testes in men and the ovaries in women; the *pineal gland,* in the upper back part of the brain; and the *thymus,* below the thyroid in young people (withering away in adulthood), with little known as yet about the last two.

The relationship between the endocrine system and the nervous system is two-way. Nerve impulses influence glands, and glands influence nerves. Emotions affect the autonomic nervous system, which in turn affects gland activity. And glands work through the nervous system and influence emotions. One example of the latter is evident in the hyperthyroid person, whose thyroid is excessively active;

he is tense, easily excited, stirred up by the slightest disturbance, nervous, irritable.

Diabetes Mellitus

A disorder in which there is some degree of intolerance for carbohydrates (sugars, starches), diabetes mellitus results from inadequate production of insulin by the pancreas or from disturbance in the use of insulin. It occurs in some children, but is far more common after the age 40, especially but not exclusively in the obese and in those with family histories of diabetes.

Symptoms include excessive urination, thirst, itching, hunger, weakness, weight loss, dryness of the skin. In children and young adults, onset of diabetes is abrupt, but in older people it is commonly subtle, with early symptoms so relatively mild that the disease may be discovered only on routine blood and urine examination.

The cornerstone of treament for diabetes mellitus is diet, with insulin or oral drugs used as needed. In adult-onset diabetics, about 80 percent of whom are overweight, the disease not uncommonly can be controlled when the excess weight is lost. For diabetics, special dietetic foods, artificial sweeteners, and special preparation are not necessary although they may be a convenience. Diet control rather involves such considerations as caloric intake, the ratio and types of carbohydrates, fats and protein, and timing of food intake. For most diabetics, the total diet is one that would be considered ideal for the general population: restricted consumption of sugar, decreased intake of animal and saturated fats, and total caloric intake calculated to maintain ideal weight.

Diabetics have an increased risk of premature coronary heart disease, stroke, kidney failure, and blindness. As yet, no certain ways of preventing these complications are known. Good control of the diabetes is considered desirable. Every effort should be made to correct other conditions—such as high blood pressure, high blood-fat levels, and kidney infections—which can contribute to the complications.

Diabetes Insipidus

Unrelated to diabetes mellitus, this less common disorder is marked by excessive urination and thirst, with as many as 5 to 40 quarts of fluid taken in and excreted daily. It is due to a deficiency of a pituitary gland hormone, vasopressin, required by the kidneys for the reabsorption of water from the urine. The disorder may be congenital or may follow injury, infectious disease, or emotional shock. If a cause can be established, it should of course be treated. Otherwise, effective control of diabetes insipidus can be obtained with pituitary gland preparations or synthetic vasopressin. In some cases, a drug such as chlorpropamide can be used.

Hypoglycemia

A condition in which the blood sugar level is abnormally low, hypoglycemia may produce, several hours after meals, any or many of a considerable variety of symptoms: flushing or pallor, chilliness, numbness, hunger, trembling, headache, dizziness, weakness, palpitation, faintness, difficulty in concentration, blackouts. It can result from organic problems such as tumors of the pancreas, liver disorders, inadequate pituitary gland function, or deficient adrenal gland secretions due to infections or other causes. It may also have functional causes such as poor nutrition or severe muscular exertion.

Diagnosis can be made by measurement of the level of sugar in the blood.

For an acute episode, sugar, candy, orange juice, or honey by mouth is valuable. Bread or other food containing protein and starch helps to prevent relapse.

If the hypoglycemia has an organic cause, that must be treated. Surgical removal of a tumor on the pancreas can be curative. If pituitary or adrenal gland insufficiency is involved, hormone replacement treatment brings control. For functional hypoglycemia, a diet high in protein and low in carbohydrate, with meals taken at frequent intervals in small servings, often helps.

Hypopituitarism

The pituitary gland, as noted earlier, releases numerous hormones involved in varied activities, including some that control the working of other endocrine glands such as the thyroid and adrenals. In hypopituitarism, one or more hormones may be deficient, leading to any of such symptoms as poor appetite, weight loss, easy fatigue, cold intolerance, diminished libido (and, in women, scanty menstruation and failure to lactate after childbirth).

The disorder can be produced by various types of brain growths, ballooning out of an artery feeding the brain, hemorrhage, shock, or other causes. When such causes are involved, they must be corrected if possible. A tumor may require surgical removal or irradiation. Ballooning of an artery may be surgically repaired.

Treatment also may include use of hormones ordinarily produced by other glands under the control of pituitary hormone secretions, and not produced for lack of the secretions. They may include thyroid and adrenal gland hormones, testosterone and estrogens, and others.

Hypothyroidism

Hypothyroidism—underfunctioning of the thyroid gland—can produce such symptoms as dry, cold skin, puffiness of hands and face, decreased appetite, weight gain, slow speech, mental apathy, drowsiness, constipation, hearing loss, poor memory. Not all symptoms are necessarily present, and the degree of those that are will depend upon the degree of gland underfunctioning.

The causes of hypothyroidism include lack of iodine in the diet, deficient pituitary functioning, shrinking of the thyroid for unknown reason, or destruction of the gland by radioactive iodine.

Various tests may be used for diagnosis and include measurement of thyroid hormone level in the blood and the capacity of the thyroid to absorb iodine.

Daily administration of a thyroid hormone preparation to compensate for inadequate production is effective treatment.

Hyperthyroidism

Only about one fifth as common in men as in women, hyperthyroidism—overactivity of the thyroid gland—can produce such symptoms as weakness, sensitivity to heat, excessive sweating, overactivity, restlessness, weight loss despite increased appetite, tremor, palpitations, abnormal eye protrusion and stare, sometimes with headache, nausea, abdominal pain, diarrhea.

The cause is unknown. There is some tendency for the problem to run in families.

Diagnosis is made by blood and other tests of thyroid function.

Treatment may consist of surgical removal of part of the gland, or use of radioactive iodine to destroy part of the gland. In some cases, antithyroid drugs such as propylthiouracil and methimazole may be employed.

Cushing's Syndrome

In this condition, with its excessive adrenal gland hormone production, symptoms can include obesity, rounding of the face ("moon" facies), fat accumulations in the back ("buffalo hump"), muscle wasting and weakness, thin and easily bruised skin, thinning of bones, formation of kidney stones, high blood pressure, mental and emotional disturbances (and, in women, menstrual irregularities, excessive hairiness and sometimes baldness at the temples).

Although excessive use of steroid hormones can cause the disorder, it is usually due to either an adrenal gland tumor (which may be benign) or excessive stimulation of the adrenals by the pituitary, sometimes because of a pituitary tumor.

Diagnosis can be made by measuring the levels of adrenal hormones in the blood and of their products in the urine. Tests are also now available to pinpoint whether the problem originates with the pituitary or adrenal gland. If it is the pituitary, irradiation of the gland may be used. If an adrenal tumor is involved, it may be removed; if necessary, both adrenals can be surgically excised. Thereafter, regular administration of adrenal hormone will compensate.

Addison's Disease

Addison's disease, with its underfunctioning (insufficiency) of the adrenal glands, may occur at any age and affects both men and women equally.

Symptoms may include increasing weakness and easy fatigability, increased pigmentation of the skin, black freckles over the forehead, face, neck, and shoulders, bluish-black discoloration of mucous membranes of lips, mouth, and other sites, appetite and weight loss, nausea, vomiting, diarrhea, dizziness, decreased tolerance for cold, and fainting attacks.

Most often, wasting of the adrenal glands from unknown causes is responsible. Less often, activity of the adrenals may be dampened by failure of the pituitary gland, or the glands may be affected by infection, hemorrhage, or tumor.

Diagnosis is made by measuring the levels of adrenal hormones in the blood and the levels of the hormone products in the urine.

Addison's disease can be treated successfully with daily use of adrenal hormones such as cortisone or prednisone.

Hyperparathyroidism

Overactivity of the parathyroid glands can produce such symptoms as appetite loss, nausea, constipation, abdominal pain, excessive urination, muscle weakness, excessive thirst, and calcium stones in the urinary tract.

In most cases, the overactivity is due to a benign parathyroid tumor; in some cases, the cause may be enlargement of the glands or a cancerous growth. Other possible causes include cancer of lung, kidney, or other organ; other endocrine gland disturbances; chronic kidney disease. Surgical removal of the tumor, if one is involved, or of some of the gland tissue, if overgrowth is responsible, can reduce the excess secretions.

Urinary

The Urinary System

Every body cell must have its nutrients and must also get rid of its wastes. And all cells deliver their waste products continuously into the blood, which in turn carries them to various centers for excretion: carbon dioxide and some water in vapor form to the lungs; salt and additional water to the skin's sweat glands; and other wastes—including water, salt, urea, and uric acid—to the kidneys.

The kidneys—each about 4½ inches long, 2½ inches wide, and 1½ inches thick, and weighing about 5 ounces—are located deep in the abdomen at about the level of the lowest ("floating") ribs. Essentially, they are filters containing intricate plumbing—a system of tiny tubes called *nephrons* whose combined length in each kidney is about 140 miles.

Viewed under a microscope, a nephron looks like a twisted worm with a huge head. The head, called the *glomerulus*, is covered with a network of capillaries that carry blood continuously into the glomerulus. The tail is the *tubule*.

In a healthy kidney, as blood enters a glomerulus, some fluid is separated from it. The fluid contains no red or white blood cells and only a trace of large protein molecules. The fluid passes along the tubule, and about 99 percent of the water, amino acids, proteins, glucose, and minerals needed by the body is returned to the bloodstream. The remaining fluid, with its waste material content, is eliminated as urine.

Every 24 hours, the kidneys filter about 200 quarts of fluid and salts. One or two quarts of the waste go to the bladder and are flushed out. Actually, the kidneys have tremendous reserve capacity and could handle nine times more fluid than they are called upon to do, which is why a single healthy kidney can readily serve the body's needs.

The kidneys act to maintain correct balance between the salts and water of the body, to eliminate any toxic substances, and to keep the body in proper mineral balance. For example, too much potassium in the blood could stop the heart as effectively as a bullet.

From each kidney, a tube, or *ureter*, leads to the *urinary bladder*, which functions as a collecting and temporary storage point for urine, expanding to accommodate increasing amounts. With accumulation of about half a pint, reflex contractions lead to a desire to urinate, or micturate. The contractions stimulate pressure receptors in the muscles of the bladder wall, from which nervous impulses go to the brain. When it is convenient to urinate, the brain sends out signals which cause the bladder's external sphincter to relax. The signals also set up a series of other events, including holding of the breath, forcing of the diaphragm down, and contraction of the abdominal wall, which increase pressure in the bladder and help it void its accumulated urine.

Normal daily production of urine may range up to two quarts. In some diseases, such as diabetes insipidus, the quantity is increased; in others, fever and diarrhea decrease it. Tea, coffee, alcohol, excitement, and nervousness increase urine output. Whatever the actual liquid output, the day's urine generally contains about two ounces of solid wastes.

The bladder empties through the *urethra*, a tube leading to an external opening called the *meatus*.

Acute Pyelonephritis (Kidney Infection)

Although far more common in women, acute bacterial infection of the kidneys can affect men, and older men are prone to it when the prostate becomes enlarged, inhibiting complete bladder emptying with resultant stagnation of urine and infection.

Symptoms may include painful urination, with frequency and urgency, sometimes with chills, fever, headache, and pain in one or both sides of the lower back.

Prompt treatment, which includes use of antibiotics or sulfa drugs, sometimes with urinary antiseptics—and, when necessary, clearing up any obstruction and draining the bladder by tube— usually leads to early and complete recovery.

Chronic Pyelonephritis

Usually the result of the acute form of infection that has not been adequately treated, the chronic form is only about one third as common in men as in women.

Symptoms are similar to those of the acute infection. There may be repeated attacks over many years. A hazard of chronic infection is eventual damage to the kidneys.

Treatment includes vigorous use of carefully selected antibacterial agents suitable for the bacteria involved. If obstruction is present, surgery may be required. Any other underlying cause must be treated at the same time as the infection itself.

Acute Nephritis (Glomerulonephritis)

This is a nonbacterial inflammatory disease of the kidneys, particularly of the glomeruli and other kidney blood vessels. It is usually related to a previous streptococcal infection of throat, sinuses, tonsils, skin, or ear. Although the strep bacteria themselves are not found in the kidneys, there is some possibility that nephritis arises as an allergic reaction to some material produced by the organisms.

The disease can occur in adults but is much more frequent in children and adolescents. It may begin during or shortly after recovery from a strep infection, with headache, appetite loss, nausea, and vomiting. Other symptoms may include blood in the urine, change in urine color, reduced volume of urine, with edema or fluid retention appearing as puffiness of the face and eyelids and later extending to the legs and other parts of the body, and blood pressure elevation.

Treatment may include bed rest, intensive antibiotic treatment for the underlying respiratory or other infection, and restriction of salt and protein intake in the diet.

Ninety percent of patients recover completely, although recovery time may range upward of several weeks.

Chronic Nephritis

Chronic inflammatory disease of the kidneys may develop in some patients with the acute form. It may occur in others in whom the acute disease was so mild as to pass unnoticed and in some cases may appear for unknown reasons without a previous history of strep infection.

Sometimes, a routine examination may reveal albumin and blood (not visible to the naked eye) in the urine, pointing to chronic nephritis even before symptoms develop. As the disease progresses, symptoms may include puffiness of the face, eyelids, and ankles and distention of the abdomen from fluid retention, breathlessness on exertion, and rise in blood pressure. There may be other symptoms: growing anemia, poor vision.

Treatment may include intensive use of antibiotics for any respiratory infections, restrictions of salt, bed rest, and measures to counteract anemia and elevated pressure.

Chronic nephritis was once almost invariably fatal, leading to heart and kidney failure, with *uremia* as wastes accumulated in the blood. Today, the outlook for survival is good. *Hemodialysis*—or use of an artificial kidney machine to clean the blood of wastes— may be needed. And the success rate with kidney transplantation is now high, in the range of 75 percent, and increasing.

Acute Kidney Failure

This may result from kidney disease, crushing injuries, severe burns or shock, septicemia (bacteria or their toxins in the blood), mismatched blood transfusion, or poisoning.

It is marked by a significant decline in urination or failure to void, sometimes with low back pain or tenderness.

In treatment, fluid intake is matched to urine output, and the intake of sodium, potassium, and protein is eliminated. If necessary, an artificial kidney machine may be used to cleanse the blood and prevent uremia until the kidneys have a chance to recover.

Kidney Stones

Occurring more commonly in men than in women, most often in middle age, kidney stones can vary considerably in many ways. Some are no bigger than a speck; others may range up to Ping-Pong ball size or larger. Some are primarily composed of calcium compounds, others of uric acid compounds. Usually, there is more than one stone, and the stones may occur in one or both kidneys.

If a stone is small and smooth, it may be passed through the kidneys, ureter, bladder, and out through the urethra without symptoms. Larger stones are likely to block the ureter, producing one of the worst of all pains—spasmodic, in the back, radiating from the kidney across the abdomen into the groin. The pain can persist for hours, with sweating, chills, nausea, and vomiting.

In treatment, medication may be used to control spasm and morphine or other drugs to relieve pain; and if the stone is relatively small, large amounts of fluid may be given in an effort to get it to pass into the urine and out. When passage is impossible, removal by surgery may be required.

Once a stone has been passed or removed, efforts are made to minimize the likelihood of formation of others. The stone will be analyzed for composition. Depending upon the composition, specific dietary measures may be prescribed. For example, for calcium oxalate stones, dietary measures may include daily intake of vitamin B complex and exclusion of such foods as cocoa, chocolate, cabbage, celery, spinach, and tomatoes, which are high in oxalates.

Bladder Stones

When a stone passes into and remains in the bladder or forms there, symptoms may include frequency of urination, painful urination, and blood, pus, and albumin in the urine. Most bladder

314 · The Complete Medical, Fitness & Health Guide for Men

stones sooner or later move into the urethra and are expelled. When a stone fails to do so, an instrument, the cystoscope, may be introduced through the urethra into the bladder for its removal.

Cystitis (Bladder Inflammation)

The bladder may become inflamed as the result of infection of the kidney or urethra, or because of urine retention induced by an enlarged prostate.

Symptoms include urgent, painful urination, with a frequent need to void but little output.

In treatment, sulfa drugs or antibiotics are used, sometimes with additional drugs to relieve pain during urination. With prompt treatment, symptoms often disappear in a week. For a permanent cure, the underlying cause must be diagnosed and treated.

Hydronephrosis (Kidney Distention)

In hydronephrosis, the kidney becomes distended with urine as the result of obstruction of urine flow in the urinary tract, causing recurrent attacks of pain in the kidney region that may be dull, nagging or sharp, sometimes with fever and with blood and pus in the urine.

The obstruction may result from stones, tumors, prostate enlargement, urinary tract infections, or cancer of the bladder, urethra, or glans penis.

In treatment, the urinary tract is drained by catheter and any infection is combated with antibiotics and urinary antiseptics. In some cases, surgery may be required to overcome blockage.

Urethritis

An inflammation of the urethra, the canal from the bladder to outside the body, urethritis may produce both increased urination and urgency, along with burning pain and sometimes a purulent discharge.

Although it often is a symptom of gonorrhea or other infection and antibiotic treatment then is effective, in some men no infection can be found.

In at least some of these mysterious cases, according to a study by Dr. Stephen M. Rous of New York Medical College, the problem may lie with a persistently alkaline, irritative urine, and vitamin C may be helpful.

When urine becomes strongly alkaline, it no longer can hold in solution, as it normally does, phosphate crystals, which then produce discomfort, much as cinders in the eye do. This appeared to be the problem in a group of a dozen men. All responded to massive doses of vitamin C (3 grams a day for 4 days), which acidified the urine, permitting it to dissolve the irritating crystals.

A Selected Bibliography

Chapter 1

Neff, W. S. *Work and Human Behavior*. New York: Atherton Press, 1968.
Lewis, H. R. and M. E. *Psychosomatics: How Your Emotions Can Damage Your Health*. New York: Viking Press, 1972.
Benson, H. *The Relaxation Response*. New York: William Morrow and Co., 1975.
Galton, L. *How Long Will I Live?* New York: Macmillan, 1976.
Journal of the American Medical Association, 223:801.
Canadian Medical Association Journal, 114:1095.
Science News, 109:54.

Chapter 2

Galton, L. *How Long Will I Live?* New York: Macmillan, 1976.
Archives of General Psychiatry, 26:463.
Medical World News, 12(5):286.
Modern Medicine, 40(17):40.
Journal of the American Medical Association, 230:1680; 227:514; 220:1745; 219:394; 228:978; 237:1569.
Science News, 111:203.

Chapter 3

The Medical Aspects of Sports, 16. Chicago: American Medical Association and The Sports Medicine Foundation of America, Inc.
Sports and Physical Fitness. American Medical Association.
Medical Evaluation of the Athlete. Chicago: The American Medical Association, 1976.
Sports medicine. *World Health*, the Magazine of the World Health Organization, July 1972.
Physical Fitness Research Digest. Washington, D.C.: The President's Council on Physical Fitness and Sports: Series 5, No. 2; Series 6, No. 2.
Newsletter. President's Council on Physical Fitness and Sports. Jan. 1976; March 1977.

InforMed: University of Arizona Health Sciences Center, Tucson, April 1977.
Journal of the American Medical Association, 223:627; 224:1655; 233:463.
Archives of Physical Medicine and Rehabilitation, 53:323.
Southern Medical Journal, 64:549.

Chapter 4

Galton, L. *How Long Will I Live?* New York: Macmillan, 1976.
New England Journal of Medicine, 294:1322; 294:1372.
Masters, W. H., and Johnson, V. E. *Human Sexual Inadequacy.* Boston: Little Brown & Co., 1970.
New Physician, Sexual Medicine, a series, 1976–1977.
Science, 186:330.
The Bulletin, New York State District Branches, American Psychiatric Association, 14:8.
Roche Report: Frontiers of Psychiatry, 2:4.
Hospital Practice, Sept. 1975, p. 126.
American Family Physician, 15(4):112.

Chapter 5

Comfort, A. *A Good Age.* New York: Crown Publishers, 1976.
Forsham, P. H. In: Do men go through a "change of life?" *Family Health,* Nov. 1972.
In Consultation. Treating menopausal women—and climacteric men. *Medical World News,* June 28, 1974.
American Family Physician, 10(6):91.
Newton, M. In: Do men go through menopause, too? *Family Health/Today's Health,* March 1977.
Schanche, D. A. In: What happens emotionally and physically when a man reaches 40. *Today's Health,* March 1973.
Galton, L. *How Long Will I Live?* New York: Macmillan, 1976.
——— Current research in aging, in *Don't Give Up On an Aging Parent.* New York: Crown Publishers, 1975.

Chapter 6

American Family Physician, 10(3):80; 11(2):166.
Journal of the National Cancer Institute, 53:335.
Canadian Medical Association Journal, 112:22S.
Medical Tribune, 17(30):23.
Galton, L. *The Patient's Guide to Surgery.* New York: Hearst Books, 1976.

Chapter 7

Miller, B. F., and Galton, L. *Freedom from Heart Attacks.* New York: Simon and Schuster, 1972.

Likoff, W., et al. *Your Heart.* Philadelphia: J. B. Lippincott Co., 1972.

Galton, L. *Save Your Stomach.* New York: Crown Publishers, 1977.

———— *The Silent Disease: Hypertension.* New York: Crown Publishers, 1973.

Lancet, 1(1973):333, 1404.

American Heart Journal, 87:722.

Chest, 68:195.

Journal of the American Medical Association, 230:130.

New York State Journal of Medicine, 77:227.

Chapter 8

RF Illustrated. New York: The Rockefeller Foundation, 1977.

Canadian Medical Association Journal, 116:468; 116:549; 116:531.

Nutrition, 27:170.

Journal of the Science of Food and Agriculture, 25:1451.

Proceedings, Nutrition Society, 32:159.

Yudkin, J. *Pure White and Deadly.* London: Davis-Poynter, 1972.

Galton, L. *The Truth About Fiber in Your Food.* New York: Crown Publishers, 1976.

———— *Save Your Stomach.* New York: Crown Publishers, 1977.

Miller, B. F. *Freedom from Heart Attacks.* New York: Simon and Schuster, 1972.

Chapter 9

Galton, L. *Save Your Stomach.* New York: Crown Publishers, 1977.

———— *The Truth About Fiber in Your Food.* New York: Crown Publishers, 1976.

Journal of the American Medical Association, 225:1243; 226:1525; 217:1359; 225:1659.

British Medical Journal, 1 (1976):424.

American Family Physician, 15 (2):158.

Annals of Internal Medicine, 80:663.

Burkitt, D. P. Some diseases characteristic of modern Western civilization. *British Medical Journal,* 1(1973):274.

Cleave, T. L. *The Saccharine Disease.* Bristol: Wright, 1974.

Painter, N. S. Diverticular disease of the colon—a disease of Western civilization. *Disease-a-Month.* Chicago: Year Book Medical Publishers, June 1970.

Chapter 10

Canadian Medical Association Journal, 111:397.

American Family Physician, 10(5):131; 6(3):92.

Friedmann, L. W., and Galton, L. *Freedom from Backaches.* New York: Simon and Schuster, 1973; Pocket Books, 1976.

Journal of the American Medical Association, 233:336; 233:364; 233:1247; 227:1373; 231:1143.

American Family Physician, 13(2):116.

Arthritis and Rheumatism, 16:139.
Arthroscope, The Arthritis Foundation Newsletter, 3:2.
Archives of Physical Medicine and Rehabilitation, 52:479.
Clinical Orthopedics, 95:9.
Medical World News, 15(16):40; 14(41):86D; 15(9):22.
Medical Opinion, 4(9):35.
Archives of Neurology, 17:503.

Chapter 11

Journal of the American Medical Association, 219:519.
Medical World News, 15(28):51.
Cutis, 9:375.
Medical World News, 14(40):14K; 17(1):89
Journal of the American Medical Association, 210:2341; 228:1004; 230:72; 224:257; 224:905; 230:878; 233:1257; 224:132; 235;237.
Archives of Dermatology, 106:200; 111:1004.

Chapter 12

Archives of Neurology, 27:129.
Archives of Otolaryngology, 100:262; 97:118; 98:10; 93:183.
Medical Tribune, 15(2):21
Medical World News, 12(39):34E; 15(9):13.
The Laryngoscope, 5:639.
Journal of the American Medical Association, 227:1165; 219:93; 227:79.
Annals of Otology, Rhinology and Laryngology, 81:611.
Galton, L. *The Patient's Guide to Surgery.* New York: Hearst Books, 1976.

Chapter 13
Miller, B. F. *The Family Book of Preventive Medicine.* New York: Simon and Schuster, 1971.
———. *The Complete Medical Guide,* 4th revised edition. New York: Simon and Schuster, in press.
The Merck Manual, 12th edition. Rahway, N.J.: Merck Sharp & Dohme Research Laboratories, 1972.
Canadian Medical Association Journal, 109:891.
American Family Physician, 6(6):60; 11(5):105.
Modern Medicine, 40(20):128.
Headache, 15:36.
Neurology, 22:366.
Archives of Neurology, 32:649.
Journal of the American Medical Association, 221:1165.
Galton, L. *The Disguised Disease: Anemia.* New York: Crown Publishers, 1975.

Index

Abrasions, first aid for, 68
Acetaminophen, 221
Acupuncture, for hearing loss, 268
Adaptation, diseases of, 17
Addison's disease, 308–309
Adult stages in life, 114–116
Aerophagics, 189
Aggressiveness, 19
Aging, see Middle years and beyond
Air pollution, 161
Air swallowing, 148, 189
Airplane ankles, 229
Alabama, University of, 158
Alcohol, 282
  meditation and, 22
  sexuality and, 82–83
Allergic purpura, 303
Allopurinol, 228
Aluminum hydroxide, 207
Alvarado Medical Center, 69
Amelar, Dr. Richard D., 104
American Aerospace Medical
    Association, 27
American Association of Sex
    Educators and Counselors, 101
American Association of Sleep
    Disorders Centers, 51
American College of Sports Medicine,
    65
American Heart Association, 55
American Journal of Public Health,
    76
American Medical Association, 65,
    101, 113, 209
  Committee on Aging, 131

Committee on the Medical Aspects
    of Sports, 65, 67, 70
American Red Cross, 209
Aminophylline, 167
Amobarbital, 297
Amphetamines, 175
Anabolic steroids, 71
Anabolism, 82
Anal itching, 203–204
Anderson, Dr. W. H., 162
Anemia, 300–302
  fatigue and, 31–32
  iron deficiency, 31, 300
Angina pectoris, 148–149
Ankles
  airplane, 229
  replacement of, 235–236
  sprained, 226
Ankylosing spondylitis, 229–230
Antacids, 197, 199, 200, 206–207
Anthracosis, 170
Antimalarial drugs, 232
Anxiety, see Stress
Aphrodisiacs, 83–84
Apnea, 45–46
Aristotle, 241
Arnold, Dr. Samuel J., 35
Arthritic joints, 230–237
  choosing a doctor, 230–231
  drugs for, 231–233
  surgery for, 234
  water exercise therapy, 233
Arthrodesis, 234
Asbestosis, 170
Aspirin, 221–222, 229–231, 257

About the Author

LAWRENCE GALTON is a noted medical writer and editor and a former visiting professor at Purdue University. He is a columnist for the Washington Star Syndicate and *Family Circle,* and his articles frequently appear in *The New York Times Magazine, Reader's Digest, Parade,* and other national publications. He is the author of more than a dozen other books.